HALO WARS

PRIMA Official Game Guide

Written by:

David S.J. Hodgson

Prima Games

An Imprint of Random House, Inc.
3000 Lava Ridge Court, Suite 100
Roseville, CA 95661
www.primagames.com

The Prima Games logo is a registered trademark of Random House, Inc., registered in the United States and other countries. Primagames.com is a registered trademark of Random House, Inc., registered in the United States.

Senior Product Manager: Mario De Govia
Associate Product Manager: Shaida Boroumand
Design & Layout: Bryan Neff & Jody Seltzer
Manufacturing: Stephanie Sanchez

ISBN: 978-07615-6181-1
Library of Congress Catalog Card Number: 2008941413
Printed in the United States of America

09 10 11 12 LL 10 9 8 7 6 5 4 3 2 1

Author Acknowledgements

To my wonderful and loving wife Melanie; Bryn, Rachel and Samuel; Mum, Dad, Ian and Rowena; The Moon Wiring Club, Laibach, Ladytron, Kraftwerk, T Power, Pendulum, and The Knife; Ron & Fez (and the Bearded Joker); And D for Dagon, Because he's one of the gods, And not for the Deep Ones, Who're just one step up from frogs.

Thanks to all at Prima, especially Mario De Govia and Shaida Boroumand for their help and support throughout this project. Thanks also to Julie Asbury, Andy Rolleri, and Alexis Scheuble.

This guide would not have been possible without the dedication, help, and support of Ensemble Studios. It was an honor and a privilege to work with such an incredible team. A huge debt of gratitude from the Author, and all at Prima Games, to the following people:

Design: Dave Pottinger, Graeme Devine, Jerome K. Jones, Tim Deen, Aaron Keppel, Joe Gillum, Vance Hampton, Jeff Brown, and Karen McMullan

Balance: Donnie Thompson and Mike Wagner

A.I. Programming: Mike Kidd

Art: Lance Hoke, Dave Kubalak, Bart Tiongson, Don Gagen, Gene Kohler, Juan Martinez, Scott Winsett, Danny Beck, Brett Briley, Matthew Burke, David A. Cherry, Won Choi, Brad Crow, Shannon Dees, Matthew Goldman, John Andy Gotcher, Bryan Hehmann, Dion Hopkins, Jonathan Jacobson, Paul Jaquays, Duncan McKissick, Jason Merck, Jeffrey R. Miller, Chris Moffitt, Thonny S. Namuonglo , Marco Nelor (Volt), Pete Parisi, Chris Pineda (Volt), Josh Powers (Volt), Jason Sallenbach, Duane Santos, Adam C. Schimpf, Alexander G. Scott, Mark Sinclair, Paul Slusser, Woody Smith, Nate Stefan, Charles Tinney, Chris Van Doren, Robert Walden, and Phil Wohr

About the Author

Originally hailing from the English city of Manchester, David began his career in 1995, writing for numerous classic British gaming magazines from a rusting, condemned, bohemian dry-docked German fishing trawler floating on the River Thames. Fleeing the United Kingdom, he joined the crew at the part-fraternity, part-sanitarium known as *GameFan* magazine. David helped launch GameFan Books and form Gamers' Republic, was partly responsible for the wildly unsuccessful *incite* Video Gaming and Gamers.com. He began authoring guides for Prima in 2000. He has written over 60 strategy guides, including: *The Legend of Zelda: Twilight Princess, Assassin's Creed, Half-Life: Orange Box, Mario Kart Wii,* and *Fallout 3.* He lives in the Pacific Northwest with his wife Melanie, and an eight-foot statue of Great Cthulhu.

We want to hear from you! E-mail comments and feedback to dhodgson@primagames.com.

CREDITS

Special thanks to the Ensemble team for creating an amazing game:

Aaron Keppel, Adam C. Schimpf, Alexander G. Scott, Andrew Foster, Angelo Laudon, Bart Tiongson, Ben Donges, Bill Jackson, Billy Ethan Khan, Brad Crow, Brad Robnett, Brett Briley, Brian Dellinger, Brian Lemon, Bruce C. Shelley, Bryan Hehmann, Capen Apple (Volt), Charles Tinney, Chris Moffitt, Chris Pineda (Volt), Chris Rippy, Chris Stark, Chris Van Doren, Clare Braddy (Volt), Colt McAnlis, Crystal Newell (Spherion), Danny Beck, Darby Hadley (Volt), Dave Kubalak, Dave Pottinger, David A. Cherry, David Bettner, David Leary, David Lewis, David Rippy, Dion Hopkins , Don Gagen, Donnie Thompson, Doug Marien, Duane Santos , Duncan Grimshaw, Duncan McKissick, Duncan Stanley, Dusty Monk, Dwayne Gravitt, Eric Best, Gene Kohler, Graeme Devine, Graham Somers, Greg Street, Harter Ryan, Ian M. Fischer, J.D. Smith, Jake Dotson, Jason Merck, Jason Sallenbach, Jeff Brown, Jeff Ruediger, Jeffrey R. Miller, Jerome K. Jones, Joe Gillum, John Andy Gotcher , John Evanson, Jonathan Jacobson, Josh Powers (Volt), Juan Martinez, Justin Hallmark (Volt), Justin Randall, Justin Rouse, Karen McMullan, Karen Swanson, Kevin Holme, Kevin McMullan, Kevin White, Lance Hoke, Lizette Atkinson, Marc Hanson, Marc Holmes, Marcin Szymanski, Marco Nelor (Volt), Mark Sinclair, Matthew Burke, Matthew Goldman, Michael Bean, Michael W. Capps, Mike Coker, Mike Kidd, Mike McGlumphy, Mike Wagner, Milo Philips-Brown (Volt), Nate Stefan, Nicolas Currie, Nique Gardner (Spherion), Oscar Santos, Patrick Hudson, Patrick Thomas, Paul Bettner, Paul Jaquays, Paul LaSalle (Volt), Paul Slusser, Paul Warzecha, Pete Parisi, Peter Chapman, Phil Wohr, Randall Woodman, Rich Geldreich, Robert Anderson, Robert Fermier, Robert Walden, Roy Rabey, Sandy Petersen, Scott Winsett, Sergio Tacconi, Shannon Dees, Shawn Halwes, Shawn Lohstroh, Stéphane LeBrun, Stephen Clayburn, Stephen Rippy, Thonny S. Namuonglo , Tim Deen, Timothy R Ruessler, Todd Ruediger (Volt), Tommy Bean, Tony Allen Goodman , Vance Hampton, Vijay Thakkar, Wallace H. Wachi, Jr., Won Choi, Woody Smith, Zane Sadler (Volt), Zeke Marks

Special Thanks to the following people from Ensemble Studios and Microsoft Game Studios for their help and support:

Harter Ryan, Chris Rippy, Graeme Devine, the Ensemble Art and Design teams, Mike Kidd, Donnie Thompson, Mike Wagner, Jim Ying, Josh Kerwin, Steve Schreck, Jason Pace, Alicia Brattin, Haley Church.

CONTENTS

3

BASICS

In this chapter, we reveal precise, battle-tested tactical knowledge, including the primary general fighting strategies you can employ. We also detail base management and upgrading. This information is designed to help you win many wars, but you are also encouraged to devise your own plans.

Welcome to Halo Wars Advanced Training

Please read through the instruction manual so you're familiar with the basics of movement, combat, and multi-player modes. The following training assumes you've learned game function and perfected the two Training missions prior to starting the Campaign mode. Can you split up your units, fast-scroll around a map, and use your Leader Powers? Then Advanced Training begins now!

NOTE

For specific information on a building or unit type, consult the "Factions" chapter.

To learn details on basic movement, unit selections, and combat, read your instructions manual.

Rock, Paper, Scissors: RPS in the RTS

In order to plan effective battle tactics, you must first learn the overriding tenets of real-time strategy games. They follow the very general format of "Rock, Paper, Scissors," where one element type counters another. The "rocks, paper, and scissors" in question are "infantry, air units, and ground vehicles." The following is a complete overview of how these advantages and disadvantages work in the UNSC and Covenant armies.

NOTE

The following revelations include two terms: "advantageous" and "highly advantageous." A unit that is "advantageous" to use when attacking another unit usually wins a battle with around 40 percent of its force remaining afterward. For example, if ten units attack ten foes they are advantageous against, expect four of the advantageous units to still be alive at the fight's end. From this point on, the term "advantageous" is indicated by the greater-than > symbol.

A unit that is "highly advantageous" to use when attacking another unit usually wins a battle with around 80 percent of its force remaining afterward. For example, if ten units attack ten foes they are advantageous against, expect eight of the advantageous units to still be alive at the fight's end. From this point on, the term "highly advantageous" is replaced with the much-greater-than symbol >>.

General *Halo Wars* RPS Facts

The following diagram shows the basic advantages each of the three unit types have over each other. This applies to all the different classes, unless specified otherwise:

Mainline Infantry Units > Mainline Air Units > Mainline Ground Units > Mainline Infantry Units

The UNSC's mainline infantry are Marines, advantageous when dealing with Covenant Banshees.

This shows that each army's mainline infantry units are highly advantageous at taking out air units. Mainline air units are highly advantageous at taking out ground vehicles. Mainline ground vehicles are highly advantageous at taking out infantry units. "Mainline" indicates the main troop type trained or built, as detailed below.

When you're dealing with a counter-unit (or an "anti" unit), the general facts are different. First, a counter-unit has a specific enemy type it is geared toward defeating. It is always highly advantageous at defeating this unit type, but unfortunately, it is also always highly disadvantageous when facing the two other mainline unit types it isn't specialized against. For example, Flamethrowers are anti-infantry, meaning they are highly advantageous at countering every other infantry type on the battlefield, but expect heavy losses when pitching them against any mainline vehicle or air unit.

The UNSC's anti-infantry units are Flamethrowers, highly advantageous when dealing with all Covenant infantry.

NOTE

For specific information on the strengths and weaknesses of individual unit and troop types, consult the "Factions" chapter.

The advantages that general unit types have over each other only occur when they are the same Veterancy level. If you're at a higher Veterancy level than your foe, expect your advantages to be more pronounced.

Veterancy on the Battlefield

A veteran Spartan adds bonuses to his own ability and to any vehicle he controls.

One advantage of troops that survive fights is that they gain in Veterancy levels, which is much more important than you may initially think. If your in-game units have star icons floating next to them, consider them preferable in many combat situations, as they have attained a rank of Veterancy and the associated bonuses that are awarded with this combat prowess.

Generally, each level of Veterancy is equal to an upgrade of a regular troop type. For example, a three-star Marine unit has about the same combat effectiveness as a raw, just-trained Marine unit with a Medic (#3) upgrade. Although statistically the following varies wildly, the following bonuses are generally awarded to Veteran units:

Veterancy Level	Additional Damage Inflicted	Additional Damage Resistance
1	+15 percent	+15 percent
2	+43 percent	+43 percent
3+	+95 percent	+95 percent

Units earn Veterancy experience (XP), which isn't revealed under game conditions and is a complex set of mathe-matics that may be tweaked continuously. However, the first points of XP are usually awarded when a unit destroys an enemy unit whose costs are equal to around twice their own. Each subsequent point costs twice the amount to earn than the previous point. Note that infantry units have a bonus that allows them to gain Veterancy faster.

The following two examples show how a Scorpion battle tank (worth 25 XP if destroyed by a single unit) and a squad of Marines (worth 5 XP) earn their Veterancy. As each squad varies wildly and the gameplay balance may change, these are for example only:

Unit	Veterancy Level	XP Needed
Scorpion	1	40
Scorpion	2	100
Scorpion	3	180
Marines	1	4
Marines	2	12
Marines	3	24

Spartans are another unique unit, as they automatically give any vehicle they are in (whether belonging to the UNSC or Covenant) a 15 percent damage and damage resistance bonus, which is augmented by another 15 percent for each upgrade the Spartan receives. So, a fully upgraded Spartan increases the vehicle they are controlling by 60 percent. A Spartan's Veterancy bonus is also added to the vehicle! This makes them incredibly useful for leading vehicles into battle.

Upgrades on the Battlefield

Upgrading your units allows for a wide variety of impressive and unique skills, as well as general combat bonuses.

Before reading the specific information on every unit's and building's upgrade path in the next chapter, it is important to understand what upgrades offer in a more general sense. Usually, a unit upgrade provides a specific ability (accessed via ❂) or function (such as a faster-rotating Turret for a Scorpion), but each upgrade also adds a +25 percent statistics boost to damage inflicted and resisted. Most units have three (or two) upgrades providing specific combat enhancements to purchase when your Tech level is sufficiently high enough. However, there is one exception: Covenant leaders' upgrades grant a 200 to 300 percent upgrade in combat performance and defense.

Scorpions, Hornets, Wolverines, Cobras, Vampires, and Wraiths are already "statistically upgraded" once prior to arriving on the battlefield. Vampires are already statistically upgraded three times prior to arriving on the battlefield. Vultures are already upgraded with additional firepower, while Scarabs appear fully upgraded.

Skills and Skulls

Grab a floating dead guy's head once you slay enough specific enemies to unlock some wild gameplay enhancements!

Aside from the main objectives throughout the Campaign mode and the Black Box hidden on each map that unlocks much of the timeline, there are more secrets to discover: the infamous Halo Skulls. There are 15 of them, and each appears only when you complete each mission's Kill objective; be sure to return to the Skull's location before ending the mission. Every Skull you collect is revealed on the menu showing your previously completed missions.

These Skulls have specific gameplay enhancements, which can help (or hinder) your attempts at a perfect score and a Gold ranking for each Campaign mission. The following table shows what enhancements to the game each Skull enables. Check these out before deciding whether to attempt a mission with this Skull turned on.

Naturally, Skulls 11 through 15 are the most useful, because they give to an in-game bonus ability as well as (not instead of) a percentage added to your Complete Score ranking.

Mission Number	Skull Name	% Added to Mission Complete Score	Description of Skull's Ability
01	Look Daddy!	None	Grunts' methane tank always explodes on death.
02	Grunt Birthday Party	None	Grunts explode into confetti.
03	Cowbell	None	Destruction physics magnification x2.
04	Wuv Woo	None	Scarabs shoot rainbow beams made of Pure Love.
05	Fog	+10 percent	No minimap.
06	Sickness	+10 percent	All player units explode into Flood units on death.
07	Rebel Sympathizer	+20 percent	Nonplayer units receive +25 percent more Hit Points.

Mission Number	Skull Name	% Added to Mission Complete Score	Description of Skull's Ability
08	Rebel Supporter	+20 percent	Nonplayer units inflict +50 percent more damage.
09	Rebel Leader	+20 percent	Nonplayer units start with extra Veterancy.
10	Catch	+20 percent	Nonplayer units recharge abilities in half the normal time.
11	Sugar Cookies	+50 percent	All player units have 50 percent more Hit Points.
12	Boomstick	+10 percent	Five percent chance any nonplayer unit blows up on death, with splash damage.
13	Pain Train	+25 percent	All player units train 50 percent faster.
14	Bountiful Harvest	+30 percent	Supplies arrive 25 percent more quickly.
15	Emperor	+50 percent	All player Leader Powers recharge in half the time.

Base Construction Tactics

NOTE

For specific information on unit names and building types, consult the "Factions" chapter.

Building the Perfect Base: UNSC

Aim to initially construct a well-built, easily defendable UNSC Fortress in a classic 2-1-2 formation.

With the UNSC, begin construction with two Supply Pads, followed by a Reactor. The Supply Pads allow immediate access to Economy, and the Reactor allows you to begin building some important structures (such as Turrets). When the third building's Reactor tower begins to glow, construct two more Supply Pads. If you're playing as Anders or Forge, it is usually safest to begin constructing Warthogs immediately and sending them on Scouting reconnoiters across the map. This allows you to defend an early enemy Rush. The first Reactor also allows you to quickly upgrade your Warthog to Gunner status, enabling combat effectiveness. You can use them now to raid enemy structures; they are excellent at destroying enemy buildings under construction. Finish your base with a Barracks, Vehicle Depot, or Air Pad, depending on your micro-tactics and changing battle environments.

Captain Cutter's base has more flexibility; he can get away with an infantry-focused 4-2 formation.

With Cutter, build an Elephant from your command center while placing four Supply Pads down in quick succession. Follow this up with two back-to-back Reactors and then a Vehicle Depot or Air Pad as your seventh structure. Cutter can train infantry from the back of his Elephant, which makes him more flexible (and powerful) in the early stages of combat. His base begins as a Station (rather than a Firebase) with seven sockets instead of the usual five.

A Typical Forge and Anders Base Progression

1 Supply Pad	2 Supply Pad	3 Reactor	4 Supply Pad	5 Supply Pad

6 Upgrade Base to Fortress	7 Reactor	7 Vehicle Depot OR	7 Air Pad

A Typical Cutter Base Progression

Construct an Elephant	1 Supply Pad	2 Supply Pad	3 Supply Pad	4 Supply Pad

5 Reactor	6 Reactor	7 Vehicle Depot OR	7 Air Pad

NOTE

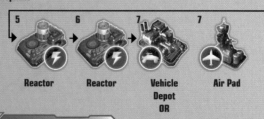

This type of base planning optimizes your initial sockets by giving you a solid Economy and giving you the room to construct troops that you cannot get at lower Tech levels.

Building the Perfect Base: Covenant

The Covenant's focus is the Temple, Warehouses, and Hot Dropping.

Tactically, it makes more sense to start your Covenant base-building with the Temple; this allows you to access your leader on the battlefield as soon as possible. You can then use him in several ways: He can Scout and gather supplies, bolstering your Economy while you then place a couple of Warehouses into your base to augment the supply collection. He can also defend your base against an enemy Rush with vicious effectiveness. In addition, his combat effectiveness is considerable, especially as you can Hot Drop friendly units directly to his side from the Covenant base's teleporter—a ruthless and excellent early Rush strategy.

CAUTION

Constructing Warthogs or Ghosts may seem like a waste of time if you're hoping to focus only on the bigger-hitting vehicles or aircraft. However, this strategy usually results in you being overrun by opponents using this very technique!

A Typical Covenant Base Progression

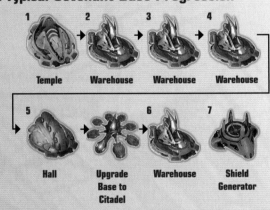

1	2	3	4
Temple	Warehouse	Warehouse	Warehouse

5		6	7
Hall	Upgrade Base to Citadel	Warehouse	Shield Generator

NOTE

Covenant base generation can vary wildly (much more than the UNSC), but this is a good template to use.

Base Control: The Rush and the Boom

A brief Scouting mission reveals a foe focused on flight. Bring this plan crashing back to earth with antiair forces!

When you bring in the human element of Multiplayer mode, exactly what to construct in terms of buildings and troops depends on your foe. The best plan is to build your base's basics while Scouting your opponent. Forge and Anders should employ Warthogs to Scout and harass your foe while your base gains buildings, specifically Supply Pads and Reactors. Change this tactic only if you spot your enemy massing an early army for a quick Rush. At this point, stop the construction of "extra" Supply Pads, and focus on building an army that can swiftly counter the troops your foe is sending out. Cutter should employ an early infantry army to gain any advantage possible, whether Economically through map Hooks or militarily through a well-executed Rush. For example, your Scouting expedition has revealed a foe building Hornets. Retaliate immediately by producing Wolverines, the key antiair unit.

TIP

The leader your foe chooses should also give you a clue of the tactics they are likely to employ: If your foe chooses the Brute Chieftain, he's probably going to Rush you. If he chooses Anders, he's likely to strike from the air. Expanded information on the unit types and abilities are shown in the "Factions" chapter.

When facing human foes while playing as the Covenant, it is almost always best to immediately construct your Temple to gain numerous additional units to choose from and to gain access to the backbone of your army: the leader. Generally, spend your Resources into building as many units as possible once your Temple is fully built. Preferred units include Banshees (due to their mobility, especially after the Boost upgrade), a mixture of Hunters and Jackals, or an army focusing on leader upgrades with Jackals sniping foes from a great distance. The real problem is ascending to a different "Age" (Tech level); it requires 1,000 points to go from Level 1 to 2, so only attempt this if you know your foe is Turtling, and you're comfortable enough to let your Economy build. However, the Temple upgrade is very useful in securing a win.

Additional Base Construction

Two bases make you doubly difficult to defeat, unless you spread yourself too thin.

The timing of constructing your next base is incredibly important and varies considerably based on the map you're on, your current strength, and your opponent's tactics. This can ultimately decide the outcome of a battle. Naturally, this means constructing a second base at different times:

- If you're attempting a Boom strategy, stake a claim on a second base as early as you can so you can build Supply Pads or Warehouses as quickly as possible. Simply put, two Supply Pad queues are better than one.

- When engaged in a Rush strategy, a second base is completely unnecessary; construct one only if you have a load of additional resources, you're at your Population maximum, or you require additional sockets for a Reactor (for army upgrading).

9

- If you're trying a Turtle strategy, use a more measured approach. Ensure your primary base is defended to your satisfaction before you even think of constructing your second base. Once you've reached the goal for your Turtle strategy (e.g., when you've gained an appropriate Tech level or a strong economy), then attempt to land-grab.

> **CAUTION**
>
> The biggest risk when taking a second base is attempting this early, and you suspect your foe is about to Rush. Your foes can easily destroy a base that's lightly defended.

> **TIP**
>
> Conversely, when your foe is engaged in attacking a neutral base or sending a convoy to take over an empty base, this is the perfect moment to strike!

> **CAUTION**
>
> If you're under heavy fire, it is always better to defend yourself and utilize all your resources to beat back your opponent than try to flee and expand to a second base. Build a second base when you're in a strong position, not a weak one.

The Economics of War: Supply Pads and Warehouses

A Supply Pad (left) and Heavy Supply Pad (right) keep your base and unit-expansion plans going.

Both the UNSC and Covenant rely on supplies to "feed" their armies, either by collecting supply crates dotted around maps or by building Supply Pads (UNSC) or Warehouses (Covenant; referred to from now on just as Supply Pads). Generally, the more Supply Pads you build, the more supplies are added to your economic totals, allowing purchases of buildings, troops, upgrades, and Covenant Leader Powers. Here are some vitally important points to remember when attempting to build Supply Pads:

- UNSC Heavy Supply Pads (a Supply Pad upgrade), or Covenant Blessed Warehouses (a Warehouse upgrade) are 40 percent more proficient than normal Supply Pads. For example, if a Supply Pad gives you 10 points per second, a Heavy Supply Pad gives you 14.

- Supply Pads have diminishing returns; the more you build, the less proficient they all become:

  Going from one to two Supply Pads increases supplies per second by 82 percent. For example, if one Supply Pad gives you 10 points per second, two Supply Pads would give you 18.2 points per second.

  Going from two to five Supply Pads doubles your supplies per second. For example, if two Supply Pads give you 18.2 points per second, five Supply Pads would give you 36.4 points per second.

  Going from five to ten Supply Pads increases supplies per second by 50 percent. For example, if five Supply Pads give you 36.4 points per second, 10 Supply Pads would give you 72.8 points per second.

> **TIP**
>
> For a normal battle, between five and seven Supply Pads is the optimal number for a return on your investment.

- The output of Heavy Supply Pads relative to regular Supply Pads is as follows and reflects diminishing returns:

  Two Heavy Supply Pads are the same as three regular Supply Pads.

  Three Heavy Supply Pads are the same as five regular Supply Pads.

  Five Heavy Supply Pads are the same as nine regular Supply Pads.

  Seven Heavy Supply Pads are the same as fourteen regular Supply Pads.

> **TIP**
>
> The break-even point for upgrading to Heavy Supply Pads happens at around seven Supply Pads; after that, Heavy Supply Pads are more profitable.
>
> Forge begins with Heavy Supply Pads automatically and doesn't need to upgrade them; the optimal number for an early Rush is three Heavy Supply Pads.
>
> It is important never to horde your resources, as any supplies you don't spend can't work to help you ultimately win the battle. Instead, work with what you currently have available, and look toward a larger investment in Tech levels and technologically advanced units only when you feel comfortable or relatively secure.

> **NOTE**
>
> Specific information on Tech levels, Reactors, and Temples is shown in the "Factions" chapter.

Main Methods of Play

Glossary of Terms

Throughout this guide, certain terms are used to describe a play style or attack plan. These are described in detail below:

Play Styles

Rushing: Building an army as quickly as possible and immediately attacking the enemy.

Booming: Expanding your economy as quickly as possible by Supply Pad, Warehouse, Supply Hook, and supply crate activities.

Teching: Attempting to obtain a higher Tech level as quickly as possible to field more powerful units.

Turtling: Using a large number of defensive structures to fend off an enemy attack.

Attack Plans and Other Terminology

Ambushes: Locking your base, fooling your foe into thinking you're building a particular unit, then attacking with another type.

Hit-and-Runs: The art of taking troops to the enemy, inflicting great damage, and retreating before casualties become too high.

Hooks: Usually prebuilt structures on a map that offer a Tech or Economic advantage when claimed.

Hot Dropping: When a unit is quickly transported across the battlefield, usually via a teleporter or Transport Pelican.

Queues: Units or buildings that are ready to be built but that are not currently being constructed.

Scouting: Immediately sending (ideally fast-moving) units to search for supply crates and spy on the enemy's movements.

Sling-Shots: In 2v2 or 3v3 battles, where one or two players send most or all their economy to bolster a single player.

Swarming: When a vast (20+) army of a single, low-level troop type moves and takes down straggling enemies.

Play Styles: Rushing, Booming, Teching, and Turtling

Rushing

A lightly defended base with no troops means victory for this ragtag band of low-Tech-level units.

A risky tactic but one that can result in an early victory, Rushing involves not creating a massive economy in favor of creating a low-Tech-Level army (e.g., consisting of Marines, Flamethrowers, or Warthogs). This army is used to attack the enemy and inflict as much damage as possible. This strategy is excellent to try on maps that have numerous Hooks; if the Rush fails, your teams can fall back and take these Hooks to quickly catch up via the economy or via your Tech level and thus access better units.

To retaliate against a Rush, begin by Scouting to see if your foe is massing an early army. Next, try the following:

A recommended UNSC Rush army: Early Flamethrower units (to scorch enemy infantry) backed up by Warthogs (with the Gunner upgrade) for support and for destroying buildings. If you're well defended against attackers, use the Warthogs to quickly reach the Hooks on the map.

A recommended Covenant Rush army: Immediately harass your opponent with your leader while Hot Dropping units that can destroy buildings (such as Grunts, Hunters, or Brute Infantry). This can be a vicious combination that drives your foes to despair!

Hide a Rush army by locking your base so your Scouting foes can't see what troops you're creating. Then send them out en masse to wreak havoc! If an enemy has a closed base door, this might indicate you should prepare for a flood of troops.

Booming

This base is in full Boom; note the large number of Supply Pads and small number of other building types.

Booming involves not creating any military in order to expand your economy as quickly as possible. Supply Pads are produced rapidly and upgraded to Heavy Supply Pads (or Blessed Warehouses), and usually a second base is utilized for the extra Supply Pad sockets. It is preferably to try Booming when you're on a map with one or two completely undefended empty bases that you can capture with a nonupgraded Ghost or Warthog and then build up quickly. Booming relies on your enemy deciding not to Rush you. If they make this mistake, your enormous economic advantage should allow for a win. Create six Supply Pads before starting to expend your capital on troop creation; however, get ready for a disappointing defeat if your risk doesn't pay off—you're extremely susceptible to an enemy Rush, no matter how feeble!

> **TIP**
>
> As you'd expect, the telltale signs of a Booming strategy is early base expansion, a secondary base, and a large number of Supply Pads with little or no troops. If you spot this, quickly try a Rush. If you're Booming, try locking your bases so your foe isn't quite sure whether you're hiding troops. Apply this tactic to the larger maps or in conjunction with allies who are trying other strategies.

Teching

A fearsome mechanized UNSC division is the ultimate in end-game tactics, crushing foes asunder!

Increasing your Tech level as soon as possible involves building a few Reactors as early as you can and becoming more technologically advanced than your opponent.

Units such as Scorpions and Hornets are commonly upgraded, but there are riskier tactics, too, such as attempting to build higher-Tech-level troops such as Vultures or the Covenant's Scarab. Teching usually requires a small defensive force or troops designed to harass the enemy and keep them occupied while you build up to the devastating units you'll be ending the game with. Teching is extremely effective in 2v2 or 3v3 multiplayer games. When attempted correctly, it can beat even the most determined Rusher. Group-harass all your foes while Teching up as soon as possible.

The Covenant are adept at building a few Ghosts at the beginning of the battle, pretending to Rush around an enemy base, and shooting at the buildings and enemy troops. While the opponent is chasing these Ghosts, the Covenant player uses the time to upgrade the Temple before sending out Locusts or Vampires.

> **TIP**
>
> The Covenant Teching tactics are initially much more difficult because you must change "Ages" at your Temple and because only one Temple is allowed. Counteract this by locating Reactor Hooks; this greatly shortens the time frame for a Teching strategy!

11

> **TIP**
>
> Once you've Teched, you may not need the Reactors. For example, a base or fully upgraded Scorpion still requires only a Tech Level 2 to construct (but requires a Tech Level 4 for all the upgrades). For this reason, you can recycle your Reactors once the upgrades are researched; upgrades still appear on your troops. You can even demolish a Vehicle Depot (or Factory), Barracks (or Hall), or Air Pad (or Summit), and rebuild it at a different location and still have the upgrade already researched.

Remember that each UNSC leader has their own unique unit requiring a Tech Level 4 to create but bringing unparalleled combat effectiveness when created. Of particular note are Sergeant Forge's Grizzly Tanks and Professor Anders's Hawks.

Turtling

Build up your four Turrets, place a Shield Generator (Covenant only), and watch your foe's Rushing plans fail.

The most effective way to counter an enemy Rush is to Turtle—essentially staying in a defensive posture and sending your Warthogs or Ghosts on a Scouting mission to check on your foe. If they have constructed a Barracks (or Hall) suspiciously early into the battle, retaliate by fixing a Turret at each corner of your base (starting with the corner closest to your foes). If you're playing as the Covenant, place at least one Shield Generator on your base. Do this prior to your foe attacking; these defenses slow down any enemy army. The ultimate plan with Turtling is to negate an early enemy force while you (sometimes secretly) either mass a large counter army, or Tech up to a stronger unit. Combine Turtling with base Locking so the troops you are training are more effective when attacking en masse.

> **TIP**
>
> A Covenant base defended by four Turrets and a Shield Generator is notoriously difficult to take down with an early Rushing army.

Play Styles: Attacking and Other Terminology

Ambushing

Place an Air Pad in your base, and your foe is likely to build antiair troops. So double bluff them with an Ambush!

A difficult tactic to try but effective under the correct circumstances, an Ambush works on the premise that you Lock your base, hiding your army from an enemy and disguising the true strength of your forces. Once you reach the maximum Population (or when you have a sizable force), unlock your base, unleash the Ambush on your enemy, and hope you can damage your foe's forces severely before they have time to attack.

> **TIP**
>
> A Covenant example of an Ambush is to build a Summit, with the Brute Chieftain as your leader and with your base Locked. Your opponent will be expecting air units and is likely to start building early antiair units such as Warthogs or Ghosts. Meanwhile, you should quietly train a Brute Infantry in your Citadel, along with a couple of Banshees (to maintain this ruse) so your foe thinks you're building only Banshees. When your Brute Infantry reach a good size, unlock your Citadel and watch as the Brutes pour out and attack your unsuspecting opponent!

> **NOTE**
>
> Locking your base's main ramp doors allows you to train troops without sending them out onto the battlefield. There are several reasons to do this:

1. It stops your foes from seeing just how many troops you have (you can send some out so it looks like you have less troops than you do), allowing you to lure your opponent in to attack you before charging out and massacring them!

2. It fools your opponents, as they don't know which plan you're attempting—you could simply be Teching with a closed door or building up a Rushing army without revealing them. Your foe doesn't know until you show them.

3. During early battles, locked doors indicate a foe is building an army they don't want you to see. As you wage more battles, it becomes clearer that base Locking is a tactic that instills fear into an enemy, unsure of how to react to you.

4. However, you should be able to judge what your foe is doing by the buildings on their base. If they are building Heavy Reactors, for example, you know they are going to be light on units. Judge by the buildings instead of the troops being assembled.

5. Naturally, you can't be sure of the troop types being built, as the Covenant Ambush example shows.

6. If a foe decides to open his base doors, time a perfect Leader Power strike when the crowd of troops appears. This can be a spectacular way to partially nullify this troop buildup!

Hitting-and-Running

A squadron of flying fiends lays into a rival's structures before fleeing to heal and then repeating this effective and annoying tactic.

Veteran players use Hit-and-Run tactics with great skill and judgment, and this is a common tactic with them. Many units are extremely effective at dashing into an opponent's stronghold, blasting it, and then retreating. For example, Hornets are excellent to try due to their maneuverability (difficult terrain doesn't affect them, as they can fly), and initial rocket attacks are effective against enemy vehicles and buildings. This allows you to send Hornets into an enemy base, unleash a missile barrage, and retreat before an enemy response. With longer-ranged units such as the Scorpion, you can flee enemy fire and strike back as you retreat, making this tank a great asset. Long range, high Hit Points, and reasonable speed are what the Scorpion offers and what any Hit-and-Run troop needs. Remember to repair your troops afterward!

Hooks

Strange obelisks and openings in the ground are remnants of Forerunner architecture and are valuable assets to your cause.

Every location on a map that augments your forces is known as a Hook, and all are shown in the "Skirmish and Multiplayer" chapter. Common Hooks include Supply and Reactor locations—essentially a remote location, sometimes guarded by neutral forces. Once you tackle these forces, you can garrison infantry units in the structure and any Sniper Towers nearby. Naturally, these locations may be attacked by your foes, so check them periodically or increase your offensive presence there. Hooks are a quicker way to, for example, quickly increase your supplies or Tech level without losing a Base Socket.

Hot-Dropping

A powerful Covenant leader flanked with an ever-expanding force of appearing foes is the bane of a UNSC player's existence.

Troops don't have to laboriously trek across the battlefield: They can be teleported or transported into the heat of battle in a couple different ways. Aside from teleporters that appear on certain maps, the UNSC player can order a Pelican via the Spirit of Fire menu to take a small group of troops and deposit them anywhere on the battlefield. This is useful when boosting the defenses of a Hook or massing forces near a Scouting unit, ready for a base attack. Meanwhile, the Covenant have a direct line to their leader via a circular teleport at the front of every base. Once the leader is active, additional units are trained as normal, then Hot Dropped, instantly moving from the teleporter to the leader's side. Highly effective in Rushes, Covenant forces can be created and Hot Dropped to soak up the damage for the leader or to quickly tackle troops an enemy attempts to stop your leader with.

Queuing

With a large enough economy, you can begin to queue different troops and buildings. Obviously, the troop and building types depend on your Population, Tech level, and Economy, so react accordingly. However, queuing can become problematic. For example, a Vehicle Depot can only create one "element" at a time. For example, you cannot create the Canister Shell upgrade for a Scorpion and a Scorpion at the same time; one of them must be queued.

Queuing becomes problematic when you're under pressure and need both upgrades and forces at the same time. Each element takes time to build, as indicated by the circular green timer around the element icon. If you've queued up seven Scorpions to build, then decide you want a Canister Shell immediately, there are two options:

1. Build a second Vehicle Depot, allowing you to construct two of each element simultaneously (assuming you have the supplies).

2. Cancel six of the Scorpions but keep constructing the one (or you're simply wasting time). Do this by hitting ✪ in the menu, queuing the Canister, and then adding the six Scorpions back into the queue afterward.

Scouting

A couple of Scouting units check out unexplored locations before gathering supplies.

It is vital that you Scout as much and as early as possible. Use your initial vehicle (a Warthog, Ghost, or Brute Chopper) to scour the entire map looking for: Supply crates (which Scout vehicles and infantry pick up); Hooks (place an infantry garrison inside); and Enemy activity (so you can plan an appropriate strategy).

The more widespread your Scouting is, the quicker you'll achieve these three objectives. Constantly Scout if you can, as a forewarned army is a forearmed one. Start off by Scouting around your initial base to locate the supply crates. If you're worried about a potential Rush, send units over to your enemy's base to check up on them. Make sure you Scout to all corners of the map. When Scouting for supply crates or Hooks, it is preferable to head deep into your opponent's territory, grabbing what you can, and then working backward (or "backfilling"), grabbing crates or Hooks closer to your starting base, so your foes have less chance to gain the upper hand. Naturally, this only works if your opponent is being overly cautious.

Sling-Shooting

The fabled Covenant Scarab: only rarely seen due to the colossal supply costs involved in its creation.

Reserved for 2v2 or 3v3 battles, Sling-Shooting involves one or two players bolstering up the economy of a third player at the expense of their own. Requiring a streamlined and competent communication between allies, Sling-Shooting only works under certain circumstances, such as when one player is close to other enemies but the two other allies are far away or have fully defended bases. The additional funds are used mainly to Tech up and deliver an impressively powerful force (such as a squadron of Hawks or a Scarab) to punch through and turn the tide for your team.

13

Swarming

Take your trusted foot soldiers and begin a mass trek across the battlefield to slay lone enemies.

One last general tactic is the Swarm, which involves either Marines or Grunts and can be extremely effective. It is much easier to execute than any other type of attack already mentioned. Swarming involves massing these low-cost units and simply overwhelming an enemy army with sheer force of numbers rather than the quality of the units. For example, a group of 20 Marines can surround an enemy Scorpion and destroy it in seconds using their Grenade ability. Once you learn to move mass numbers of highly expendable troops, you can quickly decimate a foe, although the longer the battle lasts and the greater the number of clustered enemy troops, the harder this tactic is to pull off.

Leader Powers

Leader Powers are special attacks that each of the six leaders—the UNSC's Cutter, Forge, or Anders, and the Covenant's Arbiter, Brute Chieftain, or Prophet of Regret—possess. UNSC Powers are executed as attacks from the Spirit of Fire; UNSC leaders do not appear on the battlefield (except during Campaign mode). Covenant powers are contained with the leader and are used on the battlefield, directly from the leader. Proper use of a Leader Power can dramatically change the course of a battle.

For example, if Sergeant Forge's army is being attacked by a rival UNSC force consisting of Flamethrowers interspersed with other troops, a well-placed Carpet Bomb can decimate the Marines before they can deal any damage to units vulnerable to Flamethrower attacks. A precisely timed Cryo Bomb from Anders can kill enemy aircraft and immobilize ground forces—and your own forces, so use with care! It is typically more dangerous and less effective to use the powers during a fight; there are less units for you to kill, and you won't have softened up or slain the attackers, giving them more chance to whittle down your own troops.

> **TIP**
>
> While the Covenant Leader Powers work differently, they still follow the same rules. For details on all the Leader Powers, consult the "Factions" chapter.

To become highly ranked, simply practice and try a wide variety of tactics. Play dozens of games using all six leaders, picking the best, learning exactly what your enemy is going to do, and reacting quickly to it. Find a strategy plan that works for you over and over again.

Dealing with an Artificial Intelligent Enemy

Skirmish: Reacting to the Enemy

Although this can apply to other game types, when attacking an AI player in Skirmish mode, there are some additional tactics to try. The AI enemy has six different starting strategies that can branch out depending on your actions, the map, and many other factors. These strategies range from an early Rush to a fully defensive Turtle posture. The AI also prefers to attempt a hit-and-run tactic of hitting your base or units and then fleeing. This makes tackling AI units difficult at times, especially on Legendary difficulty.

When facing an AI Covenant player, rest assured he's probably constructing a Temple first, so expect to see his leader fairly early in battle. React by building a Turret or two and creating some infantry units (such as Flamethrowers) to slow down the Covenant hero; this can withstand a Rush. Be prepared to build or train units as quickly as possible (that is, prior to accessing a Vehicle Depot or Air Pad), because the AI Rush is extremely difficult to defend against if you are unprepared.

AI UNSC players have access to the same six starting strategies but execute them in different ways, depending on the leader. One of these tactics is a Rush, involving a mixture of Marines, Flamethrowers, Spartans (who can really cause problems if they Jack your vehicles) and a few of the leader's special unique units (Cutter's Elephant, Forge's Cyclops, or Anders's Gremlins). Stop this Rush with Turrets (with Flame Mortar or Rail Gun add-ons) and anti-infantry units.

> **TIP**
>
> When facing an AI foe, amass a large force as early as possible. The largest weakness of an AI player is retaliating against or defending a well-executed Rush. So, a large infantry or Warthog/Ghost force early enough is an excellent method of taking down these foes.

AIQ: How the Enemy Reacts to You

Generally, the AI is always aware of everything going on in the battlefield. A lack of human intelligence is balanced by quick reactions and complete knowledge of how the war is going. However, the *Halo Wars* AI experiences human, or more natural, tactical styles. Usually, a human player lacks a deft multitasking ability and concentrates on only one aspect of the fight at a time (managing a fight, building up a base, Tech leveling, training units, gathering supplies, or other activities). The AI mimics this, too, shifting focus after a small amount of time, which diminishes depending on the difficulty setting.

This results in the AI at Normal difficulty having "lapses in concentration," like a beginning player. You may see a foe overly focus on fighting you while ignoring the training of replacement troops. They might send a group of troops to attack, return to base to construct buildings and Tech Level up, but forget to return to manage the battle. Scouting units may idle if a battle is happening elsewhere.

AI Thoughts

When engaged with an AI enemy, a circle on your minimap shows where the AI's focus is. When that circle is over their base, they are usually training or building. When it moves to an enemy base, they are probably sending units to attack that location. When the circle is tracking one of its Scout or attack groups, it is managing those squads and usually ignoring its base. Use this knowledge to your advantage; after a few games, you can get to know your AI foe—or friend, as allies exhibit these tendencies too.

AI Ally Command and Control

As AI allies cannot communicate via headsets, tactical plans are attempted using flares; every flare you launch is interpreted in a different way, and your AI ally reacts accordingly (with a voice to indicate this reaction):

Location of Flare	Usual AI Response	Notes
One flare into an unexplored area	Ally sends a Scout and confirms when the Scout reaches the destination	Helpful for exploring areas you cannot, or don't have time to, reach
One flare into an explored area with no enemies	Ally uses that location as its Rally Point for new squads	Useful to get ally troops together for a joint assault
Two flares into an unexplored area	Ally sets Rally Point at the unexplored location	—
Extra flare after set Rally Point	Ally disengages from any current battles and retreats to the location	—
Flare on an area that has a small enemy force	Ally sends an appropriately sized task force to engage	—
Flare on an area that has a medium enemy force	Ally sends its spare squads to attack	—
Flare on an area that has a huge enemy force	Ally respectfully declines if it doesn't have enough troops to do the job	—
Repeated flare on an area with enemy forces	Ally drops what it's doing and sends all forces to that area, no matter how scary it looks	—
Flare on a friendly base with enemies present	Ally sends a force to defend	—
Flare on an ally's Supply Pad	Ally sends you supplies if it has any available	Repeat for multiple deliveries
Flare on your Supply Pad	All allies send you supplies if available	Repeat for multiple deliveries

AI Changes and Difficulty Levels

Your AI enemy has the power to crush you instantly, or forget where you are completely, and this is due to the sliding scale of difficulty, ranging from 20 (Easy) to 100 (Legendary). When facing an AI opponent on Normal or Heroic difficulties, they receive no economic bonuses, statistic tweaks, or other bonuses. Instead, a Normal AI foe tends to periodically forget

to place buildings, or becomes overly focused on a battle and forgets to train new squads, or doesn't train units to effectively counter yours. Compare these foibles to an AI foe on Heroic difficulty, who has a much more focused game and can be considered to be playing as effectively as a human who has mastered the game.

The greater the difficulty, the more cunning, murderous, and reinforced your enemy becomes.

A Legendary AI player is akin to challenging a grand master: a tournament-level, top-ten ranked foe with an answer for every one of your choices, sometimes before you think of them! Legendary difficulty can be beaten, but only after you thoroughly master the game. Many seasoned players still win only half their battles against a Legendary Skirmish opponent. Legendary AI players receive statistic and economy boosts to reach this level of intensity.

TIP

When selecting a game, one of the difficulty options is "Automatic Difficulty," which tracks your performance and adjusts the difficulty between games so you're challenged no matter what your skill level. It begins a little tougher (40) than the Normal rating and can continue beyond Legendary rating (100) if you're a true master of this game.

Statistically, on a scale from 0 to 100, the difficulty levels are rated as follows:

Difficulty	Rating	Difficulty	Rating
Easy	0	Heroic	67
Normal	33	Legendary	100

Dealing with More Than One Foe

Adapting to more than one foe is the key to winning a 2v2 or 3v3 battle, and this comes down to understanding the specific facets of every unit. For example, if a foe erects a Barracks early, this should alert you to a potential Rush, and you should react accordingly (e.g., retaliate with Jackals or Flamethrowers or anti-infantry units). If a foe heads at you with Marines and a Scorpion, nullify these units—in this case, with a Spartan to Jack the Scorpion, or Hunters—or speak to your allies to bring in help.

In large-scale battles, a defensive play is usually best early in the fight. Construct some Turrets so you avoid enemies Scouting your base for weak points. With Turrets, a foe may have a unit advantage over you, but the power of the Turrets, combined with an attack from your Leader Power (either via the Spirit of Fire with the UNSC, or on the ground as the Covenant) overcomes this. Highly mobile units such as Warthogs, Ghosts, Hornets, and Banshees are effective when tackling multiple foes, as you can swiftly move from a defensive point to attacking a foe without losing time or becoming too vulnerable. But nothing beats good communication and teamwork (via a headset or flares). Remember tried-and-true techniques such as providing support or resources and "piling on" with multiple Leader Power attacks at the same enemy fortification or squad.

15

Tactical Tips

Part I: UNSC Forces

- The Marines' Grenade ability is useful for dealing damage to buildings or infantry.
- Flamethrowers can stun enemy infantry with their Flash Bang ability.
- Spartans can take over enemy vehicles with their Jack ability, adding their combat strength to the vehicle.
- Spartans have several upgrades that change their weapons from SMGs to a chain gun, and eventually to a Spartan laser.
- The Warthog is fast and great for Scouting and quickly gathering supply crates.
- Use the Warthog's Ram ability to knock enemy infantry units around the map.
- The main UNSC vehicle is the Scorpion. Its Canister Shell ability enhances its attack power against infantry.
- Cobras are good against other vehicles. Build them to neutralize enemy tanks.
- Cobras can lock down, which increases their range. Lock them down by enemy bases and shell the buildings from a distance.
- If you're having trouble dealing with enemy air power, try building Wolverines. They excel at taking down air units.
- The Hornet is the mainline UNSC air unit; useful at both offense and recon.
- The Vulture's Barrage ability is a deadly area attack with multiple missiles. Use Barrage against enemy groups or bases.
- The Elephant is difficult to destroy. Lock down an area. Use it as a forward base.
- When Elephants are locked down, they can train infantry. Use them to quickly get fresh troops to the front lines.
- In addition to destroying buildings, Cyclopes can pick up and throw enemy units.
- The Chain Amplifier allows Gremlins to hit up to three targets with an EMP blast.
- Professor Anders's special unit—the Gremlin—is good against vehicles.
- The Hawk is an improved Hornet, available only to Professor Anders.
- The Grizzly is an upgraded Scorpion tank that is available only to Sergeant Forge.
- Cutter's ODST serves the same role as the Marine, but he's better in every way.

Part II: Covenant Forces

- Upgrades for Grunt squads adds additional Grunts and eventually give them Needlers.
- Jackals are effective in an anti-infantry role. Use them against Marines or Grunts.
- Hunters are particularly good against vehicles, but they should be kept away from enemy aircraft.
- The Spirit Bond upgrade allows Hunter pairs to do bonus damage as long as both are alive.
- The Wraith is the Covenant's mainline vehicle. Its Heavy Shield upgrade deflects a percentage of incoming damage.
- The Covenant Locust, like the UNSC Cyclops, is primarily a building killer.
- The Locust's Overdrive ability dramatically increases its attack power at the expense of its shields.
- When a Scarab appears on the battlefield, no enemy is safe. The Scarab can only be defeated by concentrated firepower.
- The Banshee is the Covenant's mainline air unit and is effective against most targets except its direct counters.
- Use Vampires to counter enemy air units. Upgrade their Stasis ability and the Vampire will drain enemy Hit Points to heal itself.
- Engineers are the only known noncombatant Covenant race. Experts at repairing things, they heal damaged units.
- The Ghost is a fast, cheap Scouting unit. Don't expect it to go toe-to-toe with most enemy units.
- The Brute Chopper is an improved heavy scout, only available to the Brute Chieftain.
- The Brute's Electric Shot upgrade adds electrical stun damage to his weapon.
- The Suicide Grunt's high-damage special attack is effective against many types of units.
- The Arbiter's Rage power lets him cut through entire enemy armies.
- The Arbiter's Ghastly Vision upgrade enables him to permanently cloak.
- The Prophets of Regret, Truth, and Mercy came to power in 2525, usurping the power of the previous Hierarchs.
- The Prophet's Cleansing ability does lots of damage to all types of enemy units.
- Want to enhance the Prophet's mobility? Get the Divine Absolution upgrade and he becomes a full-fledged flying unit!
- Use the Brute Chieftain's Vortex to damage large groups of enemies.
- The Brute Chieftain's Destiny upgrade adds an area-of-effect stun to his attacks.
- Try slipping cloaked Elites behind enemy forces to strike at their weaker support units.
- Use the Wraith's Scorch ability to deny an angle of approach to enemy forces.
- Banshees with the Sacrifice ability will crash into a ground target when destroyed, doing area-of-effect damage.
- The Engineer's State of Grace upgrade dramatically improves its ability to heal.

Part III: Basic Gameplay Hints

- Put your infantry in cover whenever possible. Cover increases their range, line of sight, and Hit Points.
- Use ❶ to move around the map.
- Pressing ❶ will send a flare to your allies. This is useful for quickly telling an ally where you plan to attack.
- If you flare a location, your AI ally will try to help attack or defend there.
- Proper use of Rally Points allows you to get fresh units to the front lines. Try both Global Rally Points and Rally Points set from bases.
- Double-clicking ❶ will set your Global Rally Point to that location.
- Use ❶ to change your camera's rotation and zoom. Press it once to reset to default.
- Use ❍ to jump around the map quickly. Advanced players will use it more often than ❶.
- Press ❺ to quickly jump to your Covenant leader.
- Press ❻ to cycle through the last few alert messages.
- Press ❼ to jump from base to base.
- Pressing ❶ will cycle you through all your armies around the map. This is helpful when planning a multifront assault.
- Select a unit with ❹. You can also hold down ❹ to get a paint brush that will select any unit it touches.
- Group selection and management is important in *Halo Wars*. To select all the units on the screen, press ❽.
- Press ❾ to select all the units in the game at one time.
- Use ❿ to cycle through the unit types you have selected. Expert players will use this to give orders to individual unit types.
- To move around the map quickly, hold down ⓛ when you scroll with ❶ to quadruple the camera speed.
- Press ❽ to cancel a selection or close a menu.
- The primary Action button is ❽. It will command your selected units to move around the map or attack enemies.
- The Secondary Ability button is ❹. Most units have secondary abilities that dramatically alter what you can do with those units.
- At any point in the campaign, press ❾ to see your objectives.
- Pause the game with ❾. Now you can change options or turn on Skulls during a game.
- Move commands can be queued up for sequential execution by briefly holding down ❽ when giving commands.
- When you select any unit, it tells you what type of unit it is. This can be invaluable in deciding how to counter your enemy's forces.

Part IV: Battlefield Roles

- In Skirmish games, UNSC players can choose between Captain Cutter, Sergeant Forge, or Professor Anders. Each comes with several unique additions that alter play style.
- The Covenant has three leaders to choose from for a Skirmish game: the Arbiter, the Prophet of Regret, and the Brute Chieftain.
- Unlike the UNSC leaders, each Covenant leader personally appears on the battlefield.
- The UNSC army is professional and regimented. Overall, each UNSC unit is slightly stronger than each Covenant unit.
- The Covenant forces are led by charismatic leaders who drive their zealous followers to fight against humanity with little concern for any individual's well-being.
- While each Covenant unit is somewhat weaker than an equivalent UNSC soldier, the overall Covenant army size is bigger than the UNSC's.
- The Covenant leaders are the strongest units on the battlefield, though a well-managed group of three Spartans can do a lot of damage too.
- UNSC and Covenant leader powers can be upgraded with technologies. Some upgrades even add new abilities.
- Covenant leaders are upgraded at the Temple. Each upgrade increases the leader's combat power and adds interesting new passive abilities.
- Covenant Leader Powers cost few supplies to activate but require additional supplies to keep active. Be careful not to spend all your supplies on one power!
- Captain Cutter can call down the MAC Blast power from Spirit of Fire. Akin to an oversized sniper rifle, the MAC Blast is great for taking out single targets.
- Every new base Captain Cutter builds starts one level higher than normal.
- The Elephant is Captain Cutter's unique unit. He can also upgrade his Marines to ODST.
- Forge's unique power is the Carpet Bomb; the ultimate grenade for ground foes.
- With the Cyclops unique unit and the Grizzly upgrade, Sergeant Forge displays his fondness for strategies that focus on heavy units.
- Sergeant Forge's Supply Pads cost more than normal Supply Pads, but they start with the Heavy Supply Pad upgrade, resulting in a faster midgame economy.
- The Cryo Bomb is the main Spirit of Fire power for Professor Anders. It freezes ground units in their tracks and can knock flying units out of the air.
- Fancy units are the thing for Professor Anders. The Gremlin unique unit can immobilize other ground vehicles while the Hawk superunit can dominate the sky.

16

- Because of Professor Anders's science background, her research into unit and Leader Power upgrades is completed more quickly and at a reduced cost.
- The Arbiter's Rage Power channels his irrepressible evil into one long fatality string. Use ⓑ to initiate quick-jump fatalities in this mode.
- Befitting his disregard for his troops, the Arbiter's unique unit is the Suicide Grunt squad. The Suicide Grunts' special ability detonates their methane tanks.
- The Prophet of Regret can call down the massive Cleansing power. This beam of energy, even in its weakest form, is pure devastation for anything it hits.
- Elite Honor Guards protect the Prophet and serve as his unique unit. Equipped with the Cloak ability, these Elites are excellent for sneak attacks.
- The Prophet of Regret's third combat upgrade converts his floating chair into a flying chair, giving him exciting new tactical potential.
- The Brute Chieftain's power is the gravity-related Vortex. Steer it around the combat zone to pull in enemies, then unleash the stored power with ⓐ.
- Jet Pack Brutes complement the Brute Chieftain leader. These heavy infantry units can use their jet packs to cross impassable terrain.

Part V: Light Lessons in Strategy

- *Halo Wars* has a rock-paper-scissors balance between the unit types. Vehicles beat infantry, aircraft beat vehicles, and infantry beat aircraft.
- Counter-units are great at killing one type of unit but are worse against any other unit. One counter-unit example is the anti-infantry UNSC Flamethrower.
- Multitask: Units will continue to think on their own even if you're off someplace else.
- The Fog of War covers the areas of the map that your units cannot currently see. Scout frequently to make sure you know what your enemies are up to.
- You can increase the troop limit. The technologies that do this are in the UNSC Field Armory and Covenant Temple.
- If you're looking for a quick way to select your units, try either ⓡⓑ (all units on screen) or ⓛⓑ (all units in the world).
- Different units require different amounts of resources, Tech levels, and available army space to train. Stronger units usually cost more and require more army space.
- To try a Rush strategy, attack quickly and aggressively. Train military units as soon as possible, apply pressure to the enemy's base, and don't let up until you win.
- To try a Boom strategy, build only a few cheap Scouting units to take control of additional bases. Build Supply Pads in all bases to maximize your economy before building up your military.
- To try a Turtle strategy, build towers at the front of your base and upgrade your Command Center. Use the base defenses to stall the enemy until your technology allows you to train vehicles or air units.
- If you'd like access to better units and upgrades, you must improve your Tech level. Build Reactors (UNSC) or research the Temple's Age upgrades (Covenant).
- Try matching up counter-units against the units they can best kill. For instance, use Cobras to take on enemy Wraiths and Ghosts.
- Most strategies should involve building at least two types of units. This approach will give you some sort of answer for the majority of enemy units.
- For a simple strategy, build just one type of mainline unit and upgrade it all the way.
- Don't ignore postgame statistics. You can learn a lot about how to improve your game.

Part VI: Interesting Insights

- If you're playing as the Arbiter, try running him near the enemy base and then Hot Dropping Suicide Grunts to blow up a few buildings.
- If you're playing as the Covenant, try a leader Rush. Just build a Temple and Warehouses, then attack the enemy base with the leader's special ability.
- Try the Elephant Rush: Build one Elephant and then lots of Supply Pads. Lock down the Elephant just outside your opponent's base and churn out Marines.
- If you're playing as Anders, Gremlins and Flamethrowers are a devastating combination in large groups.
- Jackals and Hunters complement each other well.
- When playing as Forge, try massing Flamethrowers and then using your Carpet Bomb to kill enemies that can counter the Flamethrowers.
- One simple Boom strategy is building four or five Flamethrowers and using them to grab map-specific buildings and additional bases.
- If you micromanage the Prophet of Regret and give him time to recharge his shields, he can take out the enemies around map-specific buildings all by himself.
- The Brute Chopper is stronger than either the Ghost or the Warthog.
- Covenant buildings and bases are naturally weaker than their UNSC counterparts. Be sure to add a Shield Generator.
- To gain Veterancy, kill foe around map-specific buildings with your Covenant leader.
- Whenever you have a free building site and you're not sure what to build, a Supply Pad or a Warehouse is always a good choice.
- Garrisoning infantry in a Forerunner bonus Reactor is a great way to advance your Tech level without having to build a Reactor or purchase a Temple upgrade.
- Garrisoning infantry inside a Forerunner Supply Elevator grants a nice boost to supply resources.
- The Protector Plant offers a selection of protector units that can boost the unit you

attach them to with shields, healing, or firepower.
- You can purchase Forerunner Sentinel units, including the unit-disabling Super Sentinel, at the Sentinel Factory.
- If you have damaged units, moving them near a Forerunner Spire of Healing will quickly get them back to full health.
- Controlling the Forerunner Life Support Pod will allow you to build larger armies by increasing your Population limit.
- Garrisoning infantry in an Energy Wall will create a barrier that will deny mobility to ground units. This can help you hold ground or block choke points.
- Sending units into a Forerunner Teleporter instantly moves them to another Teleporter location. A flare on your minimap will help you see where your units have reappeared.
- The team that controls a Mega-Turret is a force to be reckoned with. Garrison infantry inside and blast away.
- Sniper Towers are great defensive structures. An infantry squad inside can stand their ground against forces that would normally overwhelm them.
- Minibase locations let you gain extra building sites by allowing you to construct a single building on them.
- Fortify areas away from your base by building on stand-alone Turret sites. Once claimed, these Turret locations will match the upgrade level of your own Turrets.

Part VII: During Your Campaign Missions

- Become proficient at cycling through selected units with ⓡⓣ: This is used to quickly single out important units, such as your Campaign Spartans, Forge, or Anders.
- Remember to consistently check your Spirit of Fire (SOF) menu (⬦). SOF Leader Powers are granted under many different circumstances, and some are free to use. Periodically check the power's timers to see what is accessible.
- Sometimes it is beneficial to let Forge or a Spartan stay down until they are fully healed.
- Remember that Spartan shields regenerate for about 10 to 12 seconds when they are away from combat. They also regenerate their shield right after they are revived from being down.
- Remember Flood Colonies (dormant for 220 seconds), Dens (dormant for 120 seconds), and Nests (dormant for 90 seconds) stop spawning while they are dormant.
- Move infantry units into cover whenever possible: It gives an enormous boost to your offense and defense.
- In Cooperative campaigns, have one player supervise the base construction, resources, and Spirit of Fire powers while the other controls the armies and fighting. This way, confusion is kept to a minimum.
- In Cooperative campaigns, there is an option in the Spirit of Fire menu that allows you to send units to each other, which is extremely helpful.
- An adept player always keeps their army at maximum Population. Having a quick and steady resource income is vital; that supply counter can never spin too quickly!
- Keep constant watch on your units' special ability (ⓥ) timers when you employ the attack. Once recharged, these abilities are exceptional and can help you survive an otherwise terminal fight.
- Scout and gather loose crates all the time. You never know when you may need 100 extra resources.
- Live your life hating, finding, and killing all Jackals. They hate you anyway.

Part VIII: Multiplayer Takedown Tactics

- Rushing is tactically much more difficult in a 1v1 match, compared to a 2v2 or 3v3 battle.
- Mobile units (such as Hornets, Banshees, Vultures, or Vampires, or to a lesser extent Warthogs, Ghosts, and Brute Choppers) are favored in team games to quickly reach long distances, whether you're raiding enemy installations or helping your allies.
- Using combinations of Covenant leader or Spirit of Fire powers is very important in team games. For example, launching Anders's Cryo Bomb makes Forge's Carpet Bomb much more damaging; launch them quickly, one after another. Have you tried sending two Covenant leaders to rampage through the same enemy base at once?
- Try sending a double (or triple) UNSC Pelican Transport of units to a foe's base for an unexpected and nasty surprise.
- Rushing is more effective and easier to attempt with allies, as you can double-team a single enemy, especially if you're both playing as the Covenant—imagine the problems if you both hack at a single foe's base and Hot Drop troops to help you!. This is even worse for the enemy if his friend is far away.
- Professor Anders is an especially impressive leader in team games. Her Cryo Bomb works well with other Leader Powers. She also has the airborne Hawk (a "Super Hornet") that rules the skies.
- It is easier to specialize in one unit type in multiplayer battles; one ally can exclusively build Hornets, the other can construct a Scorpion division, and both can cover each other's weaknesses, allowing you to Tech level up to more powerful upgrades as fast as possible.
- In 1v1 battles, specializing in one unit isn't usually successful; it is wise to upgrade at least two unit lines so you can react to every enemy your foe tries to counter you with.
- In team games, you can abandon Forerunner structures (Hooks) and give them to your ally. This enables you to, say, quickly take a Reactor Hook whether you need it or not, then step away when your ally needs it so you can both upgrade your troops without each building Reactors.

17

UNSC

COVENANT

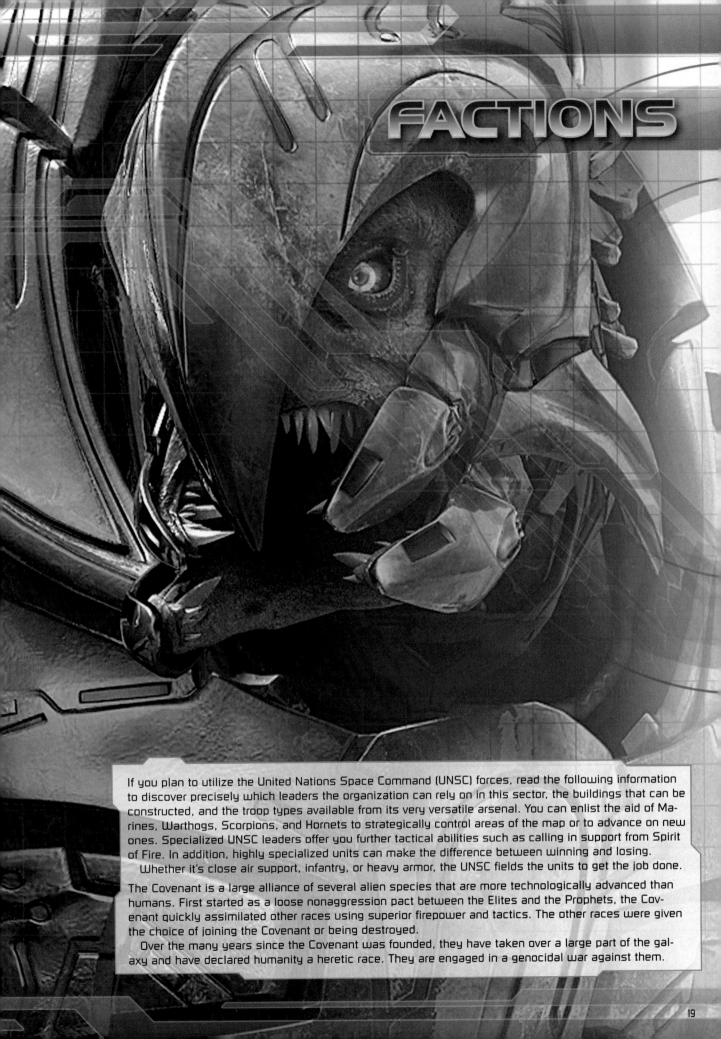

FACTIONS

If you plan to utilize the United Nations Space Command (UNSC) forces, read the following information to discover precisely which leaders the organization can rely on in this sector, the buildings that can be constructed, and the troop types available from its very versatile arsenal. You can enlist the aid of Marines, Warthogs, Scorpions, and Hornets to strategically control areas of the map or to advance on new ones. Specialized UNSC leaders offer you further tactical abilities such as calling in support from Spirit of Fire. In addition, highly specialized units can make the difference between winning and losing.

Whether it's close air support, infantry, or heavy armor, the UNSC fields the units to get the job done.

The Covenant is a large alliance of several alien species that are more technologically advanced than humans. First started as a loose nonaggression pact between the Elites and the Prophets, the Covenant quickly assimilated other races using superior firepower and tactics. The other races were given the choice of joining the Covenant or being destroyed.

Over the many years since the Covenant was founded, they have taken over a large part of the galaxy and have declared humanity a heretic race. They are engaged in a genocidal war against them.

UNSC LEADERS

Captain James Gregory Cutter

Background Details

Age: 52
Height: 6'1"
Weight: 195 lb.
Hair Color: Black
Eye Color: Blue

Captain Cutter commands Spirit of Fire; his confidence in those around him is matched by a strong loyalty amongst the crew. His stance and his voice immediately identify him as a leader, and an intelligent, unambiguous, and thoughtful one at that. His face is slightly older-looking than his actual age, and he has some gray around the fringes of his hair, but his energy and determination are that of a man half his years. Cutter is almost always at attention, listening to his advisors and crew. He is constantly on the move and has little need for pomp and circumstance. This lack of flourish may be why he is the kind of man who so many rally to, making him the perfect leader for the fight ahead.

Cutter was an officer from the start. But his demeanor was never one of a do-nothing officer like many of his class. Many of the young men had political aspirations far beyond their potential, but Cutter found it more interesting to "talk shop" in the soldier's club with the non-officers. Cutter liked his fellow officers, but he believed in "get[ting] to know and respect your men, and they'll give you 200 percent when the time comes."

But this approach had good and bad sides. Cutter had served on seven ships, two of them as captain, and had a record of service and bravery that were well known within the fleet. But it was his lack of political ambition, his unwillingness to climb the ladder of the UNSC by stepping over others, that kept him from far more. He could easily have been a general if he had ever cared to be.

Cutter was selected for the Spirit of Fire first and was the only man they wanted for the job. Where some would have seen this as a job lacking in prestige—being the supply boat of the fleet—running a 2,500-meter-long, 5,500-person juggernaut that always had an assignment with more missions waiting in the wings was something that made Cutter smile behind his morning coffee.

"I have a bridge to look after here."

Cutter looked out over the bridge and took in the view. Slipspace always reflected and lit the exterior of the ship in an unnatural and unwelcoming light. The vast size of Spirit of Fire stretched out serenely in this odd sea. The orders were quite specific: rendezvous with The Prophecy and join the fleet en route to Harvest. He had always liked the word "rendezvous" ever since he got it right on Mrs. Ash's sixth-grade spelling test. He unconsciously sounded it out and Serina flickered on.

"The Prophecy is a good ship—could have been your ship if you had taken them up on the chair," Serina quipped. She said it loudly enough that Blake looked up from his console.

"I'm happy with the seat I have, Serina." Cutter glared back.

And in truth he was. Spirit of Fire was the largest operational ship in the fleet, and while it wasn't the fastest and didn't boast the best weaponry or military complement, it was the one ship every other captain in the fleet was happy to see. Spirit of Fire brought supplies, water, fuel—and ground support to the field. More importantly for Cutter, Spirit of Fire was stationed at Reach and generally wasn't part of long tours of duty. Cutter thought of his daughter and wondered if she had a spelling test today or not. He also knew that by passing on The Prophecy command that his chances of being offered something as prestigious again were slim. In fact, he had already heard rumor to that effect. The choice had been easy, though, and he had no regrets.

"Hello! Ship AI on deck!" Serina brought him out of the moment and back to the bridge. "Well, I would have hated to break in a new captain anyway; took me long enough to get you where I want you."

"Thank you, Serina. I think. How are we doing?"

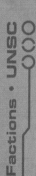

Serina could get under his skin, and she knew it. The AI was necessary to run the ship, and her sometimes flippant character didn't betray the complexity of her second-to-second duties. However, sometimes Cutter thought he could do without the running commentary.

"Loaded for bear, sir. We should exit Slipspace in thirty-two hours, twelve minutes. Professor Anders has requested better quarters and insists on seeing you. Apparently you must know the ship layout better than me because I told her—"

Cutter interrupted, "Mister Blake, please go see to our guest. I have a bridge to look after here."

Blake looked around the largely empty bridge. Lieutenant Green peered up from the flight control; he was sure Serina was looking at him smugly.

"Yes, sir!" Blake barked as he made for the door. He thought to himself that he would never be babysitting civilians if he was on The Prophecy.

Serina paused, waiting for Blake to leave. "So, Mr. Captain, sir, what do you think 'loaded for bear' actually means?"

Cutter sat down and pushed back in the chair. His mind fixated on the empty seat Blake had vacated, and he thought back to his long days as an Ensign in the fleet. His father had pushed him to get his degree and was furious that he had signed up for the UN Colony logistics office and even more furious when he applied to flight school. "Nothing more than a trucker!" He could still hear the words echo.

Piloting colony ships was mind-numbing work, but it gave him experience and eventually earned him command of the Glasgow, a colony freighter vessel. It wasn't special, but he pulled his runs, and after an incident with insurgents in the Epsilon Eridani system, he gained the attention of UNSC command.

His mind moved to his father again and the redeeming words he later said when he toured the ship with his son—the new captain on the Spirit of Fire. "I guess you knew something, after all. Your mom would be proud." This was all he said, but it was enough.

Cutter sighed. "Serina, it means that tomorrow is going to be a long day."

Leadership Qualities and Tactical Notes

Unique Troop Type: Elephant

Accessed via the Firebase, the Elephant synergizes well with Cutter's base bonus (Leadership Quality #4); this means you can save another socket and construct an Elephant instead of a Barracks if you need infantry (although the Barracks is needed to upgrade the infantry). Elephants are also excellent at Rushing early into a battle; lock it down just outside an enemy base and constantly train troops from it. Elephants are adept at defensive posturing as well; place them to the sides or the rear of your base to act as an additional turret (when Deployed using ⓨ) and to train infantry defenders in the event of an enemy Rush. Be warned: Attempting an early Rush against Cutter, who has an Elephant or two, is ill-advised!

Leader Power: MAC Blast (◊, then ◊ + Ⓐ)

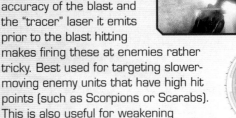

Accessing the MAC Blast from the Spirit of Fire can have devastating consequences, but the pinpoint accuracy of the blast and the "tracer" laser it emits prior to the blast hitting makes firing these at enemies rather tricky. Best used for targeting slower-moving enemy units that have high hit points (such as Scorpions or Scarabs). This is also useful for weakening buildings you're already attacking. There are less opportunities to use this power defensively.

TIP

You can upgrade your MAC Blast a total of three times to shoot four blasts—if you have the Supplies and Reactor levels! For more information, consult the "Spirit of Fire" section.

Super Unit: Orbital Drop Shock Trooper (ODST)

The most powerful non-Spartan infantry unit is the Orbital Drop Shock Trooper (ODST), an additional upgrade accessed via the Barracks. ODSTs aren't often a battle-changing advantage, as they are available only after numerous Marine upgrades, and infantry aren't as effective as vehicles and aircraft later in a battle. However, dropping ODSTs into the middle of any fight can sometimes turn the tide of a large fight. You need only line of sight for a Drop (via the Spirit of Fire), and you can release up to ten ODSTs (population permitting) to help support your army or attack enemy buildings effectively. Try splitting the ODSTs you drop from your other attacking units so your foe must split their fire to attack two sets of your forces.

Starting Advantage: All Bases Start at One Higher Tech Level

Cutter's initial Firebase has already been upgraded to Fortress level, with seven building sockets ready at the start of battle (additional bases start at one higher Tech level, giving you instant access to Turret sockets and five building sockets). This saves you time and expenses (400 Supply Points per base) and is a huge advantage early in the game, giving you extra flexibility. Without having to wait for this upgrade to build, you can elect to construct Reactors or mass troops earlier in battle without waiting around for base improvements.

Tactical Notes

The further a battle progresses, the weaker Cutter becomes of the three UNSC leaders (however, he is the strongest early on). This is because his ODSTs are not as effective as Grizzlies or Hawks, and his Leader Power is a pinpoint blast that isn't as flexible an attack as those of the other leaders. Take advantage early in the battle to secure a win, or the other leaders may eventually train units that walk all over your defenses.

21

Sergeant John Forge

Background Details

Sergeant Forge is of average height, muscular in build, and particularly formidable even in his relaxed posture. Decades of military training, discipline, and service have made his movement purposeful and reflexive, and never really relaxed. Lines on his face, especially his brow, indicate that this man doesn't laugh much. Forge has a strong jaw, a cleanly shaven bald head, and a tight mouth that is very often silent, even when he has an opinion that he wants to voice. When he does speak, his voice is strong and cadent and has an almost military precision. He is not philosophical; rather, he maintains a matter-of-fact grasp of the situation that can be a great asset if listened to. Forge has a knife that he always keeps close, and he is well trained in many different types of weapons.

Age: 29
Height: 6'3"
Weight: 215 lb.
Hair Color: N/A (Bald)
Eye Color: Blue

Forge's life has been the military. He entered boot camp at the minimum age, which was 16. There was something unique and special about him; at least, that was what the officers had told him. It wasn't that he was as physically gifted as some older cadets, though he was strong for his size and weight. It was the desire and toughness he displayed in the way he did just about everything. The fact that he was incredibly competitive and driven to succeed didn't hurt either. These qualities made him a lifetime member of the Corps. Forge was now a warrior, but that was all he was. His training and discipline had left him with a "unique" personality and method of getting things done. He had lost pretty much all contact with his family. His wife was a distant shadow in his mind, but his daughter had never really given up on him, though it had been months since they had talked.

Forge was a sergeant, but that was about as far up the ladder as he was going to go. He had been jailed at least twice (by the official record) for directly disobeying orders and for disorderly conduct. What the record didn't say was that he had saved the lives of four of his squad and that he had defended his daughter in an officer's bar. But these altercations meant little to him. Now nearing 30, Forge is a grizzled, seasoned veteran who has seen and done almost everything in a military sense. He is no-nonsense, tough, unapologetic, always on his guard, and slightly pessimistic about the universe in general.

"Spirit of Bloody Fire. Cutter. Bloody hell."

Forge opened his eyes and looked up into the sun. Quickly closing them again, he tried to remember what sequence of events had led to him waking up outside. The sounds were off, though, echoing wrong and way too quiet. He opened his eyes a second time and realized that the sun was actually a single lightbulb high up on a concrete ceiling. He sat up and looked out through iron bars.

"Bloody hell. Jail." He lay back down and closed his eyes again.

"On your feet, Sergeant!" An MP rapped the bars with his clipboard. "You've got a visitor."

Forge thought about staying down, but when a military man like Forge is told to stand, he finds himself on his feet before the thought even finishes.

"Bloody hell," he repeated. He wasn't at his best and was in civilian clothes and obviously in a military jail. The events of the previous night flooded back, and his overnight accommodations now seemed to be a luxury compared to the pain that was sure to follow.

"Admiral! Admiral Cole, sir!" Forge straightened up and stood at attention. He felt naked in these civilian clothes. His discomfort was obvious.

"Sergeant Forge. At ease."

Cole looked him over, and right away Forge knew he was in deep trouble, a ranked admiral in the cell, and Cole at that. His career flashed before his eyes. He had joined up straight from high school. His father had been in the military, as had his father before that. His grandfather once told him that the military family line could be traced all the way back to World War II. It was in his blood. He had worked his way through a stint as an MP on Mars and had done grunt time on Epsilon Eridani IV during the insurrections, but he disliked policing and jumped at the chance to be assigned to Fort Marshall. Cole quickly cut the thought off.

22

"Sergeant Forge. It took three MPs to haul your ass off that man last night. He wants you charged with assault. Is there any reason I shouldn't ship you off to Phobos penal colony right now?"

"Sir. Permission to speak freely, sir?"

"You don't normally need permission to speak your mind, Sergeant, but go on."

"Sir. That drunk—"

Cole interrupted him. "Sergeant, 'that drunk' is Lieutenant Prosser."

The penny dropped. He had assaulted a superior officer. He was dead.

"Lieutenant Prosser. Well, sir, I was just having a conversation with him about how when a lady says no, she really means no."

Cole was obviously not amused. "And that took fists, Sergeant?"

"He didn't listen too good, sir."

Cole sighed. "Fortunately for you, Sergeant, a witness came forward and verified your story. DNA evidence confirms it too. Charges against Lieutenant Prosser are being filed as we speak. She called you a hero in her statement, says you saved her life."

Forge faltered. He might be done for, but that sick bastard was going down too. "Is she okay, sir?"

Cole smiled for the first time since entering the room. "She'll be fine, Sergeant. I'm looking for a volunteer to lead a squad into a hostile environment. Very hostile environment. Can you think of anyone qualified? I can cut tape to make it happen."

Forge saw the rope for what it was. "I reckon I do, sir."

Cole smiled again. "I thought you might. Report to Captain Cutter ASAP on Spirit of Fire. I told him to expect you already. And, Forge?"

"Yes, sir?"

"You're a good father."

Cole turned to walk out. Forge saluted as he left and then sat back down on the bunk. He stared down at the floor. "Spirit of Bloody Fire. Cutter. Bloody hell."

Leadership Qualities and Tactical Notes

Unique Troop Type: Cyclops

If you're seeking other ways to heal your troops other than with the Spirit of Fire (or the high-level Medic upgrade that heals only Marines), then the Cyclops is an ideal troop to augment a platoon of tanks. Cyclops move slowly and aren't well armored, but they fight well against small amounts of infantry and are excellent at annoying foes with their impressive building-demolishing abilities. You won't cover much ground, but Cyclops can heal your own troops or hurt enemy fortifications, giving you extra flexibility in the combat zone.

Leader Power: Carpet Bomb (◊, then ◊ + ◎)

If the enemy knows you have a Carpet Bomb, they are more likely to keep their troops moving and in smaller groups. If they don't, then launch a barrage at them! Carpet Bombs are useful against enemies attempting to Rush your position; you are often able to repel a foe with two Turrets and this Leader Power. It is also great for weakening vehicles and infantry (but misses airborne units), but don't damage your own troops with it!

TIP

You can upgrade your Carpet Bomb a total of three times to lengthen the carpeting and strength of the attack—if you have the Supplies and Reactor levels. For more information, consult the "Spirit of Fire" section.

Super Unit: Grizzly

Aside from the enormous expense to upgrade to Grizzlies, this tank variant (built as the fourth upgrade for the Scorpion, but only when you're playing as Forge) is the most terrifying vehicle available to the UNSC, especially en masse or with a Spartan at the controls. These units are extremely well armored, and a full contingent of Grizzly units with a bolstered population is the most effective single-unit army available on either side. If your supplies can withstand the cost, upgrade and lay waste!

Starting Advantage: Builds Heavy Supply Pads Right Away

Sergeant Forge never builds Supply Pads; he builds only Heavy Supply Pads, effectively saving you 100 Supply Points per pad you construct. Early access to Heavy Supply Pads gives you the ultimate economic advantage once you've spent the initial 225 Supply Points on an instant Heavy Supply Pad. This bonus is useful during the middle of a battle when your economy is likely to be much improved over your opponent's, leading to quicker defenses or troop creation.

Tactical Notes

Forge's higher Supply Pad cost is also a burden during the initial stages of battle. Because you're likely to run out of supplies when constructing two Heavy Pads and a Reactor to start your base's building activity, you may be susceptible to a strong Rush by a foe early on. If you're unprepared for this, your base can be ransacked very quickly. Combat this by Scouting using Warthogs—for supplies and for any potential of a large enemy Rush. If this never comes, plan on a mechanized tank division to lay waste to your foes.

23

Professor Ellen Anders

Background Details

Age: 27
Height: 5'10"
Weight: 114 lb.
Hair Color: Dark brown
Eye Color: Brown

A scientist to the core, Anders has spent her life in the service of science and learning. This is her first experience with any kind of combat, and the lack of organization and uncertainty of war make her extremely uneasy. She has made her life a compartmentalized, mundane, and scheduled existence, and she has no personal life.

Anders, already dramatically shaken by the reality of war, is forced to be paired with Forge, and everything about him only makes her feel more uneasy. She is nervous, impatient, worried, and uncertain about her surroundings, even though matters have apparently calmed down. To help herself cope emotionally, she has focused on the one plan of action in all of this that fascinated her—the discovery of a Forerunner relic. At this point, her curiosity and scientific nature are driving her, and she is willing to do what it takes to get to the relic. However, she is not going to be an easy passenger for Forge.

"Sit down and strap in."

There was a lot more noise than Anders expected riding in the back of a Pelican. Uncertainty filled her, and for the first time in as long as she could remember, she was a little afraid. Her life at home was very strict, very organized, and very scheduled. She took comfort in knowing that every day was exactly planned to the minute and that every part of her life was familiar. How she had been talked into this unfamiliar routine was making her honestly question her sanity.

The seats on the inside of the Pelican were chipped; some had large gouges in them; and one even had tape across it, suggesting that no one sit in it. Anders wondered if the exterior was as well maintained as the interior and if she was even going to make it out in one piece. She pulled up her portable and looked again at the ship's name. "Spirit of Fire" was an odd moniker for a UNSC ship. Her inquiries as to the origin of that name from the pilot of the Pelican got her a sharp "Sit down and strap in," followed by quite a few expletives, some of which she hadn't actually heard before.

However, the promise of something extraterrestrial, and currently alive rather than dug up, was too big of a draw to ignore. Her research vindicated, fame surely to follow, and enough work to keep her busy for life, let alone the commercial profit from any kind of alien technology she might figure out...

Coming up on the Spirit of Fire, she looked out past the pilot at the large streamlined ship in front of her, its front communications beacons flashing like Christmas lights and the formidable weapons showing from every conceivable angle. It was sleek, clean, and much newer than she thought it would be.

"My lab equipment is on board already, correct, Lieutenant?"

"On board Spirit of Fire, yes, ma'am. As soon as we're past the Argosy here, you'll be able to get a good look at your new home."

The Argosy slipped on under the Pelican, and what Anders had previously considered the orbital station only now became clearly visible as a ship itself. It was as battered as the chairs in the Pelican and old; yet it was somehow elegant for its size, majestic, even. No one put much thought into exterior ship design these days, but someone obviously had for this ship.

"That ship has an FTL drive?" Anders mumbled out loud.

"Yes, ma'am. That and the best mess of any ship out here."

"Mess?" Anders had never heard the term before.

"Food hall, ma'am."

"Oh, like a restaurant!" Anders said happily. She had heard the food was going to be terrible; maybe this trip wasn't going to be so bad after all.

"Whatever you say, ma'am." The lieutenant sighed. He was going to be very happy to deliver his passenger. Civilians had no place on fleet ships, always getting in the way and disrupting the routine.

Anders settled back down and strapped in, and her mind drifted to the task ahead. If this was a new race, would it be even more advanced than the Covenant? For all she knew, it would be like her trying to talk to a human from 100,000 years ago, a caveman barely able to comprehend fire let alone the advanced society humans had evolved into today. Kind of like talking to the lieutenant up front, she mused. That made her chuckle a bit out loud and suddenly feel quite self-conscious.

More worrisome was that this was a military mission, very hush-hush, so would we shoot first and start an interstellar war, or would they actually show restraint for once? As far as she knew, she was part of a very small contingent of civilians accompanying the military on this, and her lab equipment list had been approved without question and installed within a day. This was going to propel her career for years.

She sat back in her seat and closed her eyes. The world might not be the same when she got back, and perhaps these selfish thoughts were just that. Perhaps she would also be different when she returned.

She shuddered at the thought.

Leadership Qualities and Tactical Notes

Unique Troop Type: Gremlin

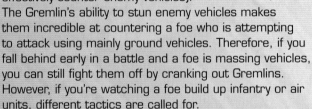

The Gremlin is an antivehicle troop and the only one the UNSC possesses that is available at Reactor Level 1 (Spartans are available at Tech Level 1, but they require melee range to effectively counter enemy vehicles). The Gremlin's ability to stun enemy vehicles makes them incredible at countering a foe who is attempting to attack using mainly ground vehicles. Therefore, if you fall behind early in a battle and a foe is massing vehicles, you can still fight them off by cranking out Gremlins. However, if you're watching a foe build up infantry or air units, different tactics are called for.

Leader Power: Cryo Bomb (⬦, then ⬦ + Ⓐ)

A devastating bomb that freezes the enemy in their tracks, this shot from the Spirit of Fire is the most powerful of the three Leader Powers, as it also allows you to completely decimate enemy air units, dropping them out of the sky and demolishing them. Even if your foe is on the ground, you can completely immobilize an enemy attack force while your other units pound on them without return fire; this is a sound strategy no matter what the enemy throws at you. Make sure you use this attack; it is particularly satisfying to freeze a Scarab and cut it down!

TIP

You can upgrade your Cryo Bomb a total of three times to increase the potency of the attack—if you have the Supplies and Reactor levels. For more information, consult the "Spirit of Fire" section.

Super Unit: Hawk

Anders further augments her antivehicle unit and incredible Leader Power by being able to produce Hawks (after you've upgraded a Hornet enough times). These are the most proficient and deadly air unit available to the UNSC. The Hawk works well with her Cryo Bomb to allow Anders the ultimate edge in airborne dogfights, but Hawks devastate all manner of troops. For this reason, Anders is the best leader when attempting a team battle; a team with her is much more mobile than a team without her.

Starting Advantage: All Unit Upgrades Are Half-Price and Research in Half the Time

With military technologies at half-price and researched in half the time of other leaders, this bonus allows Anders complete flexibility when pondering strategies she can quickly and cheaply adapt to. Whatever the situation, you have less to lose and a quick research time, allowing for upgraded troops in no time. Upgrade your Spartans, Wolverines, or Warthogs faster than you thought possible!

TIP

All upgrades listed in this chapter are halved when Anders researches them.

Tactical Notes

While Forge and Cutter have shortcomings as far as their abilities, there's no downside to playing as Anders, since she has a wide array of attributes to use. Are you being attacked by vehicles? Then crank out the Gremlins. Is your base being swarmed by air? Launch a Cryo Bomb and send in the Hawks! Whether you're playing 1v1, 2v2, or 3v3 confrontations, Anders is preferred by a wide margin due to her flexibility and inevitable late battle domination thanks to her Hawks and Cryo Bomb.

SPIRIT OF FIRE

Exitus Acta Probat

Constructed: 2473
Class: Phoenix (CFV-88)
Captain: Cutter
AI on board: Serina

The Spirit of Fire was originally a colony ship, transporting equipment and colonists in the UNSC's expansion efforts. In 2520, the ship was refitted with a Magnetic Accelerator Cannon and other armaments to serve as a warship. Huge storage bays that used to house machine parts now store everything from Warthogs and Scorpion tanks to construction supplies for Firebases that are located in front-line engagements or in rear-guard actions. We now follow the Spirit of Fire and her crew as the UNSC deals with the first deadly encounters with the Covenant.

AI Construct: Serina

Background Details

Serina is a visual representation of one of the most sophisticated artificial intelligence programs in the history of mankind. Although wholly a digital life-form, Serina, like other AI programs as advanced as she is, has developed her own personality—one of a supremely intelligent and bitingly sarcastic young woman. She has long hair, a thin figure, and a constant smirk.

Age: N/A
Height: N/A
Weight: N/A
Hair Color: Black
Eye Color: Blue

Serina, and programs like her, is one of the most important assets that the human race has in their coming struggle. Her wit and intelligence, along with her absolute candor and lack of complicated emotions, such as nervousness and hesitation, make her indispensable—that and the fact that she controls every system on the ship, including life support.

"I kissed a boy once."

Hershey looked over the medical area slowly and intently. It remained exactly the same as it had been ten minutes ago. The night shift sucked, and she now hated holo-sudoko.

"Serina? You there?" She had felt odd talking out loud in the beginning but had long ago gotten over being embarrassed about talking to air.

Serina flickered on, lighting the room and casting a blue light over the station desk. The AI turned to face Hershey. "Yes, Nurse Hershey. I'm always here."

"Call me Lulu; everyone else does."

"What can I do for you, Lulu?"

"Serina, do you dream?"

Serina looked puzzled. "Lulu, I'm an AI. I don't sleep. I'm on duty all the time."

Lulu persisted. "Yes, I know that, but don't you have moments when nothing is going on? Don't you dream about something?"

The hologram paused for a second, as if it was about to switch off. When Serina came back on, Hershey thought her color had changed a little and her voice had softened.

"I do run projected simulations for multiple events based on probabilities and known patterns."

"About...?" Hershey pressed.

"The ship, power projections and needs, crew rotation compatibility, resource management, weather patterns in LZ areas. Quite a bit actually; you would be surprised!"

"Yes, but personally, do you ever think about yourself, something girly?"

Serina could see that Hershey wasn't about to let this drop. "Well, I do try to remember what chocolate tastes like....I've actually tried to simulate the approximate chemical response within my neural network and so far have not met with any success."

Hershey was puzzled. "When have you ever tasted chocolate, Serina?"

"Lulu, don't you know anything about AIs?"

Hershey had only ever seen one other AI on a school tour of the planetary weather center. It was a lot simpler than Serina and much more function over personality.

"You're computers. Advanced, but still a computer. Right?"

Serina looked aghast. "I am NOT a computer! I just happen to live in one. My core neural network is actually cloned from a human."

Hershey was shocked. "No way!!! That's gross!"

"My network has been allowed to expand, and I am no longer that human, but I share many of her core memories."

"What do you remember...I mean, from before?"

"The identity of the human I am cloned from is unknown to me. I do remember food, the smell of flowers, the feeling of grass on my feet, and a lot of little moments...." Serina flickered and her hue changed again, this time slightly reddish. "Lulu, can you keep a secret?"

Hershey was intrigued. "Well, sure, sweetie! I'm all ears!"

"I kissed a boy once."

Hershey laughed. "Well shocker! So did I! That's not a secret!"

"I run simulations about it. Detailed simulations..."

Hershey pushed back off the station desk and giggled out loud. Of all the people on this ship, she never thought the AI would be the one she would gossip with.

"Serina, darling, you just made my day!"

Serina looked hard at Hershey. "You tell anyone and I can unmake that day pretty darn quick."

The two of them looked at each other for a second before breaking down and laughing. The night shift was never dull for Hershey from that point on.

Spirit of Fire Abilities and Tactical Notes

The Spirit of Fire is responsible for dropping in your Firebase and supplies, but it can also offer additional tactical necessities if you request them. Access the Spirit of Fire menu via ; there is a total of five (or six if you're playing as Captain Cutter) abilities or functions you can employ.

Global Rally Point (, ◉)

 All newly trained units will move to this location when training is completed. You can set a Base Rally Point to direct a specific base's units someplace else. This is incredibly useful when you're Rushing or want the entire army to converge on a single point, especially if you have multiple bases. If you plan to lay siege to an enemy fortification, place a Global Rally Point nearby so you have a constant influx of new troops.

Transport (, ◉)

 Call in Pelicans to transport a small group of units from one place to another. This is reserved for moments when you wish to whisk a few valuable units (such as veteran troops, Spartans piloting tanks, or other high-value troops) away from a battle they are losing or to quickly gain ground on a foe. Congregate your troops as close as possible, ideally outside your base, and deliver them to a Hook or for a rear-guard strike on a flummoxed foe's base.

ODST Drop (, ⬤; Cutter Only)

 This requires the ODST Upgrade, which is available once you upgrade Marines in the Barracks. Tactics for using these drops are detailed in this chapter's sections on Captain Cutter and Marines.

MAC Blast (, ⬤; Cutter Only)

 Arguably the weakest of the three UNSC Leader Powers (as it takes a while to aim and fire, especially when upgraded), the MAC Blast is still very effective at damaging very slow-moving, large targets with high Hit Points (such as tanks or a Scarab) or softening buildings while you're engaging in a base attack. It is very difficult to hit a moving unit with a MAC round.

Because this takes a while to aim and fire (especially when upgraded), you'll have more time for a foe to move out of its blast and less time for you to maneuver your troops as the attack occurs, compared to the Cryo or Carpet Bombs. The "aiming trace" of the laser also alerts all but the dimmest foes to your plans, so save this for buildings that can't move. This can be upgraded three times (for a total of four separate aiming and firing blasts) at the Field Armory.

If you're facing Captain Cutter as a foe, be sure your larger units are moving—and therefore not easily targeted. Separate your larger troops (such as tanks) so a MAC Blast doesn't strike multiple units.

Carpet Bomb (, ⬤; Forge Only)

  Compared to the MAC Blast, the Carpet Bomb is a quick and almost instant attack. It is the scourge of troops attempting to engage your forces. The Carpet Bomb is most useful against a large, grouped-together army, preferably made up of infantry units.

Be careful of the lengthy damage, and position the arrow so the Carpet Bomb strikes multiple enemy targets, especially those that have formed in a line. Try to target the bombing run to cover as much of the enemy formation as possible. Beware: this attack can

27

also damage your forces if you're not careful! Use this on Rushing enemies or when you're defending a base (especially if the enemies are close together). This can be upgraded three times at the Field Armory.

When facing Sergeant Forge in battle, employ the following tactics to ensure his Carpet Bombs are as ineffective as possible; keep your units spread apart and moving as often as possible. Also, think twice about a large army comprised mainly of infantry; Carpet Bombing can quickly erase such a force if used deftly.

Cryo Bomb (◊, ◕; Anders Only)

The UNSC's Shortsword Bomber is used to drop Cryo Bombs in an area, freezing all things for a short time. This is the most fearsome of the three Leader Powers; employ it on troops attacking your base and on airborne foes (some of which are instantly destroyed and drop from the sky), and be sure to bring on other troops that act as a backup to this power.

Cryo Bombs are also very effective when dropped on massed ground troops congregating at a tactical advantage point or outside your base. Be warned, however, that you must keep your own troops out of the blast, as they can be frozen solid too. There's nothing quite as demoralizing as a Cryo Bomb that drops your own Hornets out of the sky! This can be upgraded three times at the Field Armory.

When fighting against Professor Anders, don't attempt any strategies that heavily rely on air troops, as the Cryo Bomb can wipe out a force with this attack. When fighting, stay close to an enemy army, making the Cryo Bomb less effective because Anders's own troops are at risk.

Disruption Bomb (◊, ◖)

The Disruption Bomb disrupts existing Leader Powers and prevents new ones from being initiated in a small area for one minute. This is the key to surviving a Covenant leader's strike on your base or a battle in which UNSC forces are likely to be backed up by a MAC Blast, a Carpet Bomb, or a Cryo Bomb. If you see a Covenant leader on their way, launch this, then retaliate while they are weakened. Stripping a foe of their extra powers at a critical moment can turn the tide of a battle, so remember this attack! Beware the long recovery time if you want to use it again, and remember this affects your Leader Powers too!

Heal & Repair (◊, ◕)

Heal any units and repair any buildings in an area. This is obviously a useful ability, especially as the Covenant do not have a similar technique (but the UNSC lack shields that most Covenant troops use). The biggest shortfall is that Heal & Repair cannot be used during an attack; you must wait until the troop or building in question isn't being fired at for the healing or repairing to begin. Use this just after a major base attack or during an assault, and move wounded troops into the circle while fresh troops soak up the damage.

> **NOTE**
>
> There are three other ways for UNSC troops to heal: (1) Marines (only) can receive a Medic upgrade; (2) Spartans use regenerating armor (but when wounded, must rely on Heal & Repair to regain health); and (3) Forge's unique unit is the Cyclops, which repairs buildings and vehicles but not infantry.

Ancillary Units

Shortsword

One of the few UNSC forces not named after an animal, the Shortsword-class aircraft is a suborbital long-range bomber that UNSC command use for rapid payload attacks. It launches from the Spirit of Fire, plummets toward the ground, and delivers heavy payloads against both ground and air targets. It is not built for space combat, but it can function in outer space. For battle purposes, this aircraft is primarily seen delivering a Carpet Bomb or a Cryo Bomb.

Rhino (M-145D)

A heavy tank variant sharing some technology with the Scorpion, Rhinos are dropped onto the battlefield via Pelicans and provide siege-based heavy weapons bombardment thanks to a massive, turret-mounted 320 mm Zeus Cannon (with a 100 km range). Titanium armor allows this tank to shrug all but the heaviest enemy attacks. This vehicle is available only during the Campaign: Mission 06 Dome of Light; refer to that subchapter for Rhino tactical notes.

THE COMMAND BASE

Firebase

The UNSC Firebase combines the needs of a tactical communication command center and expansion into both a barracks and a production facility capable of assembling combat vehicles. The Firebase is a variant of the old colony starter units constructed out of polycrete and powered by a small hydrogen reactor. Because gaining a foothold quickly was key to fighting insurrection throughout the colonies, Spirit of Fire can directly deploy a Firebase's entire assembly unit, making it immediately useful. This ability has also proven invaluable in the ongoing war with the Covenant and is often considered a key advantage of the UNSC on the ground.

Firebase (Forge and Anders Only)

Building Class: Firebase
Units Trained:
    Warthog (and upgrades),
    Elephant (and upgrades; Cutter only),
    Cyclops (and upgrades; Forge only),
    Gremlin (and upgrades; Anders only)

N/A   0   500

You can request to have a small base dropped in from orbit. Eventually, you can expand that into a full base. When you destroy a neutral or enemy base, or you locate an empty base pad, you can build a Firebase if you have the supplies. It has three building pads and doesn't feature any Turret base slots. Whether this is a good idea depends on the map (as some base locations are better than others), how strong the enemy is, and what position your forces are holding. Refer to the Campaign, Skirmish, and Multi-player tactics for all the available base locations.

> **NOTE**
> You must wait 25 seconds once a neutral or enemy base is destroyed before you can build a UNSC base at the same position.

> **CAUTION**
> Firebases are extremely prone to attacks as the two large sections are being flown down from orbit. Make sure no enemies are in the area before you start to build, or your base will be destroyed before it's even been constructed!

Station

Building Class: Station

N/A   0   300

Upgrades to a Station, which adds two more building sites. Each building adds to the strength of the central structure. If you

pick Forge or Anders, this is the initial base that you begin every battle with. It is automatically constructed if you've taken over a "new" base and you're playing as Captain Cutter. It has five expansion pads and four Turret base slots. If you fear enemy attacks, it is better to upgrade from a Firebase to a Station and augment it with Turrets. It is wise to time the upgrade of this base to a Fortress so that a Fortress is built just as the last building rises up from a Station.

Fortress

Building Class: Fortress

N/A   0   400

Upgrades base to a Fortress, which adds two more building sites. Each building adds to the strength of the central structure. If you pick Cutter, this is the initial base that you begin every battle with. It has a total of seven expansion pads and four Turret base slots (although these aren't additional; it simply adds two more building pads to a Station). Judge whether the two additional pads are needed immediately; they certainly are on your initial base. It is almost always wise to upgrade to a Fortress, as the buildings allow the central command structure to absorb more damage.

> **TIP**
> The strength of the central command structure is shown as a series of white bars (from zero to seven) above your base's green damage bar; the more buildings you have attached to a base, the bigger the bar and the more damage it takes to destroy a base.

Other Base Functions

Base Rally Point

New units from this base will move to this location when training is complete. Use the Global Rally Point to override this behavior. Utilizing this flag option is extremely important, as it allows you to point to an area of your map and have any troop type head there after building or training; this effectively takes the manual labor out of this function.

Remember where your Rally Point is, in case it falls to the enemy—you don't want to send your troops straight into danger! Every base has its own Rally Point, allowing you to mass separate armies if, for example, you want to tackle a base from two directions.

29

Self-Destruct

Instantly destroy this entire base to free it up for an ally. This is really the only advantageous method of using this function; otherwise, employ this if your base is under attack so your foe doesn't have the satisfaction of destroying your base with his forces. Note that you do gain Supply Points if you blow up your own base; however, do this only if you have troops outside or elsewhere on the map that can quickly locate and build a new base. You are still at a serious disadvantage.

TIP

If you're planning to destroy a base you own, send one of your troops to an empty base elsewhere on the map so you can quickly command it without having to frantically search the map.

NOTE

All buildings can also be recycled, which destroys them and empties the base pad they stood on. Expect Supply Points (around half the building's value) to be added to your total. This happens more frequently as you remove structures for more important ones. A few examples:

If you build Reactors, upgrade units, and the units require a lower Tech level to build; this means you're overly technologically advanced now and have the luxury of demolishing a Reactor.

If you build a Barracks but no longer have any use for the troops inside (if Marines and Flamethrowers are less effective compared to your enemy's forces, and your Spartans are upgraded, alive, and on the battlefield).

If you build a Field Armory and complete all the upgrades you want. This building is now useless and can be removed for a more important structure if necessary.

CAUTION

If you destroy a base and have no other bases, you have one minute to build a new one or lose the fight.

Lock

Units train as normal but are garrisoned inside the base instead of exiting into the world. Unlock will release all the garrisoned units at once. Locking and Unlocking your base allows you to surprise a foe who is checking out your location and to keep troops that you are massing safely inside your base's protective walls. When you Unlock or Lock your base, the ramped doors clamp open or shut, respectively; also use this to determine whether an enemy's base is open or not. Usually, this means you or your foe are massing troops. However, if you get into the habit of always Locking your base, you can fool your foe into thinking you're massing troops, whether you are or not! Use this secrecy to your tactical advantage.

FIREBASE BUILDINGS

Turret

Turret defenses are available for Stations and Fortresses, while battlefield commanders must defend their Firebases with their military units. Turrets are assembled belowground and then elevated into one of four available slots. A virtually unlimited supply of ammunition flows to the turret from below the base, allowing it to keep firing as long as its exposed tower and weapon remains intact. The base turret mount supports the very versatile M202 XP Machine Gun.

NOTE

Turrets can be upgraded two times if you build the Field Armory. Information on these upgrades—which essentially add armor and a better weapon—are detailed in that building's section.

Turret: Basic

Weapon Type: M202 XP Machine Gun
Building Class: Base Defense

 N/A 0 250

Turrets are good at defending bases against all enemy targets. You can have up to four Turrets for each base (one on each corner), which allows a slightly farther line of sight. It is usually wise to build the two Turrets at the front of the base first, but this depends on where the enemy usually attacks from. Simply build the Turret and leave it to fire at enemy forces; you cannot control the Turret's aiming.

Turret: Flame Mortar

Weapon Type:
Antipersonnel Flame Mortar (KG Mk 34)

N/A 0 100

Adds bonus Anti-infantry attack to the Turret.

Turret: Rail Gun

Weapon Type: 8MJ LRG Rail Cannon

 N/A 0 100

Adds bonus antivehicle attack to the Turret.

Turret: Missile Launcher

Weapon Type:
Anaconda SAM

N/A 0 100

Adds bonus antiair attack
to the Turret.

Turrets have three unique "add-on"
augmentations that allow you to swap
out different armament types for a battle's duration.
Only one add-on can be added at a time, but each can
be changed whenever you want, and every Turret can
have one of the three options. These are well worth the
small Supply Points it takes to fit them, and you should
use them once you see what type of troops an enemy
is building or are sending your way. If you can correctly
predict (usually via Warthog reconnaissance) the troops,
it is easier to defend your base.

Supply Pad

The UNSC Supply Pad allows a base to
receive shipments from orbiting cargo
craft. The supplies are drop-shipped onto
the pads, where they are gathered by
robot cranes and brought into the base.
These crates contain the resources
needed to build units and research upgrades. Supply
Pads are the economy behind the war machine of the
UNSC and can be upgraded to produce more resources
faster.

Supply Pad: Basic

Building Class: Produces
Resources

N/A 0 100

The UNSC Supply Pad
produces the resources needed to train
units, build buildings, and buy technology
upgrades. Bases that have great
economic production might have six
Supply Pads. Only Captain Cutter and Professor Anders
can build these.

Heavy Supply Pad

Supply production
massively increased for
this Supply Pad. Sergeant
Forge builds these from the start; Cutter
and Anders must build a Basic Supply
Pad first.

N/A 1 225

 NOTE

Refer to the "Advanced Training" chapter for specific
tactics on how many Supply Pads to make and how
the different Supply Pads work. In general, try building
between 5 to 7 Supply Pads (or three Heavy Pads and
two Basic Supply Pads) for the best return on your
investment. The number of Supply Pads you build is only
limited by your base pads.

The Covenant version of the Supply Pad is the
Warehouse.

NOTE

Many maps have Forerunner structures that act as
Supply Pads. Train Marines to capture and hold these
structures, which are much more advantageous to keep,
as they free up base pads and cost less to bring online.

Reactor

Power is everything. A UNSC Firebase
is powered by a small hydrogen reactor
that allows it to operate some pretty
sophisticated systems. In order to set
up a base quickly, it has to be small,
but these power plants are modular.

As you expand your base of operations and field more
complicated weapon systems, you are going to need
more power. Base sockets can facilitate the addition
of larger hydrogen reactor units, which provide the
juice to allow you to field more and more sophisticated
weaponry. These additional Reactors built into your base
sockets are even modular and can be upgraded, at
great expense, to double their output.

TIP

Protect your base Reactors. They are prime targets for
enemy raids. When they are destroyed, you will no longer
be able to field your heavy-hitting Scorpions or Vultures.

Reactor: Basic

Building Class: Increases
Tech Level

N/A 0 250+

UNSC Reactors provide
the energy needed to access advanced
buildings, units, and technology
upgrades. High-tech bases may have as
many as four or five Reactors.

NOTE

†For each additional Reactor on its own base pad, the
Supply cost goes up 250 points. For example, your third
Basic Reactor would cost 750 points.

Reactor: Advanced

This Reactor provides
enough energy to
match the output of two
Reactors. Advanced Reactors can only
be built as an upgrade to an existing
Reactor.

N/A 0 1200

Planning the number of Reactors and how many
places they take up inside your base is crucial to winning
a battle. The following table shows the number of pads
and Supply Points it costs to reach Tech Level 4 in a
variety of ways:

31

Tech Level	Reactor (Number)	Supply Point Cost	Base Pads Utilized
1	Reactor (1)	250	1
2	Advanced Reactor (1)	1,450	1
2	Reactor (2)	750	2
3	Reactor (3)	1,500	3
3	Reactor (1) + Advanced Reactor (1)	1,950	2
4	Reactor (4)	2,500	4
4	Reactor (2) + Advanced Reactor (1)	2,700	3
4	Advanced Reactor (2)	3,150	2

As you can see from the table, the payoff of creating more Advanced Reactors is that you free up base pads for other buildings; this is useful if you're having trouble locating an additional base. The payoff for creating more Basic Reactors is that it costs less and takes less time, as you don't have to wait for your Supply Points to reach 1,250.

TIP

There are no unit upgrades that require a higher Tech level than 4. This means that you should build only to Tech Level 5 or greater if you're sure your opponent is about to launch an offensive on your Reactors and you need some "insurance." This doesn't happen often. Indeed, usually the opposite is true; it is usually better to build Reactors up to the Tech level you need (in order to upgrade the units you consider vital to the battle you're waging) and then afterward, demolish the Reactor to make way for a new building type (such as a Field Armory if you're short on base pads).

Once you've built an upgrade, you can downgrade your Tech level, as long as you remain at the level necessary to build the troops in question. One key example are Scorpion tanks: They require only Tech Level 2 for their manufacture. So, build extra Reactors, create the upgrades you wish, then demolish Reactors and move back to Tech Level 2 without losing the ability to build upgraded Scorpions.

NOTE

The Covenant version of the Reactor is the Temple, which upgrades in a different way.

Many Maps have Forerunner structures that act as Reactors. Train Marines to capture and hold these buildings; these are much more advantageous to keep, as they free up base pads and cost less to bring online.

Field Armory

The UNSC's Field Armory is where dedicated engineers and scientists create the most advanced technology for the UNSC. The UNSC can increase its population cap here, as well as improve the turrets and boost the speed of its infantry. There is also special technology that can only be researched by individual leaders. Don't underestimate the usefulness of this structure!

Field Armory (Building)

Building Class: Special Upgrades

N/A · 1 · 150

The UNSC Field Armory is a combination machine shop and high-tech laboratory. Many advanced technology upgrades can be found here.

The Field Armory is usually overlooked, as it doesn't provide any "instant" gratification (i.e., troops to defend your base). Usually, it is created in the middle of a confrontation once you've established a base (many players put one on a second base). The following upgrades are available and augment a wide variety of troops and armaments.

NOTE

All Supply Point values for these upgrades are halved if you're playing as Anders.

Reserves

Train times for all units are drastically reduced. Basically, in half the time you would normally train a squad of Marines or build a Wolverine, you receive the chosen unit if you complete this upgrade. This is pricey but helpful if you're planning a late Rush or wish to quickly bolster your troops to patrol or defend (if you have enough Supply Points amassed to handle the quicker training). If you need an army quickly and you have the Supply reserves, take this upgrade.

N/A · 2 · 800

Medium Turret

N/A · 2 · 500

Upgrades all Turrets to Medium Turrets, increasing their Hit Points and damage.

Large Turret

Upgrades all Turrets to Large Turrets, increasing their Hit Points and damage.

N/A · 3 · 800

These two upgrades instantly bulk up every Turret you've already built (or intend to build), granting an extra M202 XP Machine Gun and adding about a third more armor (Medium Turret) or two M202s and one and a half as much armor again (Large Turret). If foes are constantly hassling you at your base, this makes enemy incursions more difficult. It also sends a visual signal to your foe that your base is now much stronger and well defended. Naturally, the more Turrets you already have, the more useful these two upgrades are.

TIP

You can see the differences in the size and number of guns at the top of each upgraded Turret. This is useful when scanning your enemy's base; if there are enhanced Turrets, you know your job is going to be that much more difficult, and you can prepare accordingly (with more reinforcements or Leader Powers focused on the Turrets).

Reinforcements

Adds +10 to your army's Population cap. Aside from the 2v2 Beaseley's Plateau Map that features a Life Support Pod, this is the only way you can increase the total Population of your army from 30 to 40. For example, this means three extra Scorpions (and a Spartan to ride in one of them) or five more Hornets. Additional units are always useful, and this is a thoroughly recommended upgrade, as long as you're already nearing your 30 Population limit; if you're scrabbling around at 10 to 15 Population and under constant enemy attacks, gain a tactically stronger position and more troops first.

N/A 3 800

Adrenaline

Booster shots enable all infantry units to run at significantly increased speeds. If you want to employ an infantry Rush or take Hooks early in battle, this offers a significant advantage once you've built a Barracks and the Field Armory: This should be your first upgrade if you're focusing on an infantry-heavy army. Troops run at 1.5 times the normal speed, effectively shortening the distances they travel. Even if you're only using Spartans, this is useful, as you can run and Jack a vehicle in a shorter time and thus avoid more damage.

N/A 1 250

Medium MAC Blast (Cutter Only)

MAC Blast ammo capacity upgrade to provide two shots.

N/A 2 700

Large MAC Blast (Cutter Only)

MAC Blast ammo capacity upgrade to provide three shots.

N/A 3 1,000

Super MAC Blast (Cutter Only)

MAC Blast ammo capacity upgrade to provide four shots.

N/A 4 1,400

Medium Carpet Bomb (Forge Only)

Carpet Bomb strafe distance and damage increased.

N/A 2 700

Large Carpet Bomb (Forge Only)

Carpet Bomb strafe distance and damage increased.

N/A 3 1,000

Super Carpet Bomb (Forge Only)

Carpet Bomb strafe distance and damage increased.

N/A 4 1,400

Medium Cryo (Anders Only)

Increases the duration of the freeze effect and instantly kills more air units.

N/A 2 350

Large Cryo (Anders Only)

Increases the duration of the freeze effect and instantly kills more air units.

N/A 3 500

Super Cryo (Anders Only)

Increases the duration of the freeze effect and instantly kills more air units.

Although the exact specifications aren't available, each of the three Leader Powers (accessed via the Spirit of Fire menu, or ○) can be further upgraded, and the Field Armory is the building that provides this function. Often overlooked because these attacks are less tangible than constructing a platoon of tanks, Leader Power upgrades should be seriously considered, especially when playing as Anders (as hers are effectively half the cost of Forge's and Cutter's). The general rule here is that if you can afford to upgrade powers without your second-by-second game suffering, then go for it; Leader Powers are the perfect way to augment an attack. For specifics on Leader Powers, see the "Spirit of Fire" section earlier in this chapter.

33

Barracks

This is no UNSC academy; the Barracks is a rustic shack compared to the comforts of a real training center, but then again, a Marine in the field isn't thinking about creature comforts: They make you soft. The Barracks simply houses the raw recruits and equipment needed by field squads of UNSC Marines. A quick briefing and a visit to the armory, and you've got boots on the ground.

Barracks (Building)

 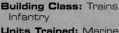

Building Class: Trains Infantry

Units Trained: Marine (and upgrades), ODST (fully upgraded Marines; Cutter only), Flamethrower (and upgrades), Spartan (and upgrades)

The Barracks trains the bulk of the UNSC infantry units. Infantry technology upgrades can also be found here. Barracks are usually built early rather than later into a battle, because infantry are less and less useful as more powerful troops become available. The Barracks has many advantages, providing quick and cheap units to instantly nullify early enemy Rushes. It also doesn't need a Tech level to be built, enabling you to set up a Barracks as soon as you wish. In addition, it trains three types of units (detailed later in this chapter). Spartans are by far the most useful of the three, as they can board your own vehicles or Jack an enemy's. Consider recycling this when ground and air vehicles become more prevalent. Finally, consider a mixture of light vehicles from your Firebase and infantry for a good combination of units at the beginning of a war.

> **NOTE**
>
> The Elephant (utilized only by Captain Cutter) also trains infantry, making it a good alternative. However, infantry upgrades are only available via the Barracks, meaning you must build one if you want ruthlessly effective infantry. Another trick is to upgrade the infantry you need, then remove the Barracks for another building type and train the infantry from the more mobile, and therefore useful, Elephants.

Vehicle Depot

A Vehicle Depot contains the heavy equipment and crew to assemble vehicle kits. Hydraulic cranes serve as the muscle to move everything from Cobra chassis, Scorpion armored plates, and the impressive selection of weaponry that these vehicles can bring to bear. The parts may take a while to arrive, but when the engine from a new Scorpion fires up in the Vehicle Depot, the rumble is felt all across the base.

Vehicle Depot (Building)

Building Class: Trains Vehicles

Units Trained: Scorpions (and upgrades), Grizzly Tanks (fully upgraded Scorpions; Forge only), Cobra (and upgrades), Wolverine (and upgrades)

The UNSC Vehicle Depot constructs the ground vehicles for the UNSC army. Vehicle technology upgrades can also be found here. Usually a player opts for either a land or air-based contingent during the middle stages of battle, although you can take a chance and ignore the Barracks and leave your base prone early on to create the two Reactors necessary to build this structure. However, once you do, your options are much more varied, as you now have access to three very impressive vehicles (which are detailed later into this chapter). A Vehicle Depot is usually placed in a base, but judge your opponent's actions to deem whether one is necessary. Naturally, many other factors should be considered, too, such as if you're playing as Forge and want to upgrade to Grizzlies, and whether your foe is Turtling and you have time to spend upgrading vehicles.

Air Pad

Air superiority can be of vital importance, not only for intelligence gathering but also for tactical strikes at your enemy's weak points. A UNSC Air Pad is a surprisingly sophisticated structure that houses the maintenance crews required to refit, repair, and rearm Hornets, and it houses banks of simulation pods to train pilots in everything from the basics to advanced tactical maneuvers. Desperate times can call for desperate measures, and on more than a few occasions, Firebase commanders have thrown any able bodies they've had at their disposal into the simulators for a crash course in operating the Attack VTOL-14. With the Spirit of Fire at your disposal to provide trained air crews, chances are you won't have to resort to these kinds of unorthodox procedures.

Air Pad (Building)

Building Class: Trains Aircraft

Units Trained: Hornet (and upgrades), Hawk (fully upgraded Hornets; Anders only), Vulture (and upgrade)

The Air Pad creates the various UNSC air units. Air-unit technology upgrades can also be found here. Opting for air superiority depends on your chosen leader (it is always recommended for Anders); on whether your foe has antiair weaponry (such as Anders's Cryo Bombs); and whether you wish to use Hornets, as Vultures are exceedingly difficult to manufacture early on due to their Tech level and Supply costs. Both vehicles are showcased later in this chapter. Another way to decide whether Air Pads are useful sooner rather than later is the topography of your map; if there are numerous gullies, narrow roads, and rocky terrain, opt for aircraft that can easily navigate over these obstacles.

FIREBASE UNITS
Warthog (M12 LRV)

Hit Points: ★☆☆

Damage Caused: ★☆☆

Movement: ★★★

Warthogs are the UNSC's fast scout units. They start with an active Ram ability but can be upgraded to get various guns for extra firepower.

Base Unit & Variant

Basic Offense: None

Starting Special Attack:
Ram ability

Upgrade #1: Gunner

Weapon Type: M41 Light Antiaircraft Gun

Adds Machine Gun attack to the Warthogs, giving them combat capability.

Upgrade #2: Grenadier

Weapon Type: XM510 Multishot Grenade Launcher

Adds a Marine armed with a Grenade Launcher to improve attack strength.

Upgrade #3: Gauss Cannon

Weapon Type: M68 Gauss Cannon

Upgrades Warthog Machine Gun to a Gauss Cannon. Improves damage and defense.

Warthog Overview

Unit Class: Scout

Strengths: Strong against small numbers of infantry and light vehicles.

Weaknesses: Weak against Turrets, most ground vehicles, and large concentrations of troops.

Accessed via: Firebase

Even the most minimal of Firebases can produce the Warthog, and for good reason: These versatile vehicles are incredibly valuable for reconnaissance and can be refitted to fill numerous supporting roles for UNSC forces. The most basic of these variants doesn't have the standard M41 Light Antiaircraft Gun equipped, sacrificing this firepower for the speed necessary for reconnaissance patrols. Firebases can add the M41 and the M68 Gauss Cannon to seriously boost this unit's firepower against armored vehicles.

Tactics

This vehicle is built and upgraded inside the UNSC Firebase, Station, or Fortress—not at the Vehicle Depot. This gives you a huge advantage early in a battle: you don't need to spend time (and a base socket) building a Vehicle Depot—simply crank out Warthogs immediately!

You always begin a skirmish or multiplayer game with a single Warthog already built.

The initial Ram ability is extremely effective in knocking down and killing enemy infantry units.

Warthogs are adept at hit-and-run tactics against enemy troops or when quickly raiding enemy buildings.

Warthogs are effective at countering some infantry units in small numbers, particularly Flamethrowers, Jackals, and air units.

It is recommended that you construct a few Warthogs during the initial stages of your confrontation, and use them to locate and grab more scattered crates; this nets you more supplies, while denying your foe those same supplies. They are the fastest unit that can grab supplies, so rely on them heavily early on. Once a Warthog grabs a group of crates, it has effectively "paid" for itself.

If a UNSC enemy if not electing to build more scout units, or if you face the Covenant with only one scout—the Ghost—on your map, then quickly attempt a Rush strategy and build multiple Warthogs; stalk the lone scout and destroy it, ideally using Ram (build Warthogs first before upgrading them). Now you have a huge tactical advantage, as you can drive to all the supplies on the map, and your foe isn't able to spy on you.

Gain an early economic advantage by using Warthogs to gather crates. In addition, use them in specific reconnaissance planning: Periodically send a Warthog to inspect an opponent's base and other operations. This allows you to gain knowledge on his strategy and enables you to quickly adapt and counter any proposed strikes or other plans. Send a single Warthog, as they are expendable and won't show your foe the full extent of your forces.

35

CAUTION

Warning! Warthogs have no ranged attack until Upgrade #1 (Gunner) is fitted; do this relatively early if you intend to use Warthogs for more than scouting.

Later into the battle, the Warthog can be adept at hitting and running an enemy base once you've upgraded to the Gunner (or other ranged weaponry). Continue the upgrades if you're continuing this plan.

A common strategy with Warthogs is to build as many as you can from the moment the battle starts. At the same time, construct one or two Supply Pads, and then a Reactor to obtain the Gunner upgrade as quickly as possible. Unless your foe decides to mass a large group of infantry early on, you can pick off small groups of enemy Marines, Flame-

throwers, Jackals, or Grunts by Ramming and shooting them. This leads to early battlefield domination. Even if your foe is infantry-focused, your Warthogs are much more mobile, allowing you to run if the fight is turning against you.

The only problem Warthogs face early on are Turrets; they cannot fight them effectively. If you run into them (as part of a neutral or enemy base), drive away quickly.

The Warthog becomes increasingly ineffectual as a battle progresses. Once out of the early phase, expect to encounter units that are tougher and more specialized and to encounter base defenses that are incredibly effective at taking out Warthogs. In a prolonged firefight, expect infantry and ground vehicles to pummel Warthogs.

Warthogs are reasonably effective against air units later in battle, but you must use the vehicle's mobility and speed to survive.

Elephant

Hit Points: ★★☆

Damage Caused: ★★☆

Movement: ★☆☆

The UNSC Elephant is a unique unit available only to Captain Cutter. It can move around the battlefield and use the active Deploy ability. Infantry can be trained out of a Deployed Elephant.

Base Unit

👤	⚡	📦
2	0	400

Basic Offense: AIE-486H Heavy Machine Gun (x3)

Starting Special Attack: Deploy Mode

Upgrade #1: Twin Engine

Weapon Type: N/A

👤	⚡	📦
N/A	1	250

Elephant speed is greatly improved by the addition of a second engine. Speed increased +30 percent.

Upgrade #2: Defense Turrets

Weapon Type: N247 GPMGT

👤	⚡	📦
N/A	2	500

Adds a light auto-cannon to all Elephants. This turret is only operable when the Elephant is Deployed (locked down).

Upgrade #3: Ceramic Armor

Weapon Type: N/A

👤	⚡	📦
N/A	3	800

An additional set of composite alloy plates boost the Elephant's damage mediation. Damage reduction is -40 percent.

Elephant Overview

Unit Class: Mobile Mini-Base
Strong Against: Enemy bases, enemies that UNSC infantry are strong against
Weak Against: Vehicles, Covenant leaders
Accessed via: Firebase (Cutter only)

A Behemoth-class troop transport, the Elephant is a mobile minibase designed for use as a passenger vessel and sometimes as a cargo vehicle. However, it is usually used to transport UNSC infantry into the combat zone. Currently, the Elephant is utilized as an armored personnel carrier, and UNSC infantry can be trained from the rear of the machine once it is Deployed. It has the added bonus of thick armor and additional turret firepower when stationary, or "locked" into position. A more mobile field Barracks, the Elephant may be ponderous, but it can wreak havoc on an unsuspecting foe.

Tactics

Think of the Elephant as two different types of unit. The the first is a mobile Barracks, allowing you to train infantry troops from a remote location on the battlefield; the second is an offensive or defensive turret.

For an Elephant to actively Deploy and train troops, it must be selected and Locked. This is also how to utilize the turret, which fires automatically. If you wish to move a Locked Elephant, Unlock it first by selecting it and choosing the appropriate icon; otherwise an Elephant remains stationary and won't move with your more mobile troops.

The Elephant's biggest shortfall is its slow and ponderous movement. It is also extremely susceptible to vehicles.

The Elephant's biggest asset is its effectiveness at quickly reinforcing an army along the front line, then supporting this force with its turrets.

The Elephant is only available to Captain Cutter and is only constructed from the Firebase command center. You can construct as many Elephants as your Population allows.

A key tactic is to construct an Elephant immediately, and move it to map Hooks (such as remote Supply or Reactor Hooks) or to a second base. Ideally, position the Elephant defensively like a Turret and quickly produce troops as needed, without having to rely on a Barracks that takes up an important base socket.

Elephants are also useful as additional "Turrets" to further complement your own base's defenses, although an Elephant doesn't feature the same add-ons as a base Turret.

Employ a Rush strategy and bring your Elephants to the front lines, maneuvering them to your opponent's base. Plant them nearby and constantly train infantry (or Spartans to Commandeer your foe's vehicles); this can really annoy a foe to the point of despair!

This unit is unfortunately very slow, expensive, and vulnerable when it isn't Locked. It doesn't fare well against vehicles or Covenant leaders.

One important point to remember is that unlike a Barracks, you cannot research infantry upgrades from an Elephant: Therefore, if you're building infantry, it is important to construct a Barracks in your base so upgrades can be accessed. Fortunately, upgrades apply to all infantry troops; even those trained in the Elephant.

Cyclops

Hit Points: ★☆☆

Damage Caused: ★☆☆

Movement: ★☆☆

The UNSC Cyclops is a unique, special infantry unit. Experimental exoskeleton suits provide incredible strength, making the Cyclops ideal for destroying buildings or other large things.

Base Unit

Basic Offense: Pneumatic Power Fist/ Plasma Riveter Combo

Starting Special Attack: Rip-off and Throw

Upgrade #1: Repair Kit

Weapon Type: N/A

Equips each Cyclops with tools to heal mechanized units and buildings. This can occur when tasked by the user or if the Cyclops is standing idly by it.

Upgrade #2: High Torque Joints

Weapon Type: N/A

Massively improved mobility systems increase the movement speed of each Cyclops. It also increases the throwing damage of the special attack.

Cyclops Overview

Unit Class: Building Killer
Strong Against: Infantry, buildings
Weak Against: Vehicles, most other units
Accessed via: Firebase (Forge only)

A special operations Marine, clad in a prototype bipedal exoskeleton, may not seem the natural choice to send into a large-scale battlefield, but tests have proved so successful that this special infantry unit has become available in limited numbers. Ostensibly an armored mechanic, its primary use is to rebuild damaged buildings and vehicles, but the armor's considerable strength also makes it a vicious attacking machine, capable of ripping portions off an enemy and using them to rudimentary, blunt, and retaliatory effect.

Tactics

This infantry unit is available only when playing as Sergeant Forge. Cyclops troops are constructed only from the Firebase command center.

The Cyclops is excellent at destroying enemy buildings and should be utilized in that manner if employed in an offensive capacity. Use one or more Cyclopes as support units, wading into enemy structures to demolish them or backing up friendly troops by repairing them.

Look closely at your Cyclops when it fights enemy troops; it has a variety of impressive fatality attacks when finishing off an enemy squad!

The Cyclops special attack allows it to use enemy units or portions of enemy buildings to strike foes with.

The Cyclops is most dangerous when it is maneuvered (by sneaking around or by employing the Pelican troop transport) to the rear of an enemy base, and then unleashed on the structure before the enemy can react.

It is also useful to build a couple of Cyclops, upgrade them so they can repair, and then have them "shadow" your key units. For example, send in a Scorpion tank with a veteran Spartan controlling it, and have a Cyclops follow to heal during the battle or after it returns from a fight.

37

This is the only other way to heal troops, aside from the Spirit of Fire's Heal & Repair ability.

Although they have impressive exoskeletons, Cyclops units are only fairly reasonable at combat. In addition, because of their speed and methodical attack style, they are ineffective if you build a large number of them, as they can be easily overcome by enemy forces.

Use them in a support capacity to heal hardier vehicles such as tanks, or employ them during the early part of a siege.

Gremlin

Hit Points: ★★☆
Damage Caused: ★☆☆
Movement: ★★☆

The Gremlin is a lightly armored vehicle that fires an EMP Direct Fire Cannon. It is good against enemy ground vehicles but less effective against infantry.

Base Unit

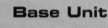

Basic Offense: EMP Direct Fire Cannon (X23 NNEMP)

Starting Special Attack: Electromagnetic Pulse (EMP)

Upgrade #1: Focusing Lens

Weapon Type: N/A

N/A | 2 | 200

Better components dramatically improve (+50 percent) laser attack damage and range for all Gremlins.

Upgrade #2: Chain Amplifier

Weapon Type: N/A

N/A | 3 | 450

EMP ability can chain to hit multiple targets (3).

Gremlin Overview

Unit Class: Combat Support
Strong Against: All ground vehicles
Weak Against: Aircraft, infantry, buildings, and turrets
Accessed via: Firebase (Anders only)

The X23 NNEMP weaponry—essentially a large Electro Magnetic Pulse Cannon—was originally designed to knock down Covenant power generators and other important relaying stations during protracted battles. However, after it was discovered that vehicles were particularly sensitive to this particular EMP pulse, the Gremlin was created. Living up to its ancient original name, this weapon on wheels wreaks havoc with all kinds of ground vehicles, and its upgrades further strike fear into those relying on land machinery.

Tactics

The low Population count needed to man this machine (one) makes this an extremely effective choice; the Gremlin is arguably the most "population-effective" unit available.

This vehicle is unique to Professor Anders. Gremlins are only constructed from the Firebase command center.

Although only lightly armored, this antivehicle unit can use the EMP ability to stun enemy vehicles, and once the upgrades have been made, it can stun multiple enemy vehicles.

This isn't the only antivehicle unit available to the UNSC. However, because Anders has access to the Gremlin earlier than to other antivehicle units, and because the Gremlin does its job exceptionally well, this is an excellent choice for countering a mechanized foe.

Unfortunately, the Gremlin's antivehicle prowess doesn't extend to air units, and it is very inadequate against enemy infantry. Therefore, the Gremlin's main role is to support an army against enemy vehicles.

Although the Gremlin's effectiveness against vehicles can't be overstated, neither can its ineffectiveness against air and infantry. However, being able to counter vehicles immediately (at Reactor Level 1 instead of 3 for Forge and Cutter) means you can react to armed Warthogs or a tank rush very adeptly by manufacturing a couple Gremlins to defend against these attacks.

The Gremlins' EMP special attack is another great trick to play on your foe, as it freezes them in place for a few seconds. If you also have Spartans, use them during this time to Jack or kill the enemy.

Think of Gremlins as the ultimate insurance or reaction against enemy vehicles. If your foe builds anything else, Gremlins become much less impressive, because they falter against all other troop types and aren't adept at destroying buildings.

BARRACKS UNITS

Marine

Hit Points: ★★☆

Damage Caused: ★★☆

Movement: ★☆☆

Marines are the main UNSC infantry unit and are good against most everything. They have an active Grenade ability that can eventually be upgraded to an active Rocket ability.

Base Unit

1 | 0 | 100

Basic Offense: MA5B Assault Rifle

Starting Special Attack: Grenade (M9)

Upgrade #1: New Blood

Adds another Marine to the squad, increasing it from four to five and increasing the squad's combat effectiveness.

N/A | 1 | 200

Upgrade #2: RPG Ability

Weapon Type: M19 SSM Rocket Launcher

N/A | 2 | 400

Upgrades active Grenade ability to activate Rocket ability. Rockets can attack from a longer range than Grenades.

Upgrade #3: Medic

Weapon Type: M6C Magnum Sidearm (Medic only)

N/A | 3 | 700

Adds a Combat Medic to the squad. The Medic heals the squad after combat.

Upgrade #4: ODST Super Unit (Cutter Only)

Weapon Type: M90 Shotgun and M19 SSM Rocket Launcher

N/A | 3 | 1,000

Upgrades Marines to Orbital Drop Shock Trooper (ODST) super units. ODSTs are better than Marines in every way. They can also be hot-dropped anywhere on the battlefield from Spirit of Fire.

Marines Overview

> **Unit Class:** Main infantry
> **Strengths:** Light vehicles, Sniper Towers, holding Hooks, grenading buildings
> **Weaknesses:** Flamethrowers, heavier vehicles
> **Accessed via:** Barracks (and Elephant)

The backbone of UNSC ground forces, the UNSC Marine Corps can trace its roots back to the United States Marine Corp, formed in the 18th century. The people behind the triggers haven't changed a great deal in all these years, far less so than the theaters of operation. Marines first started setting foot on other planets during the Interplanetary War (2160–2170), taking the fight to Mars and officially becoming the UNSC Marine Corps after their victory in that conflict. Marines come equipped with a variety of weapons but generally utilize the MA5 series of rifles. A squad of Marines can lay down some impressive firepower and can even damage armored vehicles with a volley of Grenades or Rockets if they're available. Versatile, relatively cheap to equip, and fast to get on the ground, Marines are a potentially strong force to put into action. En masse, they haul around enough firepower to put the hurt on just about anything an enemy can field.

Tactics

The Marine is the UNSC's main "go-to" infantry unit and is best suited to a variety of offensive and defensive postures.

They can hide in cover; simply locate some and order them to hold it using ⊗. They can also use Sniper Towers. In both cases, their combat effectiveness increases at the expense of movement.

Marines are trained in the Barracks but can also appear from the back of a Deployed Elephant. Upgrades are available to Marines only inside the Barracks.

Marines are excellent when used in Rush strategies; have them charge an installation and utilize their Grenade ability to destroy enemy buildings. They are also exceptional at piling on a foe by surrounding or swarming them to quickly and methodically dispose of them one at a time.

These troops fare reasonably well against enemy air units but are weak against most vehicles—that is, unless you're extremely effective at using the Marines' Grenade or Rocket abilities (e.g., to strike a target simultaneously to weaken it to the point of destruction).

Captain Cutter can field special Marines known as ODSTs. These are more powerful, upgraded via the Barracks, and can be hot-dropped anywhere on the battlefield via the Spirit of Fire menu (⊙, then ⬙).

If your battlefield includes any Hooks (such as Forerunner supplies or Reactors), use Marines for grabbing and holding these locations: Employ mainly a Marine force along with a few Flamethrowers from the back of Elephants you've Rushed in. They are useful throughout a battle for this very purpose.

39

Early in battle, Marines are recommended for tackling Sniper Towers, Turrets, Warthogs, and Ghosts, especially when they employ Grenades or RPG rounds. However, they are extremely vulnerable to Flamethrower units.

Marines are extremely slow, and it is very difficult to try Rushing tactics except on small maps. However, they can take a lot of punishment from most units and can fight off airborne foes with some degree of fortitude. They are an all-around solid unit.

Generally, Marines are used less and less as the battle progresses, as faster and more mobile units take to the field. A massive army of Marines is also very difficult to manage, because a full population of them takes up the entire screen.

Flamethrower

Hit Points: ★★☆

Damage Caused: ★☆☆

Movement: ★☆☆

Pyromaniacs to the core, UNSC Flamethrowers burn up any organic thing they can find. They excel at killing all infantry units.

Base Unit

Basic Offense: The M6334 Defoliant System (M6334/DS)

Starting Special Attack: None

Upgrade #1: Flash Bang Ability

Weapon Type: M301 40 mm Grenade Launcher

Equips Flamethrowers with active Flash Bang ability that stuns any enemy infantry for a short time.

N/A   1   200

Upgrade #2: Napalm Adherent

Slow-burning, sticky napalm burns enemies for several seconds after the initial attack.

N/A   2   400

Upgrade #3: Oxide Tank

An advanced, higher-burn-point fuel increases damage to all organic units.

N/A   3   700

Flamethrower Overview

Unit Class: Anti-Infantry

Strengths: Strong against any enemy infantry type

Weaknesses: Vehicles and air units

Accessed via: Barracks (and Elephant)

These specialized Marines are outfitted with a Napalm-spewing NA4 Flamethrower. First seeing action during World War I, flamethrowers have changed remarkably little since those early days in the trenches. These specialized Marines carry a potent mixture with them in a tank that spews the liquid through a gun onto the target. A variety of mixtures have been created to work in various atmospheric and gravitational conditions, but they are all employed for a similar purpose: to fry just about anything. Squads of Flame Marines aren't particularly common in the UNSC arsenal. Usually they are only called in to exterminate the most firmly entrenched enemies, which means they also take plenty of casualties themselves. They know it's a dirty job, but someone has to do it.

Tactics

A slow-moving, short-ranged, anti-infantry unit means Flamethrowers should be employed only on specific occasions (such as the ones listed below).

Flamethrowers are trained in the Barracks but can also appear from the back of a Deployed Elephant. Upgrades are only available to Flamethrowers inside the Barracks.

The upgraded Flash Bang ability is an excellent one to expend Supply Points on, as it stuns enemy infantry. The adherent nature of the flame liquid also damages foes continuously over time, with devastating consequences—they continuously take damage, mostly until they are killed. This is a great strategy for tagging infantry units fleeing from an attack.

Make sure you train Flamethrowers if your foe is training a large amount of infantry: They are usually favored over Marines early in a battle, because they can easily wipe out foes in neutral bases and are more proficient at defeating Covenant leaders. The best way to deal with a Rushing Covenant leader is to preempt him with some already-trained Flamethrowers locked and hiding in your base!

Unfortunately, Flamethrowers are effective only against enemy infantry. They are no match for most other units available to a foe.

Flamethrowers are reasonably adept at destroying buildings and move a little quicker than Marines. For this reason, try a Flamethrower Rush on small maps: This is especially devastating if the Flamethrowers appear from an Elephant or if your foe isn't building defenses or a collection of Warthogs.

The longer a battle wages, the less effective Flamethrowers become (unless your foe is training only infantry), as they are quickly nullified by more hard-hitting, mobile, or longer-ranged units that can easily deal with them.

Spartan

Hit Points: ★★☆

Damage Caused: ★★☆

Movement: ★☆☆

Prototype UNSC super soldiers, the Spartans possess extreme combat skills. Spartans have the ability to Jack enemy vehicles and Commandeer friendly ones, boosting those vehicles' combat power.

Base Unit

0/3   1   300

Basic Offense: Dual M7S Submachine Guns

Starting Special Attack: Jack/Commandeer

Upgrade #1: Chain Gun

Weapon Type: AIE-486H Heavy Machine Gun

N/A   2   300

Equips Spartans with two-handed auto-guns for dramatically increased damage.

Upgrade #2: Neural Implant

Improved reflexes allow Spartans to Jack enemy vehicles much more effectively.

N/A   3   600

Upgrade #3: Spartan Laser

Weapon Type: M6 Spartan Laser

N/A   4   1,000

The ultimate UNSC handheld weapon gives Spartans a distinct combat advantage.

Spartan Overview

Unit Class: Special Forces

Strengths: Ability to Jack enemy and friendly vehicles and aircraft. Regenerating shields.

Weaknesses: Vulnerable to sustained enemy fire, vulnerable while Jacking.

Accessed via: Barracks (and Elephant)

The Master Chief, John-117, didn't always fight alone. He was part of the SPARTAN-II program that started with 150 child candidates, 33 of whom made it through the intensive training and physical augmentation procedures. On November 1, 2525, the program was accelerated with the discovery of the Covenant threat, and the Spartans adopted their MJOLNIR armor. The war was under way, and the UNSC had over 30 of these supersoldiers at their disposal. Summoning a Spartan to the battlefield is not a guarantee of victory, nor is it something to be taken lightly. It requires a significant investment of time and energy to field Spartans, so they're not a commonplace sight. When they do appear on the scene, though, your opponent better take their threat on the battlefield seriously or suffer the consequences.

Tactics

Spartans are extremely hardy and are the only UNSC unit with regenerating shields. You can have a maximum of three on the battlefield at any one time.

Spartans are trained in the Barracks but can also appear from the back of a Deployed Elephant. Upgrades are available to Spartans only inside the Barracks.

In the initial stages of battle, Spartans are the UNSC's answer to enemy vehicles and aircraft.

Their main purpose (a job they absolutely excel at) is to Jack into enemy units. There's nothing more demoralizing to a foe than seeing three of their main battle tanks switch sides in the heat of battle! Remember to control these enemy units once you Jack them; if you destroy the enemy unit, attempt to maneuver the Spartan to another vehicle or flee to safety.

Spartans can also be upgraded to wield new weapons and become more efficient at Jacking enemy units—this is excellent, as the chances of death are greatly reduced if your Spartan quickly enters an enemy vehicle or aircraft.

Units that a Spartan Jacks have their combat ability increased while piloted by the Spartan. This includes your own vehicles; therefore, it is advantageous to have Spartans lead a charge, sitting inside your own vehicle or aircraft! Utilize this tactic whenever possible, and always attempt it if your foe isn't creating many vehicles but you are. This has the added bonus of making your vehicles "un-Jackable" to enemy Spartans. However, you can't exit a vehicle once you Jack into it, so survey the tactical advantages first!

Remember to check on your enemy: If they are constructing vehicles or aircraft of any sort, then maximize your Spartan troops to three immediately, and head them toward your foe.

Spartans are so adept at Jacking enemy units that the prospect of making vehicles and aircraft (especially slow-moving ones that are easily Jacked) is frightening, as they can be turned against you. Displaying a Spartan on the battlefield early can make your foe change their tactics.

If a foe is Teching up quickly to create tanks or other high-Reactor-level vehicles, simply wait and steal them without expending points Teching to Reactor Level 2 (or higher) yourself.

If you're primarily using Spartans to drive vehicles, it may not be necessary to expend the 1,000 Supply Points fitting them with the third upgrade (Spartan Laser), although this is exceptionally useful if the Spartan is on foot, including after their vehicle explodes.

41

Spartans cannot withstand sustained fire and are very vulnerable while Jacking at low upgrade levels; therefore, pump more Supply Points into upgrading them. Even at low upgrade levels, the resource and Tech swing that occurs

(you gaining vehicles your opponent has spent so much time creating) can dramatically alter the course of a battle.

Additional Spartan units are available at certain points during the campaign, but for skirmish and multiplayer confrontations, only three can be trained at a time.

VEHICLE DEPOT UNITS

Scorpion

Hit Points: ★★★

Damage Caused: ★★★

Movement: ★★☆

Scorpions are the main UNSC vehicle. They can stand toe-to-toe with the toughest enemies but are mobile enough to quickly get where they're needed.

Base Unit

Basic Offense: 90 mm high-velocity gun, M247T Machine Guns

Starting Special Attack: None

Scorpion Overview

Unit Class: Main Vehicle

Strengths: Excellent against infantry. Canister Shells exceptional against most troops.

Weaknesses: Slightly weak against air units. Highly vulnerable to Spartan Jacking.

Accessed via: Vehicle Depot

Officially known as the M808B Main Battle Artillery Tank (MBAT) but nicknamed the Scorpion, this Battle Tank is a mainstay of UNSC forces. It is a flexible weapons platform that can take a beating as well as dish out a great deal of damage, although its main gun can have difficulty penetrating some heavy-armor vehicles. Some would call it a jack-of-all-trades, but a Scorpion can truly be the ace up your sleeve when it comes to breaking through an enemy position. The Scorpion can be upgraded with a variety of technologies that make it pack more punch. Your enemy will learn to respect the Scorpion or end up under its treads.

Tactics

As the Main Battle Tank, the Scorpion is a rumbling and powerful weapon designed to pierce through enemy territory. It is arguably the most effective at destroying enemy units and is extremely efficient at defeating enemy infantry. This is a very well-rounded unit and is preferred when dealing with Covenant leaders.

Their main drawback is against air units; they can fight them but won't win any battles against them. Therefore, it is wise to pepper a force of Scorpions with other troops that are more suited to attacking the skies.

The Scorpion's Canister Shell ability is extremely effective against massed units and is recommended if you're employing hit-and-run tactics against enemy armies. It is also useful when launched at enemy buildings if you're raiding a foe's base.

Instead of charging in with Scorpions, bring them into combat, launch a barrage of Canister Shells, and then retreat while the Canister Shell ability cools down. Then repeat.

Scorpions can quickly deal with infantry troops. However, Hunters present a specific problem, as their weaponry can punch through Scorpion armor. If you spot Hunters, make it a priority to wipe them out.

Sergeant Forge can upgrade his Scorpions to Grizzly Tanks, the ultimate form of this unit, with further improvements on offense and armor.

Upgrade #1: Canister Shell Ability

Weapon Type: S1 "Grapeshot"

N/A 4 400

Equips Scorpion with a secondary Canister Shell attack. This attack is devastating to any infantry in its blast area.

Upgrade #2: Power Turret

Doubles the rotation speed for Scorpion turrets, making them considerably more responsive in combat.

N/A 4 900

Upgrade #3: Grizzly Super Unit (Forge Only)

Weapon Type: 120 mm High-Velocity Gun (x2), M247T Machine Guns

N/A 4 1,800

Upgrades Scorpions to Grizzly Super Units. Grizzlies are heavier tanks that pack a bigger punch than regular Scorpions.

Devastating against most units of a Covenant army, the Scorpion is a little less useful against UNSC forces because of its vulnerability to Jacking by Spartans. Counteract this by protecting Scorpions with Flamethrowers, and try to use this combo as early into the battle as possible.

If your foe is creating a large number of infantry units, Tech up to Reactor Level 2 and take a defensive posture. During this time, set up your base to start constructing Scorpions quickly and continuously; if you send the units onto the battlefield quickly, this can be a very adept retaliation strategy as you roll over him.

Cobra

Hit Points: ★★☆

Damage Caused: ★★☆

Movement: ★★☆

The UNSC Cobra is an incredibly effective antivehicle threat. It's fast and agile against vehicles and has an active Unpack ability that turns the Cobra into a long-range artillery unit that is excellent against buildings.

Base Unit

Basic Offense: 16 MJ LRG Rail Guns (x2; mobile)

Starting Special Attack: Unpack ability

Basic Offense: 8 MJ LRG Rail Gun (locked)

Upgrade #1: Deflection Plating

Hardened steel plates give the Cobra extra protection when locked down.

N/A | 3 | 400

Upgrade #2: Piercing Shot

Cobra Railguns gain extra power to allow them to punch through multiple targets, inflicting damage on each.

N/A | 4 | 900

Cobra Overview

Unit Class: Antivehicle

Strengths: Devastating against vehicles and buildings.

Weaknesses: Cannot fire skyward; prone to air attacks and infantry (when locked down).

Accessed via: Vehicle Depot

Although the SP42 Cobra Main Battle Tank has the ability to fill two roles, it is a specialized fighting vehicle. It has unique armored panels that are designed to deflect hardened projectiles and absorb massive amounts of damage from explosive shells. Although it is not particularly fast, the Cobra is highly maneuverable. It totes around a pair of Rail Cannons on its turret that fire a high-density slug designed to penetrate enemy armor. Alternately, the Cobra crew can choose to lock down the vehicle and Deploy the larger Rail Cannon, which fires a more high-velocity explosive artillery shell. The range advantage gained from elevating the big gun makes up for its sacrificed mobility. The artillery round is multi-purpose and can cause a great amount of damage to just about anything it hits, including enemy fortifications.

Tactics

The Cobra is most proficient when it is pounding vehicles and buildings from long range; it is particularly devastating against enemy ground vehicles.

When the Lockdown ability is employed, it can fire farther and inflict even greater damage. However, this does have drawbacks. The first is obvious: It is immobile until unlocked. The other problem is its minimum range, meaning enemy infantry and melee units can easily strike it without retaliation. Keep this in mind when using the Cobra.

The other major deficit is that the Cobra cannot attack airborne foes under any circumstances and is therefore useless against them. Also beware of infantry, Covenant leaders, and Spirit of Fire attacks directed against them; they cannot fight these attacks effectively. Therefore, Cobras are utilized with other troop types within your army; they take the role of obliterating vehicles at extreme range.

Support Cobras with other units that can tackle enemy air troops, and bolster their locked prone position.

If your opponent is mainly building infantry or air units, Cobras should be mothballed in favor of other troop types.

Because of the Cobra's major deficits, many ignore its benefits. Try the following tactic: Position a few Cobras within extreme range of your enemy's base, ideally at a place that is difficult to reach without air forces, such as the top of a cliff overlooking the base. Then shell the opposition's buildings. If you do this at an opportune moment, you can wipe out a few key installations before your foe reacts.

Cobras are a support unit and require a reasonably high Reactor level to build. It isn't usually practical to use them alone. However, if you mingle them in with a group of Scorpions, they can reduce the time it takes to bombard a base or an opponent's vehicle army.

43

Wolverine

Hit Points: ★★☆

Damage Caused: ★☆☆

Movement: ★★☆

Antiair missile pods cover the UNSC Wolverine's shell. Devastatingly effective against air units, Wolverines can also unleash a fusillade of rockets against buildings.

Base Unit

 2 | 3 | 300

Basic Offense: XM510 Multi-Shot Grenade Launcher

Starting Special Attack: None

Upgrade #1: Volley Ability

Weapon Type: Argent V Missile

N/A | 3 | 400

Enables the Wolverine's active Volley ability, which can be used to deal big damage to any ground target.

Upgrade #2: Dual Launchers I

Weapon Type: Argent V Missile

N/A | 4 | 900

An extra rocket pod gives Wolverines considerably more damage potential.

Wolverine Overview

Unit Class: Antiair

Strengths: Proficient and deadly against all airborne foes. Great to guard other troop types.

Weaknesses: Only lightly armored, problematic when fighting foes on the ground (especially without upgrades).

Accessed via: Vehicle Depot

The MAAT-9 Wolverine Main Antiair Tank (MAAT) is a fast-moving maneuverable antiair vehicle. In its arsenal are two pods of Argent V Missiles that are located on the left and right of the driver and gunner seats, respectively. These missiles are specialized to target and deliver their warhead to an aircraft with great speed and maneuverability. The missile pods are quite large and can be reloaded via a mechanical system in the Wolverine, which stores a small supply of missiles on board. The Wolverine's targeting systems and antiair capabilities are second to none, but it can also angle its missile pods to launch missiles at ground targets. Stationary targets and buildings are your best bets for actually hitting anything. Although air vehicles generally know to steer clear of the Wolverine, the Wolverine is quite vulnerable to antiarmor attacks from vehicles and heavily upgraded infantry. The driver can use an XM511 Heavy Grenade Launcher for defense from ground attacks, which can potentially wreck soft targets, but truly this support vehicle relies on heavier units to defend it from a determined attack.

Tactics

Wolverines feature only light armor but are the perfect foil for enemy air units, especially at long range. The moment you spot your foe building aircraft, counteract them with this versatile vehicle, but only build Wolverines after you see the enemy constructing air units. The Wolverine is good value as well; you don't need a great number to attack a squadron of airborne attackers.

The Wolverine can upgrade to launch a Volley: Use this ability repeatedly to bathe ground units and buildings in explosive fire.

Wolverines are the perfect complement to Cobras, as they both attack at long range, but the Wolverine has the benefit of fending off air attacks while the Cobras continue enemy base bombardment. In fact, Wolverines are the best "guardian" vehicle the UNSC builds; use them to protect against any airborne foe.

As with the Cobra, the Wolverine is clearly a support vehicle and is best used for this purpose; although it can drop a foe from the skies with ease, it is less proficient against other unit types, although it can attack both air and ground targets when upgraded.

Upgrade Wolverines to at least the Volley level, as this adds greater flexibility, and ground units can feel the Wolverine's vicious attacks. However, the vehicle is only of greater benefit to you than other troop types if you're tackling flying foes; build something else otherwise.

44

AIR PAD UNITS

Hornet

Hit Points: ★★☆

Damage Caused: ★★☆

Movement: ★★★

Hornets are the main UNSC air unit. They come armed with Gatling Cannons and explosive rockets, which give them more-than-adequate offense against most enemies.

Base Unit

2 2 250

Basic Offense: Front-mounted Tri-Barreled Chain Gun (GUA-23/A linkless feed .50 BMG rounds)

Upgrade #1: Wingmen

Weapon Type: M19 SSM Rocket Launcher (x2)

N/A 3 200

Adds a couple of Marines riding shotgun to augment damage capabilities.

Upgrade #2: Chaff Pod

Weapon Type: Class-2 Guided Munition Launch System (x2)

N/A 4 450

Hornets gain the passive Chaff ability, which is used to distract and divert incoming missiles.

Upgrade #3: Hawk Super Unit (Anders Only)

Weapon Type: Side-mounted Tri-Barreled Chain Gun (GUA-23/A linkless feed .50 BMG rounds), H6 Spartan Hawk Laser

N/A 4 1,000

Upgrades Hornets to Hawk super units. Equipped with laser beams, Hawks are fearsome combat units.

Hornet Overview

Unit Class: Main Air

Strengths: Excellent at attacking all unit types and ignoring terrain difficulties.

Weaknesses: Light armor, and susceptible to attack from a wide variety of foes.

Accessed via: Airpad

The Attack VTOL-14, or "Hornet," is a tremendously versatile, single-seat support aircraft. The Hornet is often used as close air support to UNSC forces and can also be seen flying alongside larger craft such as the Pelican. This fast attack vehicle is a versatile antiair unit, but it can also take the fight directly to the enemy's ground units. Having a few Hornets in a battle can really turn the tide in the UNSC's favor.

Tactics

The mainstay of UNSC air combat, and much easier to construct than a Vulture, the Hornet moves fast through the skies, naturally avoiding terrain that can bog down ground units.

Due to their impressive mobility, Hornets are especially useful to raid bases or to face foes with a teammate; you can send them quickly to help bolster forces or attack enemies before they realize they're exposed.

Unfortunately, Hornets suffer when attacked by a large number of other units, such as Marines, Grunts, Warthogs, Ghosts, and Wolverines. Expect heavy casualties if the enemy constructs these troop types.

Hornets have a passive Rocket ability as a special weapon, and this inflicts the largest portion of the Hornet's attack damage against vehicles and buildings. Therefore, it is important to employ hit-and-run tactics, launching a barrage and retreating to recharge.

Professor Anders can upgrade her Hornets a stage further into fearsome flying machines called Hawks, which are stronger than Hornets and have amazing offensive capabilities; they are exceptional for raiding enemy bases or quickly darting in, raking a couple of tanks and fleeing before the foe can get a shot off.

Hornets are most commonly used when playing in a defensive role; create and upgrade your Turrets to protect your base while you simultaneously mass Hornets. Once you have a small group of Hornets, chart a path to an enemy base and concentrate your firepower on their Turrets and buildings. Once the enemy begins to retaliate, retreat at speed with minimal damage to your forces.

If the enemy has multiple bases, or you're playing a team game, try flying from base to base to keep your foe guessing. While the foes are occupied blasting your Hornets, your team can increase Tech levels and build harder-hitting units.

45

Vulture

Hit Points: ★★★

Damage Caused: ★★★

Movement: ★★☆

Vultures are the most advanced UNSC war machine. Though costly to produce, Vultures dish out damage at an alarming rate.

Base Unit

6   4   900

Basic Offense:
GUA-23/A linkless feed .50 BMG rounds

Starting Special Attack: Barrage

Weapon Type: Argent V Turret-Mounted Antiair Missile System

Upgrade #1: Mega Barrage

2x

Weapon Type: A74 Sylver Vertical Missile Launcher with Anvil IV ASM Missiles

N/A   4   800

Doubles the number of missiles in each salvo of the active Barrage ability.

Vulture Overview

Unit Class: Uber Unit

Strengths: Well-armored, devastating salvos, and fearsome reputation

Weaknesses: Quite slow-moving, susceptible to the Cryo Bomb

Accessed via: Air Pad

The Vulture is one of the UNSC's most powerful units; it is a highly armed flying assault tank packed to the brim with weapons. The Vulture is the largest aircraft fielded by the UNSC and is designed to deliver massive damage to enemy ground troops after air superiority has been achieved. It is slow-moving but carries an impressive armament of two twin autocannons and rocket silos that can be used to deliver a devastating barrage to enemies in a wide area. Crewed by a highly trained UNSC pilot and gunners, the Vulture is an expensive unit and is usually reserved for difficult or lengthy battles. Being slow, it is vulnerable to antiaircraft fire and enemy aircraft, but it is surprisingly resilient.

Tactics

These flying tanks are large and slow-moving, but no more so than a Scorpion. Think of the Vulture as the UNSC's powerful end-game unit. It isn't advisable to create Vultures instead of other troop types, as the Tech level required means you'll be swarmed by all but the most timid of foes before you have a chance to use them.

Be aware of the large costs involved in Vulture creation; don't try to create one if you don't have at least six free Population!

If your foe hasn't figured out what you're doing (which is a lot easier if you're playing a map with Reactor Hooks), Vultures are a very nasty surprise and are usually hard to deal with. If you see enemy Vultures, you've let your foe build up his forces for too long!

Spartans cannot Jack Vultures, making them a good choice if you're having difficulty countering them otherwise.

Once you utilize the Vulture's Barrage ability, you'll find it excellent and effective against all ground troops and buildings, and you can employ the hit-and-run tactics favored by airborne forces.

Vultures are very slow, but this is tempered by a huge amount of armor, allowing it to last longer than any other UNSC unit under bombardment. In fact, you can lure your foe into turning all their attention to a Vulture, then using faster and sneakier units to outflank and bewilder your foe.

If you manage to acquire a complement of Vultures, they are exceptionally useful when supported by Wolverines if you're fighting the Covenant or when supported by Scorpions if you're battling the UNSC. The reason is simple: The two units complement each other and counter any combination of attacks from the opposition, allowing you to blast away the remaining units with impunity.

46

47

COVENANT LEADERS

Arbiter

Background Details

Age: Unknown
Height: 8'1"
Weight: Unknown
Hair Color: None
Eye Color: Orange

The Arbiter is a force to be reckoned with. After serving time in a maximum-security Covenant prison for crimes against the Covenant, he became the Prophet's choice to lead the battle against the human race and was anointed "Arbiter." He has killed people who serve under him for failing their tasks or bringing ill news, and he has no compunction about sending troops to their deaths if he thinks it will lead to a gain. Though extremely effective, this military savageness is what led him to jail.

The Arbiter's temper is also something of legend, and in mad fits of rage, he can summon strength and speed like no other. However, this rage is directed at enemy and ally alike, and there are several accounts of him being the lone survivor in skirmishes and that he murdered everyone while enraged.

Privilege

For him, there had never been peace, not a moment without rage. His life had been hard and difficult, and his path always murky and dark. Regret stared down at him in the cell. The plasma grid holding him back was the only light in the room, but he sat, unbeaten but purposeless.

"Have you lost your way? Does the path not illuminate your life with purpose and joy? Ripa 'Moramee, answer me. Your very life depends on these next few seconds."

'Moramee looked up; his thoughts were not of his own life but of how easily he could end this noisemaker that disturbed his penance. He focused on the Prophet, standing up and straining against the roof of the cell.

"I do not believe the Journey includes one such as I. I will be left here to rot like garbage."

Regret backed away a little, not because he was fearful but because he wanted to take in the Elite as he stood. His hulking figure was large and imposing.

"The Journey calls for one such as you."

Regret moved back in closer to 'Moramee, their faces inches apart. In the shadows behind Regret, the Honor Guards grew nervous, and their weapons rustled.

"We have need for a leader, one both cunning and savage enough to defeat a great threat to those on the path."

'Moramee thought for a second. "I have served before, and this has been my reward. Nothing has changed."

Regret laughed. "Ripa 'Moramee, you act as if you have a choice in the matter! Your fate is already decided. Your name, it is gone, expunged from the records of this facility. Rise up. I name you Arbiter."

The Honor Guards muttered and whispered. They had no knowledge of this plan.

Regret shouted, "Silence! I need not explain what the Journey demands! Now what say you, Arbiter?"

The Arbiter moved his stance. "I live only to serve Holy One. What task awaits your Arbiter?"

Leadership Qualities and Tactical Notes

Unique Troop Type: Suicide Grunt

These units are extremely specialized and expensive, compared to other leaders' unique units. They are not usually utilized on the battlefield, as Hunters can fill a similar role without the problem of exploding themselves in a greasy mess of chemicals and body bits.

Leader Power: Rage

The Arbiter's Rage ability really comes into its own once you upgrade to Defiant Rage, which allows you to regenerate Hit Points for each kill during Rage mode. The Rage ability is exceptional against massed armies, but you must be careful against the UNSC, as a Disruption Bomb can quickly hamper your progress.

When fighting against the Arbiter as the UNSC, it is preferable to engage a large force that has a strong Arbiter only after you have a Disruption Bomb ready. However, you can also use counter-infantry units (such as the Flamethrower) to deal large amounts of damage to the Arbiter. If you're playing as the Covenant against an Arbiter army, massed Jackals can help to snipe down the Arbiter before he can inflict too many casualties on your forces.

Tactical Notes

The Arbiter is more than capable of massacring an entire army by himself if the enemy is unprepared. By utilizing his Rage ability, along with the Defiant Rage upgrade, the Arbiter can constantly regenerate his Hit Points every time he slays a foe. Fortunately, slaying is what he does best, making the Arbiter a considerable force to be reckoned with. Unfortunately, as the Covenant has a generally weaker economy compared to the UNSC, you must use your leader as effectively as possible to overcome this disadvantage, or you may soon by overrun by superior troops.

Brute Chieftain

Background Details

Age: Unknown
Height: 8'5"
Weight: Unknown
Hair Color: White
Eye Color: Red

As part of the assault on Harvest, he has grown to respect humans in battle for both their savage nature and perseverance against incredible odds. Death in battle against the humans would not be without honor. The Brute Chieftain is a fearsome warrior on the battlefield. Revered by his fellow Brutes, he lives for the chaos of war.

Attacks

For just a second, the Spirit of Fire bridge was in chaos. Information was coming in too fast from the surface, and everything seemed to be falling apart. Crewmembers were running between stations. Even Blake looked flustered and confused.

Cutter stood from his chair. "All right, let's take this one step at a time. Serina, report."

Serina moved from the holopad near Blake to the one right next to Cutter, cocking her head slightly. "Sir, Alpha and Bravo teams report they are under fire by unknown combatants; satellite scans show a large number of ground-based units approaching their positions. Our remaining forces were outflanked by the Covenant." She paused. "Also, Sergeant Forge reports that they are Brutes."

Cutter grimaced. "Get him online, Serina."

"I had a sneaky feeling you would want to chat, sir. He's onscreen now."

Forge's image crackled onto the screen, a thick cloud of billowing black smoke behind him. "Captain, little busy down here. These Brutes are well organized, smart even. We'll get our asses handed to us unless Alpha and Bravo can get over here." Cutter's tone became even more serious. "Sergeant, Alpha and Bravo are under attack. I need you to secure your position ASAP. More troops are inbound to your position."

"Understood, sir. We'll improvise somehow. Forge out."

Serina crossed her arms. "My previous analysis of Brute tactics is that they are very poor ground troops, disorganized and relatively easy to contain. What do you think changed?"

"I suspect like any army, the better the leader the stronger the force. We've been lucky up until now."

Serina moved pads, back next to Blake. "Yes, because they would send their dumbest as the leading invasion forces when they attacked Harvest. All makes sense now."

Blake looked up at Serina and whispered, "How the heck do you get away with that, Serina?"

Serina smiled. "It's easy, really—he knows I control the oxygen valves."

Leadership Qualities and Tactical Notes

Unique Troop Type: Brute and Brute Chopper

Brute infantry units are extremely effective at garrisoning hooks and defending them against enemy vehicles and air units. This gives the Brute an early advantage on many maps with these building types. A good example is Blood Gulch; if you garrison one of the supply elevator hooks and the Sniper Towers around them with Brute infantry, the enemy has a difficult time taking that elevator from you. Brute Choppers are also available, taking the place of Ghosts and manufactured in the Factory. They are tough and can inflict greater damage, but they cost twice as much to build.

> **NOTE**
>
> The Brute Chieftain's grunts come with a Brute infantry leading the squad rather than an Elite, making them more effective against enemy vehicles and air.

Leader Power: Vortex

The Vortex power is an all-encompassing attack that is useful in a variety of situations. Explode the Vortex when you have enemy units that are close to death and you need to finish them off. There is no incorrect way to utilize this attack; however, proficient use makes the Vortex a lot more effective, as you're dealing damage in a short time. When you're attacking a base crowded by foes and many are wounded, let this attack rip! As with the Arbiter, counter the Brute Chieftain with the Disruption Bomb, long-range troops, or massed Jackals if you're playing as the Covenant.

Tactical Notes

The Brute leader is the least effective of the Covenant leaders in large combat. This is because the Chieftain's attacks savage only enemies in immediate melee combat, and the Chieftain must stand motionless when casting his Vortex power. This makes him very vulnerable to enemy units in many situations, as this is the best time to strike. However, the Brute Chieftain is no pushover; this beast is merciless in close-quarter combat and has more impressive Scout and infantry units than either of the other two Covenant leaders.

Prophet of Regret

Background Details

Age: Unknown
Height: 7'0"
Weight: Unknown
Hair Color: None
Eye Color: Brown

Regret's recent rise to power has propelled the Covenant's quest for the fabled Halo rings into the spotlight. After the disastrous first contact with humanity, Regret has pressed hard to ensure humankind's extermination. The Prophet of Regret leads the Covenant alongside the Prophets Truth and Mercy.

The Day Before

Regret looked out over the world rolling before him. His plans, his dreams, and his secrets were all tied to this place. This world had been found many years earlier but lay dormant and still, its treasures locked in place and unreachable with Covenant technology. But now the need for a fleet to battle the humans and find a way to unlock the world had taken precedence over all other tasks, even the search for the rings....

"This world, it is secure from the infection?"

"Yes, Hierarch, the interior is sealed. The surface outside, though, is another matter, and the Flood are nothing if not persistent." The Arbiter bowed his head slightly toward the Prophet as he talked, but he watched him carefully, like prey. His armor had been fitted properly, but it still did not feel comfortable. The prison he had been sentenced to before being anointed to Arbiter had not been kind to his body, and the armor was sharp and unforgiving.

"The treasures here and the bounty they will bring are part of a larger plan. We must not waiver."

The Prophet watched for a moment, his hand clawing at the control panel in front of him, the controls snarled reddish and faded as his hand swept over them. He quickly moved away, not wanting the Arbiter to question the limit of his knowledge. "And what of your search for the key?"

"Hierarch, we scour tirelessly. Just today I have heard word that the human planet we set ablaze has a temple hidden under the ice. I have dis—"

"You have not deemed such a find important enough for your own eyes to see? Do you fear the humans? Do you tremble at the very thought of battle with them?"

"No, Hierarch. It did not seem necess—"

"Not necessary? NOT NECESSARY?! You bask in the glow of the ancients and yet you do not understand where and what you are! You are the Arbiter. Go to the temple; bring me my key. Do our bidding!"

The Arbiter clenched his fists and reached down for his weapon but pulled back. "I will leave at once."

Leadership Qualities and Tactical Notes

Unique Troop Type: Elite Honor Guard

Elite Honor Guards suffer, as they have no long-range attack and can therefore be struck from the air with impunity. However, once they receive the Cloak upgrade, they can be an excellent sneak force, accompanying the Prophet, moving behind enemies and bases, and ambushing foes, especially those fleeing the battlefield. Keep them close and send them in to melee combat when you can.

Leader Power: Cleansing

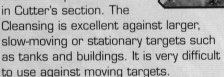

The Cleansing attack works in a similarly devastating manner to Captain Cutter's MAC Blast. Utilize it in the same way, following the tactics presented in Cutter's section. The Cleansing is excellent against larger, slow-moving or stationary targets such as tanks and buildings. It is very difficult to use against moving targets.

If you're facing the Prophet, be sure to keep your troops agile and on maneuvers so the Prophet can't target your units. Spread your units out to limit the Cleansing's area-of-effect damage.

Tactical Notes

The Prophet is a ruthlessly efficient and excellent leader early in a battle. He is best used to harass and destroy small enemy armies using hit-and-run tactics. Employ his Cleansing power against buildings, especially those currently under construction. The Prophet has few deficiencies, aside from those that all Covenant forces suffer from—susceptibility to the Disruption Bomb and the slightly weaker units compared to the UNSC.

CAUTION

All Covenant leaders can be disrupted for a minute at a time, thanks to the Disruption Bomb. This means that even if you've focused heavily on upgrading your Covenant leader, his power can be completely negated by an intelligent UNSC player.

TIP

You must spend Supply Points to use each Covenant leader power. Therefore, tactically stockpile enough supplies for such an attack, judging whether it warrants forgoing other units or buildings to give the attack greater longevity.

TIP

A good way to learn when to expect the Disruption Bomb is to play a Skirmish game and note how long it takes to receive a Disruption Bomb when playing as the UNSC. That way, you know the minimum amount of time you have to dish out damage before you're mired down.

NOTE

A complete list of upgrades (available from the Citadel) for each leader is listed next, in the "Citadel" section.

51

THE CITADEL

The seat of power in the Covenant, the Citadel is the main nerve center for the interplanetary warfare of the Covenant. It offers a modular system that makes aggressive colonization and rapid deployment of troops and armor effective. This is where the political and religious leaders of the Covenant or their underlings issue orders to the various races and cultures that create the Covenant.

Outpost

Building Class: Outpost
Units Trained: Scarab, Suicide Grunts (and upgrades; Arbiter only), Brute Infantry (and upgrades; Brute Chieftain only), Elite Honor Guard (and upgrades; Prophet of Regret only)

N/A 0 500

Use this to construct a new outpost base. Eventually, it can be upgraded to a full Citadel, increasing your ability to crush the evil enemy. When you destroy a neutral or enemy base or when you locate an empty base pad, you can build an Outpost, providing you have the supplies. It has three building pads and doesn't feature any Turret base slots. Whether this is a good idea depends on the map, as some base locations are better than others; how strong the enemy is; and what position your forces are holding. Refer to the Campaign, Skirmish, and Multiplayer tactics for all the available base locations.

> **NOTE**
> Once a neutral or enemy base is destroyed, you must wait 25 seconds before you can build a Covenant base at the same position.

> **CAUTION**
> Outposts are extremely prone to attacks during the initial construction. Make sure no enemies are in the area before you start to build, or your base will be destroyed before it's even been built!

Keep

Building Class: Keep

N/A 0 300

Upgrades base to a Keep, which adds two building sites. Unlike the UNSC leaders, the Covenant's heroes all upgrade their Outposts without any advantages over each other. The Keep has five expansion pads and four Turret base slots. If you fear enemy attacks, it is better to upgrade from an Outpost to a Keep and augment it with Turrets. It is wise to time the upgrade of this base to a Citadel so that the Citadel is built just as the last building rises up from a Keep.

Citadel

Building Class: Citadel

N/A 0 400

Upgrades base to a Citadel, which adds two building sites. Each building adds to the strength of the central structure. It has a total of seven expansion pads and four Turret base slots; these aren't additional but simply add two more building pads to a Keep. Judge whether you need the two additional pads immediately—they are certainly needed on your initial base. It is almost always wise to upgrade to a Citadel, as the buildings allow more damage for the central structure to absorb.

> **TIP**
> The strength of the central command structure is shown as a series of white bars (from zero to seven) above your base's green damage bar; the more buildings you have attached to a base, the bigger the bar and the more damage it takes to destroy a base.

Other Base Functions

Base Rally Point

New units from this base will move to this location when training is complete. Use the Global Rally Point to override this. Using this flag option is extremely important, as it allows you to point to an area of your map and have any troop type head there after building or training; this effectively takes the manual labor out of this function. Remember where your Rally Point is, in case it falls to the enemy—you don't want to send your troops straight into danger! Every base has its own Rally Point, allowing you to mass separate armies if you want to, say, tackle a base from two directions.

> **TIP**
> You can also make the Gravity Lift a Base Rally Point by clicking over it and selecting "Global Rally Point," thus sending forces directly to your leader's side.

Self-Destruct

Instantly destroy this entire base to free it up for an ally. This is really the only fortuitous method of using this function; otherwise, employ this if your base is under attack so your foe doesn't have the satisfaction of destroying your base with his forces. You gain Supply Points if you blow up your own base, but do this only if you have troops outside or elsewhere on the map that can quickly locate and build a new base. You are still at a serious disadvantage.

> **CAUTION**
> If you destroy a base and have no other bases yourself, you have one minute to build a new base or lose the fight.

52

All buildings can be recycled, which destroys them and
empties the Base Pad they stood on. Expect Warehouse
Supply Points (around half the building's value) to be added
to your total. This happens more frequently, as you remove
structures for more important ones. A few examples:

Unlike the UNSC, it is never wise to remove Temples
(the Covenant equivalent of Reactors) after becoming
overly technologically advanced.

If you build a Hall but no longer have any use for the
troops inside (if Grunts, Jackals, and Hunters are less
effective compared to your enemy's forces), recycle
the structure and erect a more useful building.

Unlike the UNSC, there are no "useless" buildings that
can be destroyed once their upgrades have been
completed, such as the UNSC's Field Armory.

Lock

Units train as normal but are garrisoned
inside the base instead of exiting into
the world. Unlock will release all the
garrisoned units at once. Locking and
Unlocking your base allows you to
surprise a foe who is checking out your
location and allows you to keep troops that you are
massing safely inside the protective walls of your base.
When you Unlock or Lock your base, the ramped doors
clamp open or shut, allowing you to know whether an
enemy's base is open. When the doors are closed, this
means you or your foe are massing troops. However, if
you get into the habit of always Locking your base, you
can fool your foe into thinking you're massing troops,
whether you are or not! Use this secrecy to your tactical
advantage.

CITADEL BUILDINGS

Gravity Lift

Actually part of the Citadel, this flat
teleporter in front of the Citadel
allows you to Hot Drop (also known
as teleporting) any Covenant troop to
your leader's location, anywhere on the
battlefield. Simply select the units you
wish to Hot Drop, select the Gravity Lift, and press Ⓐ.
This is a key advantage of the Covenant and lets you
use Rushing tactics from the first moments of battle,
allowing you to sweep through an unsuspecting enemy
immediately!

TIP

You must utilize this feature of the Citadel almost every
time in battle to bolster the support of your leader. Here
are just some of the ways Hot Dropped units can help
your cause:

1. You can provide reinforcements to a leader without
having to send them with the leader.

2. You can adjust your troop types easily and quickly,
based on what your opponent does to try and defend
against your leader. If you send your leader and
Hunters in, and your foe starts constructing Hornets,
quickly change to build Vampires and Hot Drop them
in.

3. You can cover your escape if your leader needs to
leave a theater of battle. Drop in Wraiths to block the
enemy while your leader flees to safety.

4. Drop in Engineers to heal your leader quickly and
effectively.

5. When attacking a base with Turrets, drop in quickly
trained, expendable units to soak up the Turret
damage while your leader tackles the buildings you
want demolished.

Covenant Turrets

The Covenant Citadel comes with four
Turret slots. These slots have room
for light, medium, and heavy Turrets
(upgrades the Temple provides) and
can be further upgraded with specific
antivehicle, antiair, and anti–infantry
Turrets. The Plasma Mortar, Fuel Rod, and Needler
upgrades can prove devastating against their opposing
units. Approaching enemy units would be wise to take
out Turrets quickly or risk their forces being decimated.
Turrets are expensive, and while they provide a very
effective defense, they cannot hold out forever and will
need military support in order to ensure victory. Turrets
are very effective against leader units and aircraft.

Turret (Basic)

Weapon Type: Plasma
Turrets
Building Class: Base
Defense

Turrets are good at defending bases
against all enemy targets. You can have
up to four Turrets for each base (one on
each corner), which allows a slightly farther line of sight.
It is usually wise to build the two Turrets at the front of
the base first, but this depends on where the enemy
usually attacks from. Simply build the Turret and leave it
to fire at enemy forces; you cannot control the Turret's
aiming.

NOTE

Turrets can be upgraded two times if you have the
supplies; the upgrades are located in the Temple. Information on these upgrades, which essentially add armor
and a better weapon, are detailed in the "Temple" section.

53

Turret: Plasma Mortar

Weapon Type: Plasma Mortar

Adds bonus anti-infantry attack to the Turret.

 N/A · 1 · 100

Turret: Fuel Rod

Weapon Type: Fuel Rod

Adds bonus antivehicle attack to the Turret.

 N/A · 1 · 100

Turret: Needler

Weapon Type: Needler

Adds bonus antiair attack to the Turret.

 N/A · 1 · 100

Turrets have three unique augmentations that allow you to swap out different armament types for a battle's duration. You can add only one add-on at a time, but each can be changed at any time, and every Turret can have one of the three options. These are well worth the minor Supply Points it takes to fit them. Use them once you see what type of troops an enemy is building or sending your way. If you can correctly predict (usually via Ghost reconnaissance) the troops, it is easier to defend your base.

Supply Warehouse

The Covenant Warehouse utilizes gravity lifts to bring down supplies to Covenant bases. From here, workers move the supplies to the proper area for further use by the Covenant commander. The Warehouse can be upgraded to increase the rate of incoming supplies.

Warehouse

Building Class: Produces Resources

The Covenant Warehouse produces the resources needed to train units, build buildings, and buy Technology upgrades. Bases that have great economic production might have six Warehouses.

 N/A · 0 · 100

Blessed Warehouse

Upgrade the production capacity of this Warehouse to produce more supplies.

 N/A · 1 · 225

Refer to the "Advanced Training" chapter for specific tactics on how many Warehouses to make and how the different Warehouses work. In general, try building between five and seven Warehouses (or three Blessed Warehouses and two Basic Warehouses) for the best return on your investment. The number of Warehouses you build is limited only by your Base Pads.

54

> **NOTE**
> The UNSC version of the Warehouse is the Supply Pad.
> Many maps have Forerunner structures that act as Warehouses and Supply Pads. Train infantry units to capture and hold these structures; these are much more advantageous to keep, as they free up Base Pads and cost less to bring online.

Temple (Reactor)

The Temple is the main cultural and scientific building of the Covenant. This is where Prophets go to meditate on Forerunner artifacts and on how to best eradicate humanity. The upgrades that the Covenant research here are very expensive; however, they are also very effective and powerful.

> **TIP**
> Protect your Temple. It is a prime target for enemy raids. When it is destroyed, you will no longer be able to field your more impressive vehicles, such as Vampires and Scarabs.

Temple

Building Class: Special Upgrades

Temples allow the Covenant to access advanced buildings, units, and technology upgrades. Think of the Temple as a single building structure that has the same abilities as a UNSC Reactor and Field Armory, allowing you to increase your Tech level and upgrade your troops and Leader Powers.

0/1 · 0 · 500

> **NOTE**
> You can have only one Temple no matter how many bases you own. The Temple is the only way to increase your Tech level. The maximum Tech level needed to produce all units and upgrades is three (the Age of Reclamation).

Age of Doubt

Improves all Covenant technology.

N/A · 0 · 1,000

Age of Reclamation

Improves all Covenant technology.

N/A · 0 · 2,000

Spiteful Rage (Arbiter Only)

Rage mode costs less to maintain.

N/A | 2 | 500

Blinding Rage (Arbiter Only)

Rage mode increases Arbiter combo damage and the attack power of nearby allies.

N/A | 3 | 700

Brute Chieftain (Brute Chieftain Only)

Leader of the Brute forces, the Brute Chieftain carries a Gravity Hammer capable of stunning and destroying heavy vehicles.

0/1 | 0 | 400

Inheritance (Brute Chieftain Only)

Adds a stun to the Gravity Hammer.

N/A | 1 | 400

Birthright (Brute Chieftain Only)

When the Chieftain's hammer is charged up, he will pull his enemies to him.

N/A | 2 | 600

Destiny (Brute Chieftain Only)

Adds an area-of-effect stun to the Gravity Hammer and causes fatalities on stunned enemy infantry.

N/A | 3 | 900

Tsunami (Brute Chieftain Only)

Additional enemies may be drawn into the vortex and potential damage increased.

N/A | 1 | 300

Hurricane (Brute Chieftain Only)

Additional enemies may be drawn into the vortex and potential damage increased.

N/A | 2 | 500

Temple Units and Upgrades

Although the Temple increases the Tech level of your army when created and upgraded, it is also much more than a simple Reactor. This location, much in the same way as the Hall, Factory, and Summit, has a variety of units and upgrades you can select, which are listed below.

Leader Upgrades

Arbiter (Arbiter Only)

Leader of the Covenant forces, the Arbiter is equipped with dual plasma swords for uber melee death.

0/1 | 0 | 400

Fiendish Return (Arbiter Only)

The Arbiter reflects some incoming damage back to his attacker.

N/A | 1 | 400

Vicious Blades (Arbiter Only)

The Arbiter reflects even more damage and has stronger attacks.

N/A | 2 | 600

Ghastly Vision (Arbiter Only)

The Arbiter becomes permanently cloaked and increases reflected damage even more.

N/A | 3 | 900

Defiant Rage (Arbiter Only)

Health is restored every time the Arbiter causes a fatality in Rage mode.

N/A | 1 | 300

Singularity (Brute Chieftain Only)

Additional enemies may be drawn into the vortex and potential damage increased.

| 👤 N/A | ⚡ 3 | 📦 700 |

Prophet of Regret (Prophet of Regret Only)

Leader of the Covenant forces, the Prophet of Regret also brings unique combat abilities to the battlefield. In addition to his combat strength, he can call down the Cleansing power to incinerate his enemies.

| 👤 0/1 | ⚡ 0 | 📦 400 |

Blessed Immolation (Prophet of Regret Only)

Upgrades the Prophet's Plasma Cannons to Fuel Rod Cannons, increasing damage.

| 👤 N/A | ⚡ 1 | 📦 400 |

Ancestral Perversion (Prophet of Regret Only)

Two protectors hover near the Prophet and protect him.

| 👤 N/A | ⚡ 2 | 📦 600 |

Divine Absolution (Prophet of Regret Only)

Upgrades to the Prophet's chair grant him full flight capabilities.

| 👤 N/A | ⚡ 3 | 📦 900 |

Regret's Sentence (Prophet of Regret Only)

The Cleansing Beam ability is larger and does more damage.

| 👤 N/A | ⚡ 1 | 📦 300 |

Regret's Doom (Prophet of Regret Only)

The Cleansing Beam ability is larger and does more damage.

| 👤 N/A | ⚡ 2 | 📦 500 |

Regret's Condemnation (Prophet of Regret Only)

The Cleansing Beam ability burns even brighter, doing area damage.

| 👤 N/A | ⚡ 3 | 📦 700 |

NOTE

For expanded Arbiter, Brute Chieftain, and Prophet of Regret information, consult the "Leaders" section earlier in this chapter.

Other Upgrades

Medium Turret

Upgrades all Turrets to Medium, increasing their Hit Points and damage.

| 👤 N/A | ⚡ 1 | 📦 500 |

Large Turret

Upgrades all Turrets to Large, increasing their Hit Points and damage.

| 👤 N/A | ⚡ 2 | 📦 800 |

These two upgrades instantly bulk up every Turret you've already built or intend to build, granting one extra weapon and adding around a third more armor (Medium) or two weapons and one-and-a-half as much armor (Large). If you're being constantly hassled by foes at your base, this makes enemy incursions more difficult. It also sends a visual signal to your foe that your base is now much stronger and well defended. Naturally, the more Turrets you already have, the more useful these two upgrades are.

TIP

You can see the differences in the size and number of guns at the top of each upgraded Turret. This is useful when scanning your enemy's base; if there are enhanced Turrets, you know your job will be that much more difficult, and you can prepare accordingly (with more reinforcements or Leader Powers focused on the Turrets). Also note that it costs one less Tech Level to upgrade Covenant Turrets compared to UNSC ones.

Forerunner Shield

Augmented with even more repurposed Forerunner technology, all Covenant shields now recharge much faster. This Covenant-only upgrade affects every unit and structure that uses shielding

| 👤 N/A | ⚡ 2 | 📦 500 |

(such as the Shield Generator you use to help protect the Citadel, and the Wraith's shields), allowing them to withstand enemy gunfire. Effectively doubling the speed of the recharge after combat, this is a great upgrade if you're using Wraiths in hit-and-run tactics.

Reinforcements

Adds +10 to the population cap of your army. Aside from the 2v2 Beaseley's Plateau map, which features a Life Support Pod, this is the only way you can increase the total population of your army from 40 to 50. This means, for example, three extra Wraiths and Hunters to protect them, or five more Ghosts. Additional units are always useful, and this is a thoroughly recommended upgrade as long as you're already nearing your 40 Population limits; if you're scrabbling around at 10 to 15 Population and under constant enemy attacks, gain a tactically stronger position and more troops first.

N/A   3   800

> **NOTE**
>
> Covenant forces are generally slightly weaker than UNSC equivalents but have a higher Population cap. Take advantage of this!

Other Buildings
Shield Generator

Building Class: Base Protection

N/A   1   200

Generates a large bubble shield to protect the base. Multiple Shield Generators can be built in a base to increase the Shield's strength. This is a unique building that the Covenant can rely on (the UNSC cannot construct shield protection buildings). Usually built toward the front of the structure, as the enemy can attack these without much economic or technology losses, it is wise to invest in at least one of these Generators per base. Essentially adding a layer of shielded protection, this adds valuable time to an enemy's attack, allowing you to retaliate or add Turrets. Add a second Shield Generator to toughen up the base again. Once a foe has been fought off, the Generators automatically recharge, much like a Spartan's armor.

> **TIP**
>
> You may wish to invest in the Forerunner Shield upgrade (accessed via the Temple), with faster recharge rates that apply to Shield Generators too.

Hall

The Covenant Barracks is home to the well-trained and numerous infantry of the Covenant Forces. Grunts led by Elites, Jackals, and Hunters are trained here. The different races are housed separately according to their status in the caste system. Grunts, the lowest of the caste system, perform many of the more demeaning tasks. The lone Jackals tend to socialize only among themselves, while the solitary Hunters communicate with each other via their collective consciousness. The powerful Covenant upgrades are researched here as well, augmenting the Covenant infantry with better energy weapons and armor.

Hall (Building)

Building Class: Trains Infantry

N/A   0   150

Units Trained: Grunt Squad (and upgrades), Jackal (and upgrades), Hunter (and upgrades)

The Covenant Hall rallies infantry units to the cause. Upgrades for infantry units are also housed here.

Halls are usually built early rather than later into a battle, as infantry are less and less useful as more powerful troops become available. The Hall has several advantages: It can provide quick and cheap units to instantly nullify early Rushes from the enemy. It also doesn't need a Tech Level to be built, enabling you to set up a Hall as soon as you wish. However, Covenant Factories and Summits don't need Tech levels, so you are free to build any type of unit as early as possible. The Hall trains three types of units (detailed later in this chapter), and all have their uses and hindrances in the combat zone. Consider recycling this when ground and air vehicles become more prevalent.

> **NOTE**
>
> The specialized units particular to a leader are not trained in the Hall; they are trained in the Citadel.

Factory

The Factory is the manufacturing facility for Ghost Scouts, Wraith Tanks, and Locust Walkers. This building serves as a sophisticated warehouse for all the land-based vehicles in the Covenant's arsenal, and the powerful upgrades for all the units are researched here. The Covenant can build the Factory from the get-go without having to upgrade the Citadel, giving them early land-based firepower.

57

Factory (Building)

Building Class: Trains Vehicles

N/A   0   150

Units Trained: Ghost (and upgrades), Wraith (and upgrades), Locust (and upgrades)

Most Covenant vehicles are pieced together and upgraded at the Factory.

Usually a player opts for either a land- or air-based contingent during the middle stages of battle, but a Covenant player has more flexibility in the early stages of battle, because this structure doesn't require a Tech level, unlike the UNSC's Vehicle Depot, which requires a Tech level of two. Once you build a Factory, you have access to three very impressive vehicles (Ghost, Wraith, and Locust, which are detailed later into this chapter). A Factory is usually placed in a base, but judge your opponent's actions to deem whether one is necessary. Naturally, many other factors should be considered, too, such as if you're playing as the Arbiter and want to concentrate on Suicide Grunts trained in the Citadel, or whether your foe is Turtling and you have time to spend upgrading vehicles.

Summit

The Summit is the roost for all the Covenant's powerful air force. The quick Banshees, the deadly Vampires, and the versatile Engineers are all built here. The upgrades that make the Covenant air force even more fierce are available at this location.

Summit (Building)

Building Class: Trains Aircraft

Units Trained: Engineer (and upgrades), Banshee (and upgrades), Vampire (and upgrades)

N/A   0   150

Covenant aircraft are constructed at the Summit. Aircraft upgrades are also

in this structure. Opting for air superiority depends on the topography of the map and the actions of your foe, such as whether they have weaponry designed to take down aircraft (such as Anders's Cryo Bombs) and whether you wish to use Banshees or Vampires. Engineers are the only way to heal troops easily in the battlefield if you're playing as the Covenant, so building a Summit is essential if you want extra longevity for your troops.

The difference between UNSC infantry, vehicle, and aircraft structures is that UNSC buildings require a Tech level of 2, whereas the Covenant ones can be built and troops accessed from the very beginning. This is important, as it allows the Covenant to Rush or Hot Drop near a leader incredibly early during a battle.

CITADEL UNITS

Scarab

Hit Points: ★★★
Damage Caused: ★★★
Movement: ★★☆

The Covenant super unit. These massive assault vehicles have a devastating beam that can tear apart virtually anything.

Base Unit

20   3   3,000

Basic offense: Heavy Mining Laser, Antiaircraft Plasma Cannons
Starting Special Attack: None

Scarab Overview

Unit Class: Uber Unit
Strengths: Incredible firepower. Excellent armor. Almost invincible when paired with Engineers.
Weaknesses: Slow. Vicious swarms of many enemies attacking simultaneously.
Accessed via: Citadel

The Scarab is the most frightening weapon in the Covenant arsenal. Repurposed heavy mining equipment, the Scarab's mining laser can inflict massive damage across the battlefield. It also has antiair turrets on top and a colossal laser, and it can climb over any terrain. Although it is slow, it is often the center of any battle it finds. Incredibly expensive and slow to build, the Scarab is often seen late in battles and is often a deciding factor. A Lekgolo colony directs the Scarab from within. Something as big and expensive as the Scarab is already functioning at maximum offensive capacity, so there are no upgrades available.

Tactics

The Scarab is an immense titan of a ground unit but is relatively slow-moving. Due to the Population and Supply costs, only two of these behemoths can be active at once.

This is the Covenant's powerful end-game unit and is even more powerful than the UNSC's Vulture. It is unmatched in its strength and power. It can devastate armies and bases with equal effectiveness.

Accessing the Tech level and supplies to build a Scarab is difficult and expensive, but once on the field, it is almost impossible to stop before it destroys your foe's bases.

With everything you invested in creating a Scarab, keep it going for as long as possible; use Engineers to accompany the Scarab when you send it off to enemy bases.

The Scarab tears through enemy strongholds so quickly that your foe usually can't react fast enough to stop you, and it is even more difficult if Engineers are keeping the Scarab healthy.

Scarabs are also useful on maps where there are several Reactor Hooks: Keep your opponent under a constant struggle by sending your leader to fight while you control the Reactors yourself; claim two Reactors and suddenly you'll find it much easier (and cheaper) to produce one, as the supplies you needed to upgrade your Temple aren't necessary. Pull off this cunning tactic, and you're almost impossible to stop, especially if you attempt this strategy as early as possible.

Suicide Grunts

Hit Points: ★☆☆

Damage Caused: ★☆☆

Movement: ★☆☆

Suicide Grunts are a perverted variant of the already dangerous Grunts. They can sacrifice themselves on enemy targets using the Suicide ability.

Base Unit

Basic offense: Plasma Pistols

Starting Special Attack: Suicide Mode

Upgrade #1: Zeal

Suicide Grunts are faster in Suicide mode.

Upgrade #2: Defile

The Suicide Grunt's explosion splashes enemies with burning chemicals.

Suicide Grunt Overview

Unit Class: Special Forces

Strong Against: Taking down buildings in a mass assault.

Weak Against: Flamethrowers, heavier vehicles. More expensive than regular Grunts if you aren't interested in the Suicide ability.

Accessed via: Citadel (Arbiter only)

Certain numbers of Unggoy troops are cultivated to provide the ultimate sacrifice for the Arbiter's cause and are trained in the art of suicide. Strapping volatile chemicals to their backs, they waddle off to their doom, ready to burst for the greater good of the hive.

Tactics

Unique to the Arbiter and available only through the Citadel, these Grunts are additional to regular Grunt infantry. They are slow-moving units designed to destroy buildings.

The Suicide Grunt squad has a main mission: to engage in Suicide mode and throw all squad members into enemy units and explode. The resulting explosion is very effective against both enemy vehicles and buildings.

A useful technique to master is running your Arbiter around to the rear of an enemy base, and then teleport in a large group of Suicide Grunts. With a large army of these maniacs, you can inflict crippling damage to an enemy installation before your foe is aware of what happened.

Other than this daring death plan, Suicide Grunts aren't the best for regular fighting. The only reason to train them is to send them into an enemy base to explode, removing a particular building, such as an upgraded Temple or Warehouse.

Suicide Grunts cost a lot to produce compared to the specific role you need them for. If you have the economic advantage over your foe, using them to destroy enemy structures is a useful delaying tactic.

Brute Infantry

Hit Points: ★★☆

Damage Caused: ★★☆

Movement: ★☆☆

Specialized, heavy infantry with powerful Brute guns, these squads dish out lots of damage.

Base Unit

Basic Offense: Brute Gun

Starting Special Attack: None

Upgrade #1: Jump Pack Ability

Enables the Jump Pack ability, allowing Brutes to quickly cross the battlefield.

N/A | 2 | 500

Upgrade #2: Electric Shot

Weapon: Brute Gun (Electrified)

The Brute Shot causes electrical stun damage when it hits.

N/A | 3 | 800

Brute Infantry Overview

Unit Class: Special Forces
Strong Against: Fleeing or slow-moving foes. Able to leap to Map Hooks and hold them with ease, once upgraded.
Weak Against: Flamethrowers, heavier vehicles.
Accessed via: Citadel (Brute Chieftain only).

Known colloquially as the Jiralhanae, Brutes are part of the Covenant's main forces and have a justified reputation for bloodshed, savagery, and incredible strength. With thick, sinewy gray hides and sharp fangs, they are the blunt instrument that the Brute Chieftain uses to great effect while in the service of the Prophet.

60

Tactics

A special operations unit designed as a ranged special-operations force of infantry units, Brutes don't amaze their leaders with any stand-out abilities, but they are reasonable at all forms of combat.

Initially, Brutes are slower than most troops in the Covenant army but are a recommended supplement to your mix of units. The reason to choose them becomes clear once you upgrade to their Jump Pack ability.

The Jump Pack ability increases the Brutes' mobility both horizontally and vertically, making them extremely useful if you want to tactically head behind enemy lines or move in front of escaping enemy armies to "round them up" or launch a surprise attack.

Better yet, you can utilize the Brutes' Jump Pack to leap up and over scenery. This isn't anywhere as proficient as a flying unit, but there's no other unit that can easily reach a Map Hook and then guard it as well. This alone is incredibly useful.

Another upgrade is the Electric Shot, which can actually stun enemies if an attack hits. If you're mopping up forces, upgrade to this.

A recommended tactic when utilizing the Brutes is to construct a Temple as early as possible, and train your Covenant leader quickly, moving him to the enemy's base and then Hot Dropping Brutes to the front lines. Your opponent will have a very hard time dealing with this force in his base at such an early point during the battle.

Elite Honor Guard

Hit Points: ★★☆
Damage Caused: ★★☆
Movement: ★☆☆

Speciality troops that guard the Prophet. These stealthy infantry wield powerful plasma swords capable of shredding any target.

Base Unit

1 | 1 | 125

Basic Offense: Plasma Sword
Starting Special Attack: None

Upgrade #1: Cloak Ability

Enables Cloak ability.

N/A | 2 | 500

Upgrade #2: Personal Shield

Adds a personal shield that decreases incoming damage.

N/A | 3 | 800

Elite Honor Guard Overview

Unit Class: Special Forces
Strong Against: Infantry, most foes at extremely close range, cloaked ambush attacks.
Weak Against: Air units (useless), any enemy at range.
Accessed via: Citadel (Prophet of Regret only)

The finest Sangheili troops seek to protect High Prophets, and these veteran melee combat specialists are the finest, most vicious, and calculating foes instilled with a great degree of honor. Currently duty-bound to protect the Prophet of Regret, there is currently a murmuring among the Elites that some were chosen not for their undying loyalty, but as a way to silence those who dared to disagree with some of the Prophet's edicts. A battle or two should see who remains fervently supporting the Prophet....

Tactics

A special-operations unit armed to tackle other infantry units in melee combat. Note that they cost 25 fewer Supply Points than the other unique units.

Elites are very useful when they gain their Cloaking ability, as this is their main use. Naturally, your opponent cannot see the ghostly form that you can just make out. Watch out when you decloak and cloak near enemy turrets, though; they can easily cut you down even when you return to a cloaked form.

The Elite Honor Guard isn't particular weak or strong against any enemy, although they are useless at fighting air units (they cannot strike them, as they carry only Plasma Swords).

While cloaked, the Elite Honor Guards gain a defensive bonus against enemy fire, but this cloak can also be used to sneak in behind enemy troops to tackle the weaker enemies that may be hiding at the back of an enemy army. Normally these would be tough to reach, but not anymore!

Elite Honor Guards are also great for pincer maneuvers, with a visible force luring a foe to fight them (perhaps playing the role of a weak collection of troops). As the enemy closes, attack en masse with your Guards and your visible troops and crush your foes in a sandwich of seething plasma weaponry!

A recommended tactic involves constructing a Temple as early as possible so your Prophet appears quickly. Then move him to the enemy's base while you're training Elite Honor Guards. Hot Drop the Guards to the front lines to fight alongside the Prophet, and watch your foe mill around, unable to withstand this early and vicious battering!

HALL UNITS

Grunt Squad

Hit Points: ★★☆
Damage Caused: ★★☆
Movement: ★☆☆

The Covenant's mainline troops, Grunts are slow and fire short-ranged weapons, yet still have the best returns per cost in combat.

Base Unit

Basic Offense: Plasma Pistols

Starting Special Attack: Plasma Grenades

Upgrade #1: Peons

Grunt squads have one additional Grunt. N/A 1 200

Upgrade #2: Needler

Weapon Type: Needler
Grunt squads are now equipped with Needlers. N/A 2 400

Upgrade #3: Deacon

Inspires the Grunt squad, improving their combat abilities. N/A 3 700

Grunt Squad Overview

Unit Class: Main Infantry
Strengths: Strong against light vehicles, Sniper Towers, holding Hooks, grenading buildings, and Rushing.
Weaknesses: Flamethrowers, heavier vehicles.
Accessed via: Hall

The Grunts, or Unggoy, are the foot soldiers of Covenant ground forces. Used in large numbers to overwhelm enemy positions, Grunts are weak as individuals but are a force to be reckoned with in groups. Almost always led by a higher-caste Covenant infantry unit, such as a Brute or an Elite, they can wield most Covenant weapons. The methane tanks they breathe from sometimes explode, often with hilariously violent results.

Tactics

Grunts are the most versatile of the Covenant's main units. Their role, strengths, and weaknesses are very similar to the UNSC Marines. Consult the Marines tactics; those strategies apply to both units.

Grunts are very useful if you're planning a Rush strategy, as their Plasma Grenades are effective. Grunts can also swarm enemy units.

Grunts differ from UNSC Marines in that they are a little more viable during a Rush, simply because they can be Hot Dropped to the Covenant leader's position. This eliminates their greatest weakness: slow speed.

> **NOTE**
>
> The Brute Chieftain's Grunts come with a Brute Infantryman leading the squad rather than an Elite. This makes the Chieftain's grunts more effective against enemy vehicles and air when compared to the standard Grunt squad.

Jackal

Hit Points: ★☆☆

Damage Caused: ★☆☆

Movement: ★☆☆

Counter-infantry unit, often armed with sniper rifles, Jackals can make quick work of enemy infantry.

Base Unit

👤	⚡	📦
1	0	100

Basic Offense: Slug Beam Rifle

Starting Special Attack: None

Upgrade #1: Defense Gauntlet

Adds extra shielding to deflect incoming projectiles.

👤	⚡	📦
N/A	1	200

Upgrade #2: Beam Rifle

Weapon Type: Particle Beam Rifle

Jackals are now equipped with Particle Beam Rifles.

👤	⚡	📦
N/A	2	400

Upgrade #3: Supreme Gauntlet

Jackal shields do not collapse when taking damage.

👤	⚡	📦
N/A	3	700

Jackal Overview

> **Unit Class:** Anti-infantry
>
> **Strengths:** Strong against any enemy infantry type.
>
> **Weaknesses:** Vehicles and air units.
>
> **Accessed via:** Hall

The Kig-Yar, or Jackal, is an Avian species often seen with shields and longer-range weapons. They make up the bulk of the Covenant ground forces (after the Grunts). The Jackals are often used in scouting or sniping roles, using their superior senses to their advantage.

Tactics

When you require a long-rang, anti-infantry sniper unit, Jackals are the choice. The Jackal has lengthy and superior range, and inflicts high damage on targets it strikes.

Jackals have a major drawback: They are physically weak with low Hit Points and are therefore unable to stand against units that aren't infantry; vehicles and air units shrug off the Jackal's attack and easily dispatch them. Therefore, it is wise to employ Jackals when your opponent is creating a mostly infantry-based army. They are most useful executing hit-and-runs against enemy foot soldiers.

Jackals are very adept at defeating the neutral forces that guard Hooks. They are worth positioning on any Sniper Towers that surround these hooks or that are dotted around the landscape. They are unmatched in this capacity.

Jackals share the same advantages and disadvantages of Flamethrowers and fill the same role, except Jackals are a little more adept at fighting off air units.

To be most effective against enemy infantry, Jackals must use their long range to maximum advantage, whittling down foes as they close so only a weakened force is present when close combat occurs.

Hunter

Hit Points: ★★☆

Damage Caused: ★★☆

Movement: ★☆☆

Counter-vehicle unit, powerful Fuel Rod Cannons are a credible threat even against tanks.

Base Unit

👤 2 ⚡ 1 📦 250

Basic Offense: Fuel Rod Cannon

Starting Special Attack: None

Upgrade #1: Bonded Shield

Weapon Type: Special Hunter Shield

👤 N/A ⚡ 1 📦 200

Equips each Hunter with a huge shield that can deflect many projectiles.

Upgrade #2: Spirit Bond

Hunters get a big damage boost while both bond brothers are alive.

👤 N/A ⚡ 2 📦 400

Upgrade #3: Assault Beam

Weapon Type: Fuel Rod Cannon (Override Capacity)

👤 N/A ⚡ 3 📦 700

Equips Hunters with a devastating beam-based weapon.

Hunter Overview

Unit Class: Antivehicle

Strengths: Incredibly effective against vehicles, particularly Warthogs and Scorpions.

Weaknesses: Slow, ineffective against infantry and air units. Cannot attack air units at all.

Accessed via: Hall

The Hunters, or Mgalekgolo, are massive colonies of small worklike creatures known as Lekgolo. These colonies of many smaller creatures take the form of huge, heavily armored bipedal infantry. Carrying a massive shield and a Fuel Rod Gun, Hunters occupy a strong antivehicle role. Always appearing in pairs, they are more than a match for most UNSC vehicles.

Tactics

The Hunter moves at a slow, lumbering pace, which becomes more of a hindrance as the battle progresses. However, during the early stages of a fight, Hunters absolutely decimate UNSC Warthogs and Scorpions. If you spot your opponent manufacturing these units, counteract with Hunters.

Hunters are also excellent when utilized alongside Jackals, allowing your Covenant forces to effectively deal with several vehicle and infantry combinations. If your foe doesn't immediately start constructing a number of Hornets or Banshees quickly, you can overrun his base and claim an early victory.

Hunters cannot attack enemy air units; this is a major issue if you're facing a foe flying in Hornets or Ghosts. Hunters perform poorly against any other troop type except perhaps buildings. They are reasonable at attacking buildings but are not recommended for this task.

Hunters are a highly specialized force; train them only if your opponent is building ground vehicles, or create a few Hunters as an insurance against them. For example, if your foe is Sergeant Forge (who has the Grizzly Tanks as a special vehicle), he is likely to build vehicles, so you know you're more likely to counteract them with Hunters.

63

FACTORY UNITS
Ghost

Hit Points: ★☆☆

Damage Caused: ★☆☆

Movement: ★★★

Fast assault recon unit.

Base Unit

👤 1 ⚡ 0 📦 100

Basic Offense: Plasma Cannons (2)

Starting Special Attack: None

Upgrade #1: Boosted Ram Ability

Weapon Type: Chassis Ram

N/A | 1 | 200

Enables the Boosted Ram ability on Ghosts, allowing them to effectively ram their targets.

Upgrade #2: Strafe

Allows Ghosts to more effectively dodge incoming grenades and rockets.

N/A | 2 | 400

Upgrade #3: Scout Shield

Adds an energy shield to Ghosts that deflects some incoming damage.

N/A | 3 | 700

Ghost Overview

Unit Class: Scout

Strengths: Strong against small numbers of infantry and light vehicles. Fast.

Weaknesses: Weak against Turrets, most ground vehicles (prior to Strafe upgrade), large concentration of troops.

Accessed via: Factory (Arbiter and Prophet of Regret only)

The Type-32 Rapid Assault Vehicle, called the Ghost by the UNSC, is a very common Covenant scout vehicle. It is lightly armored and carries twin Plasma Cannons

for armament. It is quick and excellent for harassing infantry; even UNSC tanks have trouble hitting it since it is so agile. Piloted by an Elite, it is very effective as a light vehicle. The Ghost has very powerful upgrades such as a Boost ability; additional thrusters, allowing it to strafe and juke incoming enemy fire; and an energy shield that deflects incoming assaults.

Tactics

The Covenant's answer to the Warthog, the Ghost shares many similarities to the UNSC Scout unit but begins with a ranged weapon and must upgrade to a Ram ability, compared to the Warthog's initial Ram and Gunner upgrade.

The Ghost is a fast, lightly armored reconnaissance unit. it fills exactly the same role as the Warthog and has almost all of its strengths and weaknesses. Consult the Warthog section for further details.

As the Ghost can fire long range, it is immediately able to tackle foes that fire back.

As you progress along the Ghost's upgrade path, the Strafe upgrade allows the vehicle to automatically dodge some enemy fire, making them fairly effective against most units. They still explode with alarming regularity, though—that armor isn't thick!

The Ghost differs from the Warthog in that it must be produced in a Factory (the Covenant equivalent of a Vehicle Depot), compared to the UNSC's Firebase.

The Ghost is arguably even more useful at the very start of battle, as you can begin production with a Tech level of zero (compared to needing Tech Level 1 for Warthogs). This enables you to construct a Factory immediately, producing ten or more Ghosts and destroying enemy Scouts, collecting crates in all different directions, and harassing enemy bases. This is the same tactic the Warthog uses, but the Ghost can get this done even more quickly.

Brute Chopper

Hit Points: ★☆☆

Damage Caused: ★★☆

Movement: ★★★

Fast assault recon unit.

Base Unit

2 | 0 | 200

BRUTE CHOPPER
Scout

Basic Offense: None

Starting Special Attack: Ram

Upgrade #1: Autocannons

Weapon Type: 35 mm Autocannons

N/A | 1 | 200

Adds front-firing 35 mm guns, improving the Chopper's attack.

Upgrade #2: Stabilizers

Improves autocannon accuracy and damage.

N/A | 2 | 400

Upgrade #3: Ramming Target

Increases damage inflicted when the Chopper runs over enemies and decreases the damage taken.

N/A | 3 | 700

Brute Chopper Overview

Unit Class: Scout
Strengths: Strong against small numbers of infantry and light vehicles. Fast.
Weaknesses: Weak against some ground vehicles (prior to Autocannon upgrade), large concentration of troops.
Accessed via: Factory (Brute Chieftain only)

The Type-25 RAV (Rapid Assault Vehicle) is a ground vehicle used exclusively by the Brutes and is known colloquially as the Brute Chopper. It is a heavily armored two-wheeled Recon and assault bike, able to tangle with light vehicles and easily dispatch infantry with its twin Autocannons. It sacrifices nothing compared to the Ghost and is one of the greatest scouting craft ever to see combat action.

Tactics

The Brutes' answer to the Ghost and Warthog, the Brute Chopper shares numerous similarities (and tactics) with these two scouting vehicles. Unlike the Ghost, it begins with a Ramming ability and can fire only long-range after the Autocannon upgrade. The Brute Chopper can also run over enemies with the final upgrade, increasing the ramming damage severely. (Consult the Warthog and Ghost sections for further details on the strengths and weaknesses of this type of craft.)

Opt to use most, if not all, of the Ghost's tactics, but beware the additional Population and supplies it takes to construct each Chopper; it is twice as expensive to build.

However, it is much more battle-tested. Three Choppers can comfortably take down a neutral base, and Choppers can hold their own against light vehicles. This allows you to try some aggressive initial tactics, such as Rushing the enemy using Choppers with Autocannons to tear through a loosely defended base.

The Chopper's armor can withstand a reasonable amount of battering, even from a Turret, allowing the vehicle to survive for a greater period of time than a Ghost. Expect to take more territory if you're driving this Recon vehicle.

Wraith

Hit Points: ★★★
Damage Caused: ★★★
Movement: ★★☆

Mainline battle tank, good speed and excellent range combine to make this a powerful ground vehicle.

Base Unit & Variant

Basic Offense: Plasma Mortar Cannon
Starting Special Attack: None

Upgrade #1: Heavy Shield

Adds an energy shield that deflects some incoming damage.

Upgrade #2: Scorch Ability

Weapon Type: Plasma Mortar Cannon (Override Syphon)

Enables the Scorch ability that superheats an area of terrain for extra damage.

Upgrade #3: Plasma Modulator

Greatly increases the damage of the Wraith's Plasma Mortar.

65

Wraith Overview

Unit Class: Main Vehicle
Strengths: Excellent against infantry. Scorch ability exceptional against most troops. Shields when upgraded.
Weaknesses: Slightly weak against air units. Highly vulnerable to Spartan Jacking.
Accessed via: Factory

The Type-25 Assault Gun Carriage, also known as the Covenant Wraith, is the Covenant's main battle vehicle. Heavily armored, it functions more like a tank than the attached artillery-like cannon would suggest. It fires a Heavy Plasma blast at targets, causing area-of-effect damage and melting through enemy armor. The Wraith is fairly quick and can devastate enemy armor columns and infantry at range. It is also equipped with antipersonnel Plasma Cannons. They carry thick armor that is almost invulnerable to small-arms fire. Upgrades include a heavier shield that provides more defensive strength; a Scorch ability that allows it to set the ground on fire, causing extra damage; and a plasma modulation upgrade that vastly increases the main gun's firepower.

Tactics

The Covenant's main ground vehicle, the Wraith tank's role, strengths, and weaknesses are essentially the same as the UNSC Scorpion's.

Used in nearly identical tactical plans as the Scorpion, the Wraith's first upgrade is shielding, but it can still launch devastating salvos with its Scorch ability.

The Wraith differs from the Scorpion in that its upgrade path allows shields. When upgraded, the Wraith is now a little more adept at hit-and-run tactics; trundle into an enemy encampment and fire away, then back out of range before your shields are completely depleted, and repeat this tactic.

The Wraith's Scorch ability effectively burns foes with a Plasma Burn attack, wounding or damaging them over time. This means foes feel the effects of a Wraith's attack afterward; this is another benefit for hit-and-running.

Locust

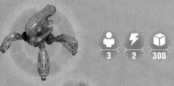

Hit Points: ★★☆

Damage Caused: ★☆☆

Movement: ★★☆

Counter-building vehicle, very slow and best set to destroying unprotected enemy bases.

Base Unit

Basic Offense: Charged Plasma Cannon

Starting Special Attack: None

Upgrade #1: Overdrive Ability

Weapon Type: Charged Plasma Cannon (Overdrive)

Enables the Locust Overdrive ability, which uses the Locust's shield generator output to overcharge its beam weapon. Attack power is drastically increased at the expense of the Locust's shields.

Upgrade #2: Shield Amplifier

Locust shields regenerate much more quickly.

Locust Overview

Unit Class: Building Killer

Strengths: Devastating against buildings. Long-range attacks.

Weaknesses: Cannot fire skyward, prone to all enemy attacks, weak against all enemy types (except Turrets).

Accessed via: Factory

The Locust, like the Scarab, is another mining vehicle repurposed for military use. The Locust uses a powerful mining laser to inflict great damage to buildings. Although slow and expensive, the Locust is a serious threat to UNSC forces and buildings. It has incredible range and can hit enemy forces when even their longest range units cannot strike back. Once upgraded, a pack of Locusts can quickly decimate an enemy base in only a few seconds. The Locust has two upgrades that can make it a more effective fighting machine: Overdrive, which increases movement speed, and Shield Amplifier, which increases how much punishment it can take.

Tactics

This "mini Scarab" is a slow, long-ranged artillery unit. The Locust's biggest drawback is that it isn't very effective against enemy units, as its primary role is taking out enemy structures. Utilize the Locust for just this purpose; stride toward an enemy building but attack from the farthest range possible (which is usually longer than a defender's attack). This gives you as much time as possible to lay waste to an enemy base.

Locusts can be upgraded to receive the Overdrive ability. This optional secondary attack removes the Locust's shields in favor of increasing the damage it causes; naturally this is viable when you aren't being attacked by enemies or when you wish to sacrifice a Locust that has almost destroyed a building and needs a boost of attack power to finish the job.

The Locust is like a UNSC Cobra, with all the building-striking tactical advantages. However, it doesn't have the Cobra's antivehicle power and is therefore less of a threat to ground troops. The damage a Locust causes to enemy units is very low.

Do not build Locusts if you are primarily interested in attacking foes or defending from enemy troops; build them only if you plan on taking down enemy structures quickly and from long range. Even then, you don't need many, and they can fill specific roles, such as destroying enemy Turrets while your other forces engage the enemy.

SUMMIT UNITS

Engineer

Hit Points: ★☆☆
Damage Caused: ☆☆☆
Movement: ★★☆

A support unit that repairs and heals nearby allied units.

Base Unit

Basic Offense: None (primary "attack" is healing any Covenant unit)
Starting Special Attack: None

Upgrade #1: State of Grace

 Increases repair rate.

Upgrade #2: Harmonious Digestion

 Increases movement speed.

Engineer Overview

Unit Class: Support Unit
Strengths: Excellent at healing and regenerating friendly units that are under constant and heavy enemy barrage.
Weaknesses: Slow prior to upgrades, and with no offensive capabilities whatsoever.
Accessed via: Summit

The Engineer, known as the Huragok by the Covenant, is a race of gas-filled alien creatures created by the Forerunners to perform maintenance on Forerunner structures. Engineers are the only way the Covenant can repair their buildings and vehicles during combat, and they are very effective, especially once upgraded. They automatically search out damaged machinery to repair. They have no defenses or weapons and are easily killed, although they can repair each other but not themselves. They can be upgraded to State of Grace, which increases their repair rate, and to Harmonious Digestion, which increases their movement speed. The Engineers can easily take apart random technological objects and can put them back together exactly how they found them. This is probably their way of studying and understanding new technologies.

Tactics

Without the orbital Heal & Repair that the UNSC counts on, the Covenant's main source of troop regeneration is the adapted Forerunner repurposed entity known as the Engineer.

This slow-moving airborne creature is supremely adept at healing. However, Engineers are unable to attack enemy units or buildings; they have no offensive capabilities whatsoever.

Use Engineers to float behind your main attack line, repairing units that you've pulled out of combat. Or, have Engineers float near friendly units already engaged in combat to keep them attacking for as long as possible. The enemy usually doesn't know whether to attack the Engineer or the unit the Engineer is healing. It is best to remove an offensive unit first.

Remember that Engineers can also heal buildings, which can be helpful if you're in a defensive or Turtling position.

Construct a mass of Engineers with the sole role of buffing up a Covenant leader or a Scarab; this is a very effective strategy. With enough Engineers (the number varies depending on difficulty), you can heal a leader or Scarab faster than they receive damage, although this depends on the type and number of foes they are fighting. Effectively turning your best troops "invincible" is the key asset this troop can bring to the battlefield.

67

Banshee

Hit Points: ★★☆

Damage Caused: ★★☆

Movement: ★★★

Mainline air unit, Banshees are armed with both Plasma Cannons and Fuel Rod Cannons.

Base Unit

Basic Offense: Twin Plasma Cannons

Starting Special Attack: None

Upgrade #1: Boost

Enables Speed Boost ability.

👤 N/A	⚡ 1	📦 200

Upgrade #2: Repeating Cannon

Increases the rate of fire for the Banshee's weapons.

👤 N/A	⚡ 2	📦 400

Upgrade #3: Sacrifice

Banshees attempt to crash into ground targets and inflict damage when destroyed.

👤 N/A	⚡ 3	📦 700

Banshee Overview

Unit Class: Main Air

Strengths: Excellent at attacking all unit types and ignoring terrain difficulties. Once Boost is available, extremely adept at raiding.

Weaknesses: Light armor and susceptible to attack from a wide variety of foes.

Accessed via: Summit

The most frequently seen Covenant air unit is the Type-26 Ground Support Aircraft, or Banshee. Carrying one pilot, this versatile and nimble aircraft is used to scout and harass enemy forces. Carrying Twin Plasma Cannons and a Fuel Rod Cannon, the Banshee can deal serious damage to both ground and air forces. It also has a speed boost ability.

Tactics

- The Banshee is the Covenant's main air unit and fills the exact same role as the UNSC's Hornet. Read strategic advice for the Hornet, as it is applicable to the Banshee as well.

- The only difference between the Banshee and the Hornet is the upgrade. One of the Banshee's upgrades is the Boost, a secondary ability that increases its speed for a short amount of time.

- The Boost ability is extremely useful if you're employing Banshees to raid enemy structures or escape from combat. Simply employ the Boost to quickly act on an intended target faster than your foes can counteract, or use it to speed away more quickly than your opponent's defenses can follow you—unless, of course, your foe is using upgraded Banshees!

- Think of the Banshee as a Hornet but with better raiding capabilities thanks to its Boost.

Vampire

Hit Points: ★★☆

Damage Caused: ★☆☆

Movement: ★★☆

Antiair aircraft, heavy Needler turret can track and engage enemy aircraft in a large area.

Base Unit

👤 2	⚡ 2	📦 250

Basic Offense: Heavy Needler

Starting Special Attack: Stasis Cannon

Upgrade #1: Stasis Drain

Stasis ability now drains target Hit Points and heals the Vampire.

👤 N/A	⚡ 2	📦 400

Upgrade #2: Stasis Bomb

When a target is drained with the Stasis ability, it explodes, doing area-of-effect damage.

N/A 3 700

Vampire Overview

Unit Class: Antiair

Strengths: Devastating against enemy air units. Self-healing when attacking after a Stasis Drain upgrade.

Weaknesses: Weak against ground troops, both infantry- and vehicle-based.

Accessed via: Summit

The Vampire is the mainstay of Covenant antiair aircraft. With a heavy Needler turret, the Vampire can quickly overwhelm enemy air forces with a large barrage. Very effective in groups, it can bring down an opposing aircraft in seconds. When upgraded, the Vampire can drain enemy aircraft of their energy and cause it to crash; however, this makes the Vampire take damage as well. The Vampire's upgrades can be a game-changing element in air battles. The Stasis Drain can lock down enemy air units while the Stasis Bomb can freeze enemy ground units for Covenant forces to pick off.

Tactics

A slow-moving airborne antiair unit, the Vampire is the Covenant's answer to any air unit your foe may be fielding.

It is incredibly effective against massed enemy air units; if your foe is creating Hornets, Vultures, Hawks, or Banshees, begin to counter this by stepping up your Vampire production. One Vampire can decimate around four Hornets if used cunningly.

The Vampire's Stasis ability can completely immobilize an enemy air unit. It can be further upgraded to drain the Hit Points from enemy air units that are already trapped by Vampires. Vampires are arguably the finest force for dropping enemy air units from the skies, immobilizing them, destroying them, and taking little or no damage in the process.

Vampires have extreme vulnerabilities, though; they are poor at combat when attacked by ground troops.

Counteract the Vampire's problems by pairing them with units that have weaknesses to air troops, such as Wraiths, Jackals, and Hunters. With a flexible army of this nature, you can rely on (and bring to bear on your opponents) your forces' strengths and none of their weaknesses.

69

CAMPAIGN · ACT I

The Covenant threat grows by the hour. A chosen soldier named Forge braves inclement weather conditions to help save a remote out-post named Alpha Base from the encroaching Covenant Hordes. In the process, he discovers a source of activity; his enemy has located an ancient Forerunner structure. After battling to a Relic structure, Forge and scientist Anders are pinned down by cloaked ambushes, and must be extricated under heavy fire.

01: ALPHA BASE

Control Sergeant Forge in his Warthog as you travel and usurp the Covenant forces from Alpha base, rallying four squads of Marines to your detachment, and attacking scattered Covenant forces along the way, before driving all enemies from inside the Base itself.

OBJECTIVES

Win Condition:

All Primary Objectives met, and all Covenant units within Alpha Base are neutralized.

Loss Condition:

All UNSC Units defeated, and Forge is down.

Par Time:

05:00–12:00

■ Eliminate Covenant within Alpha Base
Completion Score: 500 Points

Alpha Base is the key UNSC installation on Harvest. Covenant forces have completely overrun the facility. Defeating these units in the area is a top priority.

■ Optional: Find and Rescue Pinned Marines[4]
Completion Score: 500 Points

Scattered pockets of Marines are isolated and under attack near Alpha Base. Locate as many as you can and kill the Covenant forces that are attacking them; the Marines will be needed to retake Alpha Base.

■ Use Marines to Destroy Barrier Power Source
Completion Score: 500 Points

The Covenant have erected an energy barrier across the pass leading to Alpha Base. The barrier will block vehicles, but Marines can move through and destroy the power source beyond.

■ Optional: Kill 100 Grunts[100]
Completion Score: 500 Points

Grunts, called *Unggoy* in the Covenant language, are cowardly but dangerous in large numbers. Methane-breathers, they are commonly seen in Covenant infantry squads. Counter them with your own infantry or with flamethrowers.

■ Fight Your Way to Alpha Base
Completion Score: 250 Points

Alpha Base is in the northern section of the map. It has been overrun by the Covenant; get there and take it back.

Waypoint
Black Box
Look Daddy Skull

Difficulty Modifications (compared to Normal)

Easy: All enemy units have 50 percent less Health Points and inflict 50 percent less damage.

Heroic: Additional Shade Turrets. Additional enemy forces at Alpha Base. Two Spirit of Fire Heal & Repairs instead of one.

Legendary: All enemy units have 25 percent more Health Points and inflict 25 percent more damage. One Spirit of Fire Heal & Repair. One Carpet Bomb provided by Captain Cutter once inside Alpha Base instead of two.

MISSION COMMENCEMENT

1 Select ⊗, (LB), or (RB) to control Sergeant Forge and drive him northwest (ahead) over the ramp, where the first of four pinned Marines are battling a small Covenant force. Attack the Covenant using Forge's mounted Gauss Cannon (⊗), or Ram (Ⓨ) the Jackals, ideally from medium range (to avoid the Warthog missing its target). Pay particular attention to the Shade Turret—this is your most dangerous adversary and takes precedence. After the battle, use (LB) to select the UNSC Marines once they climb into their Warthog, then ride east.

Legendary Tactics

A good way to minimize the damage to your Warthog is to Ram the Jackal on the barricade's right side, then immediately destroy the Shade Turret before tackling any remaining Jackals.

2 Cross the bridge; look east and locate the three Grunts on the snowbank between the bridges. Target one with regular fire (⊗), then Ram the other. Continue north along the second bridge section.

TIP

Always try to lead with Forge's Warthog, as it has many more Health Points, and the Gauss Cannon inflicts much more damage than the Marines' vehicles.

3 Look ahead around the long left turn; from range, take out two Grunts on the icy road, then concentrate firepower on a Shade Turret that sits atop an icy embankment. After blasting it, deal with two remaining Grunts before continuing.

Legendary Tactics

Keeping both Warthogs is tricky on higher difficulties, so try either of the following tactics: First, park your troops on the inside of the snow wall to the left while you slay the first two Grunts; this keeps you hidden from the Shade Turret. Second, you may find the Marine Warthog (which is less tough than Forge's) is always destroyed at this point. Either park the Marine Warthog (before it comes into the enemies' line of fire) and bring it into the fray only after you destroy the Shade Turret, or (after taking down the first two Grunts) accelerate past and around the Shade Turret, park both Warthogs on the snow "step" below and behind it, and then finish it off from this location where it can't hit you.

NOTE

This walkthrough is based on Legendary difficulty. On easier difficulty settings, less enemies are in your path. If you didn't spot a Shade Turret, increase the difficulty level!

CAUTION

If you want to improve your time, ignore and race past the first few Grunts. Take care, though—you can miss the "Kill 100 Grunts" objective if you ignore too many!

73

Mission 01 Mission 02 Mission 03 Mission 04 Mission 05 Mission 06 Mission 07 Mission 08 Mission 09 Mission 10 Mission 11 Mission 12 Mission 13 Mission 14 Mission 15

Basics   Factions   Campaign   Multiplayer   Appendices   Art Gallery

Picture 1

Picture 2

4 Continue onto the ice and toward a group of two Marine squads dug in and battling two circular Covenant barricades. Spread your fire out by taking your two Warthogs along the south wall (Picture 1) and aiming your ranged weapons at the southern barricade. After strafing all Grunts and Jackals, Ram (Picture 2) into the Grunt squad outside the other barricade before blasting the remaining foes inside. The Marines you're rescuing will help you.

TIP

There are highly explosive methane barrels dotted about these barricades (and all over Alpha Base). Aim at these for a large and impressive explosion, which quickly kills more foes than gunfire alone and shaves seconds off your combat time (also shown in Picture 2).

Legendary Tactics

Forge's Warthog and the first Marine Warthog may be severely damaged by now. Summon the Spirit of Fire's Heal & Repair (⬡, then ⬤) either here or after securing Waypoint 5. If you can, save as many Warthogs as possible, but also save the Heal & Repair until as late as possible. Don't forget you need to be parked inside the green healing circle!

5 Climb the snowbank and from a distance, easily dispatch a Jackal on a supply plate before accelerating down

onto a snowy plateau. Split your quartet of Warthogs into two (using ⓡⓑ), and set one duo to Ram the first cluster of Grunts and the other to Ram the second cluster. There are two more hiding behind a burning Warthog to finish off, too.

NOTE

If you've Rammed most of your Grunts up to this point, try killing 50 in this manner to unlock the Achievement "Everything's Better with Bacon."

6 Finish your fight on the snow plateau by edging forward (west) until you reveal a Ghost. Destroy it—ideally before you reveal another Shade Turret at the bridge entrance (as it doesn't fire on you until the Fog of War is lifted).

7 Drive and leap the gap in the bridge, make a right, and locate the third set of Marines to rescue. Attacking the Covenant defenses is easy: Group your Warthogs and drive them all up to Ram the cluster of Grunts behind the barricade nearest the precipice (as shown). Next, shoot the Shade Turret inside the raised platform, then target the second Shade Turret before mopping up any Grunt stragglers.

Cooperative Advice

Getting behind the Shade Turrets—by using nearby rocky cover or by splitting up and attacking from two different directions—can nullify a Turret's deadly firepower.

TIP

The Marines you rescue are on foot, and if you cluster your infantry and vehicles together, your Warthog's top speed is compromised. Remedy this by immediately learning and employing the "Unit Cycle" (ⓡⓓ). Use it when you need to control just one unit type.

Picture 1

Picture 2

8 Rake the two Grunts on either side of the overturned Warthog as you cross the bridge, and blast any Grunts you can as they flee through the barrier. Ignore the remaining ones that are fleeing for a moment, and instead use a Warthog to Ram it into the cluster of Grunts pinned down by two squads of Marines (Picture 1). The Covenant have erected a power barrier at the entrance to Alpha Base, so quickly select all your infantry units, swing the camera around (with 🅞) so you can see the barrier's power source, and march your Marines into the Grunt fire. Shrug off the Grunt fire; blowing up the power source with Grenades (🅨) is of paramount importance (Picture 2).

Look Daddy!

Although you have to enter Alpha Base and defeat 100 Grunts before the skull appears, don't complete the mission until you've backtracked (ideally using a single Warthog) to the location where you rescued the fourth squad of Marines, just before the Alpha Base entrance. Collect the **Look Daddy! Skull**.

Black Box 1

While you're in this vicinity, head down the ramp near the last bridge you crossed. Underneath is **Black Box 1**.

Picture 1

Picture 2

�929 Now that you're inside Alpha Base, you must contend with a small but powerful (and scattered) Covenant strike force. You can easily be overwhelmed, so take a methodical approach. Stay to the base's edge, moving your forces to

the two sets of Covenant infantry behind cover near the burning UNSC tanks. Strike them down, and get your infantry behind this cover. Concentrate your firepower on advancing Covenant infantry, and stand your ground, even in the face of an incoming Wraith. Cutter radios in, granting you a Carpet Bomb, which takes out the Wraith in a peppering of explosive fire (Picture 1). Stay where you are, and command all forces to destroy any Ghosts hovering around with the Covenant infantry before cutting down the Jackals and Grunts.

Now advance into the middle of the base, splitting a couple of Marine infantry units to deal with the small cluster of Grunts behind the curved concrete cover. The majority of your forces should blast away at a secondary Wraith (Picture 2); this tank is the target of a second Carpet Bomb on certain Difficulty levels. Use the Marines' Grenades (🅨) constantly, alternating with their small arms fire as they recharge.

TIP

Staying in the initial base cover, letting the Covenant forces come to you, and requesting a Heal & Repair from Spirit of Fire is a great plan, if you haven't used this yet. Employ this strategy just after using the Carpet Bomb.

Cooperative Advice

Split your forces once inside Alpha Base, then try to pull as many enemy units as possible into the Carpet Bombs' line of fire. However, watch out if you haven't killed 100 Grunts yet, as those nullified in the Carpet Bombing aren't included in the total!

Finish This should leave only a couple of Covenant infantry clusters left to take down; separate any remaining Warthogs (using 🆁🆃) and charge Grunts standing in exposed areas (as shown), blast any explosive barrels, and continue until the "Base Clear" tab appears on your screen.

Awards and Summary

GOLD	SILVER	BRONZE	TIN		Best Objective Score	Best Combat Bonus	Best Time Bonus
27,000+	18,000-26,999	12,000-17,999	0-11,999		2,250	x10 (22,500)	x5 (11,250)

	Theoretical Best Score	36,000 (2,250 + 22,500 + 11,250)

Mission 01   Mission 02   Mission 03   Mission 04   Mission 05   Mission 06   Mission 07   Mission 08   Mission 09   Mission 10   Mission 11   Mission 12   Mission 13   Mission 14   Mission 15

Basics   Factions   Campaign   Multiplayer   Appendices   Art Gallery

75

02: RELIC APPROACH

Build up the small Firebase inside the walls of Alpha Base; your forces cannot emerge until a series of basic buildings are constructed. After this, you must battle your way to the Relic and destroy a Detonator that is in danger of destroying this most sought-after location.

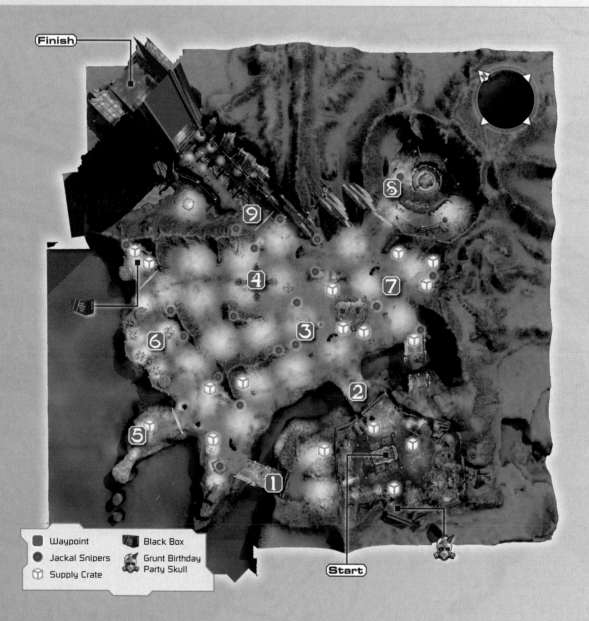

Legend:
- ■ Waypoint
- ● Jackal Snipers
- ⬠ Supply Crate
- ▦ Black Box
- 🎉 Grunt Birthday Party Skull

Difficulty Modifications (compared to Normal)

Easy: All enemy units have 50 percent less Health Points and inflict 50 percent less damage. No Hunters. Jackal Snipers greatly weakened. Fewer preplaced units.

Heroic: More Spirit attacks on Alpha Base; some Shade Turrets erected.

Legendary: All enemy units have 25 percent more Health Points and inflict 25 percent more damage. Shade Turrets erected.

OBJECTIVES

Win Condition:
All Primary Objectives met.

Loss Condition: All base buildings and units are destroyed or defeated, Forge is down, and there are not enough supplies to recover.

Par Time:
15:00–30:00

PRIMARY OBJECTIVES

■ **Get Alpha Base Online**
Completion Score: 250 Points
The Covenant attack has heavily damaged Alpha Base. Get it back up and running by building Supply Pads and military buildings.

■ **Build a Supply Pad**
Completion Score: 250 Points
A Supply Pad is a key component of any military base. Stockpiling supplies will let us build additional buildings and train military forces.

■ **Build a Barracks**
Completion Score: 250 Points
A Barracks at Alpha Base will allow military units to be trained there.

■ **Train Five Marines [5]**
Completion Score: 250 Points
With enough boots on the ground, Alpha Base will be safe once more. After the Marines are trained, patrols can be sent out and the surrounding area secured.

■ **Fight Your Way to the Structure in the Ice**
Completion Score: 1,000 Points
The Forerunner Structure is north of Alpha Base, past the Covenant forces. You will have to fight your way through enemy forces to get there.

■ **Enter the Structure**
Completion Score: 250 Points
The Covenant were after the secrets buried in the Forerunner Structure. Enter and learn what you can.

■ **Destroy the Detonator**
Completion Score: 700 Points
The Covenant are planning to destroy the Forerunner Structure. Take out the Detonator.

OPTIONAL OBJECTIVES

■ **Destroy the Covenant Base**
Completion Score: 1,000 Points
A Covenant base is between our forces and our primary objective. Destroying it will secure the path to the Forerunner Structure.

■ **Kill 20 Jackal Snipers [20]**
Completion Score: 500 Points
Jackals are birdlike aliens who serve as Covenant scouts and sharpshooters. Lacking durability, they often carry energy shields. Counter them with armed Warthogs or Flamethrowers.

■ **Destroy the Covenant Methane Refinery**
Completion Score: 1,000 Points
The Covenant are refining methane on Harvest to supply their Grunt squads. Taking out the refinery would slow them down.

■ **Rescue All Trapped Warthogs [2]**
Completion Score: 1,000 Points
Several UNSC units are trapped. Rescue them to bolster your forces.

MISSION COMMENCEMENT

(Start) The moment action begins, select "Base Build Site" (with Ⓐ) and follow Serina's instructions exactly. While the two sections of base are flown in, select each of your four units (three sets of Marines and Forge's Warthog), and send them to collect the four piles of supplies to the north, east, south, and west. Since Forge has a Warthog and is thus faster, send him to the west, as those supplies are farthest away (at the top of a lookout point between the base and west gate [Waypoint 1]). The base gates are closed until you build the Supply Pad and the Barracks and train five Marines.

TIP

Keep your cursor over the Barracks so you can train Marines the instant the building rises and is accessible. Every second counts! After the gates open, build at least two more Supply Pads (ideally enhancing them to Heavy Supply Pads) so your resource stream is steady. More tactical advice is detailed in the latter part of this mission walkthrough.

NOTE

You can now move freely about this snowy hellscape. The remainder of this walkthrough is divided into two sections: the first section provides advice on each waypoint, and the next section deals with battle tactics involving initial base enhancements and advantageous routes to take.

Mission Waypoints

① West Gate - This is an often-overlooked but advantageous exit to this base (and where Covenant Ghosts periodically attack Alpha Base if you haven't explored this region). Consider driving a small contingent of Warthogs over the broken bridge to a Pelican landing pad. Dispatch the light resistance (including two Jackals on the pad), and a Pelican pilot lands, bringing two Warthogs and three Marine squads as reinforcements; this is excellent if you need infantry and aren't creating them. This also allows you to easily maneuver north along the western flank, ignoring the more dangerous central zone.

Mission 01 Mission 02 Mission 03 Mission 04 Mission 05 Mission 06 Mission 07 Mission 08 Mission 09 Mission 10 Mission 11 Mission 12 Mission 13 Mission 14 Mission 15

Basics   Factions   Campaign   Multiplayer   Appendices   Art Gallery

77

2 North Gate - Closer to the Firebase you're constructing, this offers a more direct (but dangerous) path northwest toward the central zone. There's a light force of Grunts on the natural rock bridge. If you take this route, edge forward and destroy them early.

3 Central Zone - This route is more dangerous but offers more options than the western route out from Alpha Base, as it provides easy access in all directions. The middle part of this zone has a small complement of enemy infantry, some Shade Turrets, and a new threat—Jackals on three Sniper Towers. Concentrate your firepower on the turrets and towers first. Don't venture too far northwest past this medium-sized threat unless you wish to engage the Covenant at their base (Waypoint 4).

> **NOTE**
>
> The use of cover here (curved barricades and the wreckage of crashed Warthogs and Pelicans) significantly protects your infantry units and helps keep them active longer.

> **CAUTION**
>
> For this mission, avoid breaking off an infantry unit and placing them in an empty Sniper Tower; Flamethrower units can't fire from this height (so never send them to these perches), and your forces are better placed continuously pushing north rather than statically guarding a previously searched area.

4 Covenant Base - The Covenant Base guards the entrance to the Forerunner Structure, and although you can maneuver

around it, it is a dangerous source of enemy troops; it is difficult to tackle if you let the enemy forces build up there, especially on higher difficulty levels. Encounter it early enough (by employing the Warthog Surprise! tactic detailed below), and the Covenant Base has only three building pads attached to it. However, if you wait, even

for a medium-sized UNSC force to be trained at Alpha Base, the Covenant Base will grow larger and become more unmanageable. Tactics for taking down the base are detailed later in this mission walkthrough.

5 Trapped Warthogs (West) - Expect minimal resistance (a few infantry Grunts), which you can ignore, while your infantry steps through the barrier wall and lobs Grenades (Y) at the power supply. Of more pressing concern are the Jackal Snipers on the rock ridges to the northeast; have vehicles deal with them so you're multitasking. Expect two additional Warthogs; select them to finish off their captors as soon as they are freed. Optimally, head from Waypoint 1, although you can split your forces to quickly free the Warthogs from Waypoints 2 or 6.

6 West Flank (Covenant Methane Refinery) - Pay careful attention to the guide map, as it shows the total number of buildings to optionally demolish if you decide to tackle this area. The Covenant Grunts offer little resistance (especially if you're using Warthogs and Scorpions), but make sure to destroy the six separate buildings (four sets of giant methane tanks and two refinery pods); it's easy to miss one and your objective. Approach this area from any direction; it is lightly guarded, so a small exploratory team (a few infantry units and vehicles) can split from your main force to secure the area.

> **TIP**
>
> Notice the three landing pads along the map's western edge. Destroying each of them severely impairs the enemy from landing reinforcements at your base or the Covenant Base. This is another (recommended) way to stop enemies from coming and to defend bases with Turrets.

7 East Flank - This area is best explored after securing Waypoints 2 and 3 and is optional. The main reason to trundle through this area is for the supply crates, some light enemy infantry and Ghost combat, and some

78

occasional Jackals. However, this can waste valuable time, unless you're sneaking around to Waypoint 8 and avoiding the Covenant Base.

8 Trapped Warthogs (Northeast)

- Warthogs and a small enemy infantry force are sealed behind a barrier near a large and inaccessible circular shaft, send in a couple of Marine squads (and Forge if he's without a vehicle) to blow the power; then use the trapped troops inside to massacre the small groups of Grunt guards. There are some supply crates in here but little else of interest. As with Waypoint 5, you can peel a small strike force off from your larger contingents to do this job.

9 Structure in the Ice (Entrance)-

You thoroughly explore this area during the Final Push tactic (detailed later); reaching this location involves passing near the Covenant Base. If you aren't interested in destroying the base (as it isn't a necessary mission objective), sneak in a few infantry units to destroy the barrier power, and

have your main strike force of vehicles out of base range. Next, send them in, straight through to the Forerunner Structure entrance, which appears to be a massive relic with a Detonator to take out.

Grunt Birthday Party

Located just in front of the sealed southern gate, from which you entered Alpha Base, this **Skull** is visible only after you complete the "Kill 20 Jackal Snipers" objective. As the majority of your forces are likely to be to the north, leave or quickly train a single Marine squad or a Warthog (as it can quickly collect the Skull), then join your main force.

Black Box 2

Located in the northwest area and blocked by a barrier that requires an infantry insertion and Grenading, **Black Box 2** is guarded by two Jackal Snipers on a platform embedded in the rocks above; don't let them pick off your Marines.

> ### TIP
>
> Both the Skull and Black Box take time to collect; you may wish to skip them if you want an impressive score on a higher difficulty.

Mission Tactics

> ### TIP
>
> Global Rally Points (⬡, then ◉) are incredibly useful, as you don't have to manually select and point newly trained forces to an area outside the base. Instead, choose an automatic location for the forces to appear, such as Waypoints 2, 3, or 4 if you're pushing up toward the Covenant Base. Consider choosing a safe location for the Rally Point so you can build up forces instead of sending them one at a time into danger, because this method of attack is obviously flawed.

You don't have to kill every Jackal emplacement; as long as you complete all optional objectives and strike the two-Jackal disc platforms on the rock ridges, this is an easy objective to finish, because more Jackals arrive during the final push into the Forerunner Structure. The only issue is having a unit back at Alpha Base to claim the Skull afterward but before the mission is complete.

Jackals are located in the following areas:

- On the circular disc platforms dotted around the higher rock ground.
- Occasionally on the ground, backing up Grunts.
- On some Sniper Turrets.

Some Jackals are also trained by the Covenant Base, are dropped into the base, or are coming out of the Forerunner Structure.

> ### CAUTION
>
> Your forces move at the rate of their slowest unit. For this reason, split your forces into an "advance" team of vehicles (ideally Warthogs and Scorpions) that can travel quickly, especially when investigating uncharted parts of the map.

> ### Cooperative Advice
>
> Have one player constantly enhancing Alpha Base while the other controls the main exploratory forces. Later, split your forces into two sizable groups, either by type (for example, Scorpions and Marines) or direction (for example, so you can mount an attack on the Covenant Base from two directions).
>
> Another good tactic is for the player controlling the base to send a small energy barrier-demolition infantry group to Waypoints 5 and 8 while the other player concentrates on the main objectives.

> ### NOTE
>
> Complete the **Endless Fun Achievement** (involving the destruction of every Methane Tank), by visiting the entire map, including the corners and other areas your forces normally ignore. Blow up the small barrels dotted about.

Mission 01   Mission 02   Mission 03   Mission 04   Mission 05   Mission 06   Mission 07   Mission 08   Mission 09   Mission 10   Mission 11   Mission 12   Mission 13   Mission 14   Mission 15

Basics   Factions   Campaign   Multiplayer   Appendices   Art Gallery

Alpha Base Buildup

The following units and buildings can be constructed during this mission. What follows is tactical advice for building and training each of them.

Firebase Station

| N/A | N/A | N/A |

This offers only five building pads, so upgrade it as quickly as possible.

Fortress

| N/A | 0 | 400 |

This now offers seven building pads; try three or four Supply Pads, two Reactor Pads, a Barracks, and a Vehicle Depot.

Warthog (Scout)

| 1 | 0 | 150 |

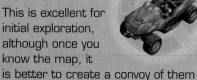

This is excellent for initial exploration, although once you know the map, it is better to create a convoy of them and send them to a Rally Point.

Grenadier Upgrade (Warthog)

| N/A | 2 | 500 |

Adding a passenger equipped with a Grenade Launcher increases the damage considerably; upgrade as soon as possible if you're using Warthogs.

TIP

Remember you can demolish buildings, too! You may not care for or need infantry, so remove the Barracks and replace it with a Supply Pad.

TIP

As long as you have the supplies, remember you can create troops from your Firebase or Fortress (Warthogs) at the same time as those from the Barracks or Vehicle Depot. Training twice the number of troops allows you to swarm enemies faster!

Although not recommended—because Forge is better suited in his enhanced Warthog—if Forge is down after his vehicle is destroyed and revived, have him tackle any power sources behind the energy barriers; this cuts down on infantry you have to train and send.

Supply Pad

| N/A | 0 | 100 |

Immediately place a second Supply Pad, then a Reactor, and then an additional (or more) Supply Pad into your base.

Heavy Supply Pad

| N/A | 1 | 225 |

Always upgrade your Supply Pads, although there may be more pressing matters to attend to (such as building Turrets) first.

Barracks

| N/A | 0 | 150 |

Although they are very important, infantry move slowly, they are much more lightly armored, and you may end up recycling the Barracks for a purely vehicular force.

Marine (Main Infantry)

| 1 | 0 | 100 |

Marines are vital for stepping through the Covenant energy barriers.

New Blood

| N/A | 1 | 200 |

Adding another Marine to the squad is vital and should be done as soon as you can if you're using infantry.

RPG Ability

| N/A | 2 | 400 |

This allows your Marines to tackle the energy barrier power supplies from longer range.

Flamethrower (Anti-Infantry)

| 1 | 0 | 100 |

The majority of the forces you encounter are enemy infantry, making Flamethrower troops a better bet than Marines, especially on higher difficulty levels where you fight Hunters.

Flash Bang Ability

| N/A | 1 | 200 |

Stunning the Covenant infantry is a superior upgrade; choose it at once!

Napalm Adherent

| N/A | 2 | 400 |

Another great upgrade, this kills off foes more quickly due to the extra damage the sticky napalm inflicts.

Turret (Base Defense)

| N/A | 0 | 250 |

Turrets are vital on higher difficulty levels. Place one at each corner, and then upgrade them if playing on Heroic or Legendary.

Flame Mortar

| N/A | 0 | 100 |

These are adept at destroying infantry but appear only from Spirits; therefore, ignore this upgrade.

Rail Gun

| N/A | 0 | 100 |

This destroys vehicles, which occasionally appear from the west gate. This augmentation is not recommended.

Missile Launcher

| N/A | 0 | 100 |

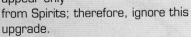

Build four of these as soon as possible when playing on Legendary; they defend the base amazingly well so you don't have to!

Reactor

| N/A | 0 | 250/ 500/ 750/ 1,000 |

Make sure the first of these is erected after your second Supply Pad; make this the second building you build. The more Reactors you build, the more supplies it costs. You need only a maximum of three for this mission.

Advanced Reactor

| N/A | 1 | 1,200 |

These cost a colossal amount, but they allow you to keep two Tech Levels on a single build pad. If you want enhanced vehicles, build a Reactor and an Advanced Reactor at your base.

Vehicle Depot

| N/A | 2 | 150 |

This is a good (and arguably better) building compared to the Barracks, but make sure you quickly build your Reactors to access the Depot.

Scorpion (Main Vehicle)

| 3 | 2 | 500 |

This is the stalwart of your army and vital if you want domination and enough firepower to cripple the Covenant Base. Enhance this vehicle with a Canister Shell, then optionally recycle the extra Reactor for another Heavy Supply Pad.

Canister Shell Ability

| N/A | 3 | 400 |

Worth constructing an Advanced Reactor for, this ability culls infantry and is excellent on the Scorpion's main enemy—the Hunter. Attack with this ability (Y) and you don't need Flamethrower troops.

Cobra (Antivehicle)

| 2 | 3 | 350 |

The Covenant has a few scattered Ghosts but little else, making the Cobra a less desirable choice compared to the Scorpion.

Deflection Plating (Cobra)

| N/A | 3 | 400 |

Because of the constant stream of enemy infantry reinforcements, you need mobility around the Covenant Base, and clamping down on the ground makes this a sitting target. Only use when flanked by Flamethrowers or Scorpions, ideally from range and to the west or east of the Covenant Base.

Legendary Tactics

Here's how to build a perfect Alpha Base: Once the fifth Marine unit is trained, instantly build four Turrets at each corner, and be sure you have at least two (ideally four) Supply Pads. Don't enhance them yet; select each Turret once it is built, starting with the two on the eastern side, and augment them with Missile Launchers. Even on Legendary, these usually decimate the incoming Spirits and keep your base almost completely secure. Now you can concentrate on building up your forces.

81

Mission 01 | Mission 02 | Mission 03 | Mission 04 | Mission 05 | Mission 06 | Mission 07 | Mission 08 | Mission 09 | Mission 10 | Mission 11 | Mission 12 | Missio | Mission 14 | Mission 15

Basics | Factions | Campaign | Multiplayer | Appendices | Art Gallery

Warthog Surprise!

This is a classic tactic that helps you crush the Covenant before they gain a foothold: As soon as you've trained your fifth Marine, immediately create four Warthogs and a Global Rally Point at Waypoint 1. Bring Forge and trundle over the bridge, neutralize the Pelican Pad, and bring the two additional Warthogs north, speeding through (and ignoring gunfire) the Methane Refinery and around to attack the Covenant Base from the west.

If you build up your base or are waylaid by fighting, the Covenant Base is much stronger (as shown) and impossible to destroy using this tactic. Immediately attack the base's main central part, Ramming it so your Warthogs are close enough for a Heal & Repair. Keep this up until the base falls, Ramming (O) any Hunters the Spirits drop in. This breaks down the Covenant, as long as you can hold ground long enough to build a second UNSC Firebase.

TIP

While securing the Pelican Pad near Waypoint 1 and driving through the Refinery to Waypoint 4, make sure you continuously upgrade Alpha Base with Supply Pads and a Reactor, and leave the Marines there to help defeat the incoming foes.

Legendary Tactics

On Easy and Normal difficulty, you can bring down the Covenant Base with just infantry, as long as you maintain a steady flow of reinforcements. On Heroic and Legendary, you must make larger vehicles to bolster your army by the time you reach Waypoint 3. It is also very important to train Flamethrower Marines to partner with vehicles; the infantry burns Hunters while the vehicles tackle the base.

Western Flank Attack

This is a more leisurely version of the **Warthog Surprise!** Build a small Warthog force outside the west gate (Waypoint 1), and move them to secure the Pelican Pad. Then journey north to the first trapped Warthogs (Waypoint 5) and rescue them with the Marines Serina awards you at the Pelican Pad. Mark this general area with a Rally Point, continue to build your

preferred units, and move them up to claim and destroy the Refinery (Waypoint 6). Turn east, then engage the Covenant Base for a longer battle, watching for Spirits dropping extra infantry on the base's eastern side. You might wish to bombard the central base hub from the west and east to maximize your chances of success (using elements of the **Eastern Flank Sneak** plan). With the Covenant Base destroyed, quickly build up your force so there's enough to withstand the charge into the Forerunner Structure.

Or, you can park your vehicles away from the base, sneak in some infantry at Waypoint 9, and charge through, shrugging off gunfire from the base.

CAUTION

The object here isn't to create two massive and well-defended bases and a squadron of ten Scorpions with Canister Shells; this takes too long, and you will lose Time Bonus Points if you don't continue pressing into the Forerunner Structure.

TIP

When attacking the Covenant Base on Heroic and Legendary, it is especially important not to let the Covenant build up their forces for too long, or the mission becomes a protracted problem. Attack as soon as you can muster a significant force, and keep up the pressure until you raze the enemy base! It is better to sacrifice all troops and obliterate a base than fall short and retreat.

Central Zone Firefight

This is one of the most hard-fought slogs, severely testing your multitasking capabilities on higher difficulties. Tearing up the map's middle (from Waypoints 2 to 3 to 4) requires your Marines to hunker down at the barricades for cover while Warthogs run down the infantry, and all your forces concentrate fire on the two southern Sniper Towers. Don't venture too far north (to the third Sniper Tower) or you'll attract Covenant attention from the base. Instead, build up your forces and place a Rally Point at Waypoint 3, then bring a sizable force to attack the Covenant Base (try attacking from two directions). As the base is bombarded, quickly use a Heal & Repair so your troops last longer. Aim for Hunters if you see them, then concentrate all firepower on the central base hub. The trick here is to continuously pump more vehicle units up to Waypoint 4 before the initial forces are wiped out (which usually happens on Legendary). Use Heal & Repair as often as possible!

TIP

This cannot be understated: Bring a large army—ideally maxed out to 30 troops, plus those you rescue along the way—and continuously build and train reinforcements as you advance.

Eastern Flank Sneak

Begin by sending a light force to tackle the Grunts outside Waypoint 2, and make your Rally Point the area just over the natural bridge. Ignore the center, send the majority of your forces around to the northeast (Waypoint 7), and build up your vehicle population here. At the same time, you can organize a quick attack squad of Marines to complete both the Warthog and Refinery objectives. Finally, break through the Forerunner Structure barrier (Waypoint 9), ignoring the Covenant Base.

Secondary Base Building

Assuming you're demolishing the old Covenant Base, keep the enemies at bay until you can order a Firebase installation from above. Depending on the troops you want, immediately build Barracks and a Vehicle Depot while upgrading them. Train all troops to appear from this location, effectively turning Alpha Base into a giant Supply Pad with Reactors; optionally demolish the old Barracks in favor of more supplies. Keep Alpha Base well defended with Missile Launcher-enhanced Turrets, and focus fully on the base at Waypoint 4.

With supplies streaming in to the south, concentrate on building your favored enhanced units. Optimally, at least four or five Scorpions is a good idea, supplemented by Warthogs and perhaps Flamethrower troops, since they can tackle the Forerunner Structure's energy barrier and help overcome Hunters, which are a problem for your Scorpions. Finally (and if you have the supplies), place Turrets at each corner, augmenting two with Missile Launchers and two with Flame Mortars to deal with any remaining stragglers. But don't do this if you haven't maximized your forces yet.

Legendary Tactics

Remember! You can crank out Scorpions two at a time if you build a second Vehicle Depot at this location! Do this if you're having trouble meeting a fast time requirement.

TIP

One Optimal Route: Determined to complete all objectives and claim Gold on Legendary? Then the best route involves no backtracking. Move through Waypoints 1 and 5, rescuing the first Warthogs. Move through Waypoint 6, destroying the Refinery and tagging the Jackals on the circular platforms. Attack and destroy the Covenant Base with your main force (attacking from the west is easier, as you're less open to attack from other directions) while a secondary force secures Waypoint 8, rescuing the second Warthogs. Then push forward into the Forerunner Structure (Waypoint 9).

The Final Push

With a sizable force (at least ten Warthogs or five Scorpions is recommended; more is preferable), send in any infantry you have (or send in Forge if his Warthog has been destroyed), and bring your entire force lumbering into the upper road leading northwest. Use the Heal & Repair here to help your infantry survive the final barrier takedown. Ignore the earth ramp leading down to a Spirit drop zone; simply pause to attack foes here, then edge forward. Continue this encroachment to the massive doorway, where two Shade Turrets may be activated. Attack each Turret one at a time, ideally with Scorpion or infantry secondary fire (🅨).

Pour through the doorway, optionally swinging the camera around for a better view of the Detonator, and concentrate all firepower on it. Use Heal & Repair to ensure the vehicles remain intact during this barrage, and throw everything you have at the Detonator, ignoring enemy forces. Keep this up until you complete the mission.

TIP

Make sure all optional objectives are complete before the final push. If you don't have infantry and need to destroy the power cable to the barrier at Waypoint 9, Serina sends a Pelican down with squads of Marines for this task. This means you only need to train Marines for the optional objectives or if you prefer to use them over vehicles.

When edging forward, aim for Hunters (as they are tank-killers), Ghosts, and then enemy infantry. Concentrate firepower on one or two specific threats at a time.

83

Awards and Summary

GOLD	SILVER	BRONZE	TIN	Best Objective Score	Best Combat Bonus	Best Time Bonus
✦	✦	✦	✦	✓	✊	⏱
70,000+	50,000-69,999	30,000-49,999	0-29,999	6,450	x10 (64,500)	x5 (32,250)

Theoretical Best Score 103,200 (6,450 + 64,500 + 32,250)

Mission 01 Mission 02 Mission 03 Mission 04 Mission 05 Mission 06 Mission 07 Mission 08 Mission 09 Mission 10 Mission 11 Mission 12 Mission 13 Mission 14 Mission 15

Basics   Factions   Campaign   Multiplayer   Appendices   Art Gallery

03: RELIC INTERIOR

The Spirit of Fire drops two formidable Grizzly full-battle tanks at the entrance to a Forerunner Relic filled with Covenant forces. Fight your way to where Forge and Anders have been ambushed. Extract them to the Landing Zone (LZ) without delay.

OBJECTIVES

Win Condition:
All Primary Objectives met.

Loss Condition:
Both Grizzly tanks are lost before Forge and Anders are rescued. Forge and Anders must both stay alive after the rendezvous.

Par Time:
08:00–18:00

PRIMARY OBJECTIVES

■ **Fight Your Way to Forge and Anders' Location**
Completion Score: 500 Points

Forge and his troops can hold off the Covenant for only so long. They will need support, rescue, and extraction.

■ **Cover Anders as She Hacks the Bridge Controls**
Completion Score: 500 Points

Anders will need time to activate the hardlight bridge. Keep the Covenant forces at bay until she succeeds.

■ **Escape the Chamber with Forge and Anders**
Completion Score: 0 Points

Get Forge and Anders to the exit. The Covenant will overwhelm you if you wait too long.

■ **Get Forge and Anders to the Marked Landing Zone**
Completion Score: 500 Points

It is vital that Anders returns to the Spirit of Fire with the information from the Forerunner Structure. Get her and Forge to the Landing Zone ASAP.

OPTIONAL OBJECTIVES

■ **Use the Bridge to Kill Covenant Units**
Completion Score: 700 Points

Deactivating the bridge will drop any units trying to cross it into the chasm below. Use this information to your advantage.

■ **Kill 45 Hunters [45]**
Completion Score: 700 Points

Hunters are collective colonies of small creatures packed into assault armor. Strong and fast, Hunters typically travel in pairs and are used to destroy enemy vehicles. Counter them with infantry or air power.

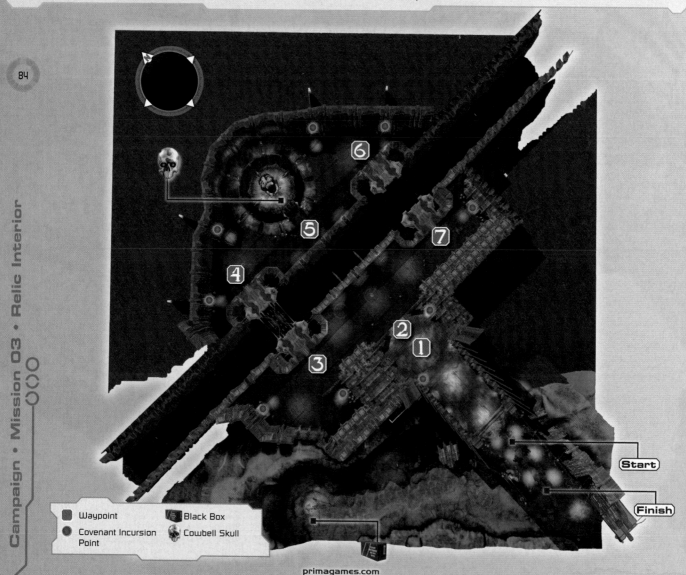

	Waypoint		Black Box
●	Covenant Incursion Point		Cowbell Skull

Difficulty Modifications (compared to Normal)

Easy: All enemy units have 50 percent less Health Points and inflict 50 percent less damage.

Heroic: All enemy units have 10 percent more Health Points and inflict 10 percent more damage. Hunters have one upgrade.

Legendary: All enemy units have 30 percent more Health Points and inflict 30 percent more damage. Hunters have two upgrades.

MISSION COMMENCEMENT

(Start) Once the Pelicans drop off your two Grizzly tanks, trundle into the Forerunner Relic entrance. To achieve the Time Bonus, keep your speed up; the UNSC troops at the massive doorway help defeat the encroaching Covenant infantry. Your tanks' exceptional battle armor shrugs off most Covenant small-arms fire, but pay attention to any Elite Honor Guards clutching their plasma swords; a couple appear as you head through the doorway.

1 Move down the main passage, making sure you deal with the ragtag Covenant threat as you head deeper into the Relic Structure. As you reach Waypoint 1, where you must deal with a cluster of Grunts and Hunters, you're prompted to utilize your Grizzlies' Canister Shell capabilities (**Y**). This is advisable, as the ensuing barrage destroys the Hunters, who are the number-one threat to the health of your vehicles.

CAUTION

Hunters, which you can easily spot due to their large size (for an infantry unit), have the ability to travel in pairs. Their Fuel Rod Cannons, which emit a bright white light, pose a real and ever-present danger to your tanks: Hit them quick and hard, ideally with a Canister Shell barrage.

Legendary Tactics

With the additional damage caused by the Covenant, it is even more imperative that your tanks survive. For this reason, keep both tanks moving side by side; if the Covenant concentrates their fire on one tank, it won't survive for long!

2 Continue your slow but steady pace to the end of the large passage, which opens up into a gigantic dome. Concentrate on the Elite Honor Guards and two Covenant Shade Turrets. As you may have spent your Canister Shells at Waypoint 1, aim your turret weaponry on the cluster of barrels behind each turret; they explode and take down all foes much more easily than aiming at the Shade Turrets and troops. This is the key to defeating the Covenant on higher difficulty settings. Finally, aim both weapons at the Sniper Turret and take a small breather.

Legendary Tactics

You can now choose to head left or right; left is preferable, as the troops to the right (including a Wraith tank) impact your tanks' armor, which means you may not reach Forge and Anders with both vehicles intact on Legendary difficulty.

Cooperative Advice

On lower difficulties, you can split the two Grizzlies, with one player mowing down foes exclusively near Waypoint 7, while the other player follows the critical path. This quickens progress but shouldn't be attempted on higher difficulties.

CAUTION

You should also pay close attention to Grunt Bombers; their attacks also considerably damage tanks and knock down your infantry.

85

Mission 01 Mission 02 **Mission 03** Mission 04 Mission 05 Mission 06 Mission 07 Mission 08 Mission 09 Mission 10 Mission 11 Mission 12 Mission 13 Mission 14 Mission 15

Basics   Factions   Campaign   Multiplayer   Appendices   Art Gallery

3 Trundle left (west), dealing with a few stragglers before you reach the span of a hardlight bridge. The Covenant burst through two openings here; quickly deal with the threats to the south (aim at the barrels to help your cause), but launch a Canister Shell on the Hunters that may appear from the west. Cross this bridge only after you eliminate these foes or you'll be attacked from behind.

4 Quickly set your tanks to reach the bridge's opposite side. Keep them moving, nullifying a few troops and a

Shade Turret to the left. As you reach the bridge's other side, turn right and concentrate your fire on a second turret. Then tackle the infantry and those foes in the Sniper Turret. More enemies pour out of an incursion point to the north.

> **CAUTION**
>
> There's no end to the Covenant reinforcements heading out from the incursion points; therefore, keep moving or your tanks eventually succumb to these relentless attacks!

Picture 1

Picture 2

5 Continue to the rendezvous point; train both tanks to destroy the next Shade Turret, then launch a Canister Shell at one of the two pairs of Hunters that have Forge, Anders, and some Marines pinned down (Picture 1). After you defeat these Hunters, fire at the other pair before worrying about the Grunts or other infantry foes, which have less-powerful weaponry. Once you've contained the immediate threat, the UNSC infantry, Forge, and Anders head toward the protection of your tanks. Immediately select Anders and have her repair both tanks (❤; Picture 2). This is imperative!

Cooperative Advice

■ With the benefit of a second player, have one control Forge and Anders (keeping Forge close to her for protection) and the infantry, while the other deals with both Grizzlies.

6 Move to the span of the other hardlight bridge, which is deactivated. Listen for instructions, as Anders realizes the bridge can be hacked (Picture 1); move her to the bridge controls and start the hacking as soon as possible. You now have a minute to repel all foes—a

Picture 1

Picture 2

mixture of Grunts, Jackals, and the odd pair of Hunters—which constantly appear from two incursion points to the north and from Waypoint 5. Spread out a little (especially the tanks), and let your forces do the firing; save Canister Shells for Hunters and any large groups of foes (Picture 2). With about ten seconds to go, move all your units (ideally with the tanks in front) to the edge of the bridge span.

Picture 1

Picture 2

After Anders activates the bridge, immediately roll all your forces south, across the bridge. Ignore any remaining foes to the north. Although the foes to the south are numerous and include Hunters, launch a Grizzly Canister Shell bombardment (Picture 1) to clear out the majority of the threats, and let the Marines do the rest. Move all your forces off the hardlight section of the bridge, and then deactivate the bridge (using Ⓐ, then ⓛ at the console just right of the tank shown in Picture 2). Any foes chasing you from the north plummet to their deaths!

86

NOTE

Complete the **Covenant Hot Drop** Achievement by ensuring five foes fall to their doom before you continue.

TIP

The bridge cannot be deactivated if your troops are still on it. Either head off the bridge and wait for foes to stream down from the north before deactivating, or stay on the north side, watch as enemies head onto the hardlight section, and drop them into the chasm below.

7 As you head off the bridge, you're greeted by a Covenant Wraith and infantry foes barging in from an eastern incursion point. Immediately deal with the Wraith and the initial wave before quickly moving left (west), ideally positioning both Grizzlies on point, with Forge and Anders in the middle and the Marines on rear-guard detail.

Legendary Tactics

If both Grizzlies look like they're about to explode, remember to send in Anders a second time: Utilize her repair talents!

Picture 1

Picture 2

[2, then **1**]** Return to Waypoint 2, and watch for a door to the right explode off its hinges. A pair of Hunters pours out. Attack them swiftly (Picture 1), and save your Canister Shells for a group of three more pairs of Hunters waiting at Waypoint 1 (Picture 2). Concentrate your Grizzlies' firepower on them and on more Hunters flooding out of an incursion point to the left, which explodes as you reach it. Take your infantry past this incursion point, but keep both Grizzlies nearby to launch barrages (and Canister Shells, once replenished) at this steady stream of Hunters until you kill 45 of them.

Cowbell

As soon as you defeat the 45th Hunter, send all your infantry, plus Anders and Forge, to the Relic's entrance doorway. Take a single Grizzly, and retrace your route from Waypoint 1 to 5; then enter the circular "island" where you rescued Anders and where the Relic is located. The **Cowbell Skull** resides here! Head back over either bridge span, making sure the hardlight bridge is activated!.

TIP

Another (quicker) way to grab the Skull is to leave a squad of Marines behind in a Sniper Tower near the Relic, and order them to collect it once the 45 Hunters are killed.

Black Box 3

At the same time as you head for the Skull, take some Marines past the LZ, and down the rocky path to the west (don't place Anders near the finish point, for obvious reasons!). They travel northwest along it, eventually reaching a downed Pelican with a Jackal guarding it. Grab **Black Box 3** here.

TIP

Both the Skull and Black Box take time to collect. You can still achieve Gold and grab both of them; try heading to them at the same time with different units (or players).

(Finish) The moment you obtain both the Skull and the Black Box (or after you kill 45 Hunters if you aren't interested in the collectibles), move Anders and Forge to the Landing Zone, marked with a circle of lights. Forge sends up a plume of smoke, and a circling Pelican extricates both of them.

Awards and Summary

GOLD	SILVER	BRONZE	TIN	Best Objective Score	Best Combat Bonus	Best Time Bonus
45,000+	35,000–44,999	25,000–34,999	0–24,999	3,200	x10 (32,000)	x5 (16,000)

Theoretical Best Score	**51,200** (3,200 + 32,000 + 16,000)	

Mission 01   Mission 02   Mission 03   Mission 04   Mission 05   Mission 06   Mission 07   Mission 08   Mission 09   Mission 10   Mission 11   Mission 12   Mission 13   Mission 14   Mission 15

Basics   Factions   Campaign   Multiplayer   Appendices   Art Gallery

87

CAMPAIGN · ACT 2

MISSION 07

pg. 102

The once-peaceful planet of Arcadia is now a disastrous pyre of displaced citizens, desperately fleeing the advancing Covenant armies. After a valiant stand in Arcadia City, Forge and his remaining troops are forced to the outskirts and grimly hold their position against overwhelming odds. The tide begins to turn when proto-soldiers known as Spartans are hot-dropped to aid Forge's beleaguered forces. Soon afterwards, a secret ONI base is found, protected by a massive Covenant energy dome. Once the dome is punctured, the Covenant's secret is revealed.

04: ARCADIA CITY

Covenant forces are invading the main city on the planet Arcadia. A large number of civilians are attempting to flee to Evac Cargo Transports at three landing pads around the city. You must protect the citizens of Arcadia, guarding them as they escape and saving as many as possible.

OBJECTIVES

Win Condition:
At least one Evac Transport must survive until the timer runs out.

Loss Condition:
All Evac Transports are destroyed.

Par Time:
21:00–23:00

PRIMARY OBJECTIVES

▪ Protect Civilians and Cargo Transports until Launch
Completion Score: 500 Points

The civilians will head toward the transports on their own. At least one of the transport ships must survive; the city's population has no other way to evacuate the area.

▪ Clear Covenant from Subway Exit
Completion Score: 500 Points

Eliminate the Covenant forces around the subway exit so the civilians have a clear path to the transports.

OPTIONAL OBJECTIVES

▪ Establish a Base
Completion Score: 500 Points

A base in the city will let you train more units to protect the civilians and transports. If you can assemble enough of a force, it might even be possible to launch a limited counterattack against the Covenant.

▪ Kill 50 Elites [50]
Completion Score: 500 Points

Elites, also known as Sangheili, are often seen leading Covenant forces into battle. Using their cloaks and energy swords to surprise and overwhelm their enemies, Elites are challenging opponents.

▪ Establish a Second Base
Completion Score: 500 Points

Establishing a second base will provide additional supplies for our troops and help hold back the Covenant forces.

▪ Rescue 500 Civilians
Completion Score: 1,000 Points

Rescue 500 civilians; at least this amount must leave on board the one surviving Cargo Transport.

▪ Rescue 1,000 Civilians
Completion Score: 1,500 Points

Rescue 1,000 civilians; at least this amount must leave on board both surviving Cargo Transports.

■	Waypoint
●	Arcadian Police Watchtowers/ Covenant Sniper Towers
●	Civilian Entrance Point
🛆	Supply Crate
▨	Black Box
☠	Wuv Woo Skull

Difficulty Modifications
(compared to Normal)

Easy: All enemy units have 50 percent less Health Points and inflict 50 percent less damage. There is no Covenant Mega-Turret.

Heroic: Covenant Mega-Turret attacks any UNSC forces during the last leg of the mission.

Legendary: All enemy units have 25 percent more Health Points and inflict 25 percent more damage. Covenant Mega-Turret attacks any UNSC forces during the last leg of the mission.

MISSION COMMENCEMENT

NOTE

Before you begin, familiarize yourself with the different units a base can train and build (see the "Factions" chapter of this book); the following tactics concentrate on the optimal forces for the job, but you may wish to try other vehicles and troop types.

(Start)
After Forge's Warthog is dropped from the Pelican, you must clear the immediate area of encroaching Covenant. On the guide's map, notice that you're near Waypoint 6; this is where you'll build your first base—but not yet. Instead, take your entourage of Hornets across the grassy area and defend the Arcadian Police Watchtower from the milling Covenant forces, Ramming the Grunts near the initial plaza area.

1 Your first port of call is the initial plaza, where a group of Elites are slicing and dicing the citizens attempting to flee. Your Hornets and Sergeant Forge should make short work of these foes, temporarily securing the plaza area. Expect citizens to stream in from this location (check the guide map for other locations they will enter from). Once these citizens are relatively safe, you are free to roam about Arcadia's streets, clearing paths for citizens with 20 minutes to go before the evacuation is complete. An advantage route is shown below:

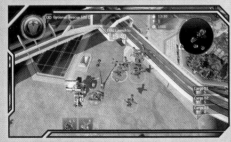

2 Head north, around the greenery to a paved area near a glass floor. There's likely to be some Covenant

activity here, another Arcadian Police Watchtower (which may be manned by Grunts), and a Wraith heading along the streets. Your airborne forces should make a quick sweep of this area and the forecourt of the building to the west before heading northwest toward the second Evac Transport ship. Kill anything that isn't human.

TIP

Your optional goal to kill 50 Elites starts immediately; use Forge's Warthog to ram them, and finish them off with your Hornets. Concentrate on personally slaying as many as possible so other friendly troops don't take your kills.

3 Swing around and eliminate your foes (usually an Elite or two), and temporarily clear the area near the canal

bridge of enemies. You may spot your first Evac Transport here, which is guarded by Spartan Red Team. Help them throughout this mission, but focus your immediate attention to the southwest.

[4 and **5**]**
Take your platoon (which should still be without casualties if you've maintained precise combat takedowns) and move them southwest, around the building near Waypoint 3, then to Waypoint 4,

91

Mission 01　Mission 02　Mission 03　**Mission 04**　Mission 05　Mission 06　Mission 07　Mission 08　Mission 09　Mission 10　Mission 11　Mission 12　Mission 13　Mission 14　Mission 15

Basics　　　Factions　　　Campaign　　　Multiplayer　　　Appendices　　　Art Gallery

where Grunts man a Watchtower on either side of the bridge. Cut them down, as well as any roaming Elites on the ground; then cut a path for the citizens to flee along. Continue this until Evac Transport #3 makes an ill-advised takeoff attempt and is shot down by Covenant forces. Your plan to save Arcadia City begins now!

Immediately take any remaining Hornets up to the entrance to Evac Transport #2 while Forge drives back to the grassy area near the starting position. Serina has located two possible spots at which to construct a Firebase.

6 As a matter of urgency, begin to build a Firebase at Waypoint 6. It is near the majority of the corridors the

citizens are fleeing along, and it allows you to quickly train any troops (except Vultures) you may need. Follow the instructions for base-building from the "Advanced Training" chapter, choosing the number of Reactors and Supply Pads that suit your play style—but don't neglect your other duties!

NOTE

From this point on, the mission takes on a free-form nature as you patrol the streets and tackle wave after Covenant wave emanating from a shielded base on the city's eastern edge. You don't need to visit the following waypoints in the order we present.

7 While your first base has its initial buildings being constructed, take the majority of your forces to this main

thoroughfare. Your Hornets can quickly reach this location, where you'll run into Covenant incursions and more citizens frantically attempting to flee. Lay waste to this area immediately, but don't stay too long; there's some quick thinking that needs doing (see Tip).

TIP

Drop everything if you hear from one of the two remaining Evac Troop Transports or from Spartan Red Team; fly in to help them, checking the minimap to see which transport is having the hardest time. Spartan Red Team does sterling work attempting to keep the Covenant off the transports, but when the battlefield gets too hot, head in to help. Remember, you can use your Heal & Repair from Spirit of Fire to heal the transports (and Spartans), but only after combat is over; otherwise the friendly troops take more damage! Finally, be sure to heal Spartans and revive them by moving close to them; they are a tremendous help when they're active!

8 After briefly purging Waypoint 7 of Covenant scum, move quickly and directly to Waypoint 8 while multi-tasking and creating a Barracks and Marines at your first Firebase. If you're fast enough, you can place a second base at this location. Do so immediately, and begin to construct Supply Bases until you reach the "sweet spot" mentioned in the "Advanced Training" chapter.

Legendary Tactics

Be quick about your base deployment at Waypoint 8; on harder difficulties, the Covenant may already have built their own base here, which wreaks havoc with your plans, as you must destroy the base before helping citizens. Don't expect a gold medal if you leave this base for too long!

You must now fortify both your bases. The first Firebase (at Waypoint 6) is likely to be attacked by a few

Covenant infantry, heading in from Waypoint 4. Build a couple Flame Mortar Turrets to keep them away. Fortify your other base at Waypoint 8 with Turrets that can bring down both infantry and air units, as the area to the north has Spirits flying in to deposit additional troops. You're also attacked by a few infantry units and Ghosts from the stepped area to the southeast; all are annoyances you must overcome. Turrets are also good at cutting down Elites, helping you satisfy that objective.

Cooperative Advice

If you're playing with a friend, once Serina pinpoints your two bases, split your management skills accordingly: Have one player in charge of base-building, upgrades, training, and constructing units, and Spirit of Fire powers (Heal & Repairing transports). The other should solely concentrate on roaming the streets, fighting the Covenant.

There are two plans to try in order to maximize the number of citizens you free and to keep a constant vigil on the encroaching Covenant. Build a Barracks at your first base as soon as possible, and train three or four squads of Marines. Spread them out over the streets, sending each to a specific Arcadian Police Watchtower or Covenant Sniper Tower. All are marked on the guide's map.

This gives you a great view of the battlefield, and you have a line of sight of all the paths the civilians take to reach the transports.

Although this becomes increasingly difficult on Legendary setting, you can beat back the Covenant quickly and effectively if you've upgraded your Marines to at least RPG Launcher status, have them in every Watchtower and Sniper Tower, and create a few fast-moving vehicles to help catch higher concentrations of foes.

TIP

Watch for battle warning icons (red "x") on your minimap; these indicate Marines in Watchtowers being attacked; use this warning to send your mobile forces here to help out.

Legendary Tactics

On higher difficulties, upgraded Warthogs or, more importantly, Hornets (which don't have to deal with moving around buildings) are your best bet to swing the battle in your favor. A highly mobile army allows you to rapidly deploy them to the transport ships, or to citizens, or to split up your Hornet squadron and do both. You must fully upgrade the Hornets to using Chaff Pods, as your supplies allow.

TIP

Make sure you leave a few Hornets to help automatically defend each transport ship, as enemy Hunters and Locusts are very adept at destroying the transports more quickly than it takes to lumber your entire army across the map.

[9] and [10]
The area to the north and northeast of the second base location is extremely dangerous. You'll find a

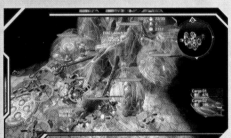

mass amount of Covenant Wraiths, Ghosts, Locusts, Elites, and Hunters to contend with, which is relatively straight-forward to avoid but suicide if you venture toward Waypoint 10, the Covenant base. This base features shielding and Turrets, as well as a Mega-Turret that slices through your

troops with ease. Unless you're adept and playing at a lower difficulty level, there's no real reason to mess with the Covenant base. Instead, keep the streets free from foes until the timer counts down to zero and the transports launch.

TIP

As the battle wears on and the countdown reaches the five-minute mark, keep the streets clean of Covenant forces, and watch for more and more Spirits flying in from the north and northeast. Watch for them constantly throughout this mission, and rake the enemies that drop out long before they kill citizens or damage the transport ships. You can shoot down the Spirits before they land, giving you an excellent (and easy) increase to your Combat Bonus. Missile add-ons on your bases help too.

Black Box 4

The Black Box on this map is simple to acquire and is located to the north of the starting point, at the base of a building. At the building, look for a lone individual cowering on a glass walkway. Select (A) the building console at the structure's base, and free this citizen. His name is Adam, and once he flees to a transport ship, you complete **The Real Winner** Achievement. You can take the Black Box whether you free Adam or not.

CAUTION

Because Adam dies if struck once, be sure you have at least three minutes remaining on the clock and have complete control of the streets between the Black Box and the transport ships before freeing him.

Wuv Woo

Once you've defeated the 50th Elite, send a vehicle (ideally Forge in his Warthog) around the back of the second UNSC base you built, to the stepped area south of and adjacent to the Covenant base; search the grass for this Skull.

NOTE

Citizens appear in six groups of five at a time. Only one citizen freed is necessary for victory, but at least one of the final two transports must take off. Between 1,200 to 1,300 citizens flee, meaning you must be very vigilant if you wish to rescue 1,000.

Awards and Summary

GOLD	SILVER	BRONZE	TIN	Best Objective Score	Best Combat Bonus	Best Time Bonus
50,000+	40,000-49,999	30,000-39,999	0-29,999	5,000	x10 (50,000)	x5 (25,000)

Theoretical Best Score	80,000 (5,000 + 50,000 + 25,000)

Mission 01 Mission 02 Mission 03 Mission 04 Mission 05 Mission 06 Mission 07 Mission 08 Mission 09 Mission 10 Mission 11 Mission 12 Mission 13 Mission 14 Mission 15

Basics   Factions   Campaign   Multiplayer   Appendices   Art Gallery

93

05: ARCADIA OUTSKIRTS

After retreating from Arcadia City, Forge and the remains of his forces attempt to usurp a large, defendable crater to the south and rally his troops. After establishing two bases and surviving numerous Covenant onslaughts, reinforcements push back north to destroy a Covenant base.

OBJECTIVES

Win Condition:
All primary objectives met.

Loss Condition:
All buildings and units destroyed, and heroes downed.

Par Time:
21:00–23:00

PRIMARY OBJECTIVES

■ Retreat to the Southern Crater
Completion Score: 250 Points

Covenant forces are closing in. Get to the southern crater and try to hold out.

■ Secure the Area By Killing All Covenant in the Crater
Completion Score: 250 Points

Covenant forces are swarming all over the crater. Take out all the enemies and create a safe zone.

■ Defend the Crater until Omega Team Arrives
Completion Score: 750 Points

Additional UNSC forces are on approach to your location. The crater is excellent defensive terrain; hold fast, maintain a base in the crater, and wait for help.

■ Destroy the Covenant Base and Its Guards
Completion Score: 1,000 Points

If the Covenant base is destroyed, the UNSC position on Arcadia will be secure. All of the base buildings and any nearby Covenant units must be eliminated.

OPTIONAL OBJECTIVES

■ Construct a Second Base
Completion Score: 500 Points

More production capacity would give you a fighting chance to defeat the Covenant. If the crater is secure, try to claim an additional base.

■ Kill Five Wraith Tanks [5]
Completion Score: 750 Points

The Wraith is a heavy vehicle equipped with a plasma mortar. Used at the forefront of ground assaults, they are a critical component of the Covenant arsenal.

▢ Waypoint	⌂ Supply Crates
◆ Mega-Turret	▨ Black Box
☢ Reactor	☠ Fog Skull
⊞ Covenant Base	

Difficulty Modifications (compared to Normal)

Easy: All enemy units have 25 percent less Health Points and inflict 25 percent less damage. Banshee assaults are less common. The Covenant Mega-Turret cannot hit the crater base and has limited Health Points. There are less Covenant units, with no enemy upgrades.

Heroic: All enemy units have 25 percent more Health Points, inflict 25 percent more damage, and are upgraded. Covenant Mega-Turret will bombard the crater base and is more resistant to damage.

Legendary: All enemy units have 50 percent more Health Points, inflict 50 percent more damage, and are almost fully upgraded. Covenant Mega-Turret will bombard the crater base and is even more resistant to damage. Banshee assaults are frequent.

MISSION COMMENCEMENT

NOTE

By now, you should be very familiar with the different units a UNSC base can train and build, and with the strengths and weaknesses each has against the Covenant. If necessary, check the "Factions" chapter before continuing.

(Start) Now is not the time for standing your ground and fighting, especially because Serina has picked a place to set up a Firebase as you're chased away from Arcadia City by heavy Covenant forces. Your ragtag collection of units should be able to continue in a south-easterly direction, fighting (but not waiting around) the small defenses along the way. You pass a large open concrete area to the east; this is where the Covenant set up their base later in this mission.

CAUTION

Don't waste your time or units trying to fight the Covenant chasing you; the situation soon becomes hopeless. Retreat!

1 Trundle onward, ignoring the ramp to your southwest. You need to establish a base of operations before you begin to search this ruined part of the Arcadia outskirts. You're retreating to a crater south of the starting point (Waypoint 4), and as you pass Waypoint 1, ignore the temptation to head down the ramp into the grassy area; you can explore and search that location in a moment. You need almost all of your fighting force to defeat the Covenant waiting farther down the road.

TIP

As you head down the road, keep your pace slow and steady: One of your Spartans, not the Scorpion tank, should lead the entire contingent to the crater. If you lead with the Scorpion, it is usually destroyed as you punch through the Covenant defenses, and you lose a great deal of firepower at this crucial time.

[2 and 3] However, as you reach Waypoint 2, the gap leading to a shallow slope to the east appears, leading to a small cluster of abandoned buildings. One of them is a Reactor Hook, effectively adding to your Tech level by one when it is manned. There's only one infantry unit for this job; peel off one of your Spartans at this point and have them enter the Reactor. You're now functioning at Tech Level 1 before you even reach the southern crater!

TIP

When the Spartan is garrisoned in the upper Reactor Hook, he can typically defend the area for a great deal of time. Check on him periodically or if you see combat breaking out at this location on your minimap. The biggest threat to this Spartan is a Wraith firing on the Reactor. Retaliate with a MAC Blast from the Spirit of Fire; it's actually more proficient than peeling other troops from their positions.

4 Progress past Waypoint 2, then punch through the Covenant troops down into a massive crater, where Serina has signaled that a Firebase is incoming. Reach this point (Waypoint 4) as early as possible. While the dropships swoop in with the two Firebase halves, split your entire

95

Mission 01 Mission 02 Mission 03 Mission 04 **Mission 05** Mission 06 Mission 07 Mission 08 Mission 09 Mission 10 Mission 11 Mission 12 Mission 13 Mission 14 Mission 15

Basics　　　Factions　　　Campaign　　　Multiplayer　　　Appendices　　　Art Gallery

infantry and any Warthogs into collecting the scattered supply crates. Increase the size of the base to a Fortress and add in your desired number of Supply Pads, but make sure you don't increase your Tech level by more than two (that means fitting two Reactors, or a Reactor and an Advanced Reactor); the other Reactors increase your Tech level to 4 (the maximum necessary).

TIP

Continue your base's progress while sending your infantry to the various cover points scattered around your crater. You may want to point your vehicles in the direction of Waypoint 7 to tackle a Mega-Turret the Covenant are about to build.

After a couple minutes of frantic building and Supply Pad grabbing, your base should look something like this. Note the Air Pad, which allows you to build Hornets. There are a couple reasons why Hornets are great to utilize on this map: First, the Covenant doesn't build the one unit the Hornets are weak against—Vampires. Second, the Hornets can ignore all terrain obstacles and fly anywhere, cutting off Covenant troops as they try to swarm you. More details are shown later in this mission.

Also of note are the Turrets. Expect constant attacks from the Covenant, and if they move past the defenses on the crater's northern slope, you want to strike them down before they destroy your base. Add on a Flame Mortar, a Railgun, and two Missile Launchers for a good mixture of augmentations to strike down the Covenant no matter how and which direction they attack you.

TIP

Having fully upgraded Turrets on both bases (particularly Waypoint 4) by using the Field Armory to research Heavy Turrets simplifies your base defense and allows you more time to survey the battlefield. If you can afford the upgrades, try them!

5 In your early supply crate hunting, search the grassy embankment to the east of the main highway path, which is sometimes patrolled by enemy Wraiths. You can work your way around the outer edge of the building cluster where your Spartan is holding the Reactor, grabbing more crates before looping around to Waypoint 2. However, expect fierce Covenant resistance if you try this; it is better to edge no farther north than Waypoint 2.

6 You now have Covenant heading in your direction from a few different locations. The first location is the abandoned freeway structure (shown in the picture) that runs along this map's western edge, one section of which trails into the crater (the freeway was the source of the bomb that created the crater). Covenant infantry head along this structure.

Employ infantry-culling troops at this point; it is wise to fly Hornets or move troops along the freeway to the defenses on the map's far western edge and hold off the Covenant there with a few squads of upgraded Marines. If you can take cover behind this wrecked Pelican on the overpass, you can shut down all Covenant attacks from this side, allowing your other troops to deal with the Mega-Turret and main pathway incursions.

7 The second location is the sunken area. Expect more Covenant vehicles, which are ripe for Jacking, and foes coming down from the overpass. Try the following:

Aside from Jacking vehicles, place Spartans (and Infantry) in cover, as they defend these positions well.

The **He's Got the Jack** Achievement is available once you commandeer six vehicles: Destroy a minimum of three vehicles so the Spartans disembark and try again.

Spartans can Commandeer and strengthen UNSC vehicles.

Lock Cobras inside the crater to provide covering fire against Wraith tanks.

Cooperative Advice

Once you reach the southern crater and build the base (keep both Reactors in UNSC hands), have one player build up the structure while the other controls the troops. Or, each player can control a base if you've attacked the Mega-Turret. Then let one player deal with enemy incursions nearby, and on the overpass, while the other pushes up the main path.

7 [continued] While the base is being fortified, waste no time in sending a sizable squadron down past Waypoint

7 (place a squad of Marines inside the second Reactor, and have a couple additional units nearby to help out if they're attacked), and head toward a small congregation of Covenant intent on building a Mega-Turret.

8 The second base location is impossible to hold if the Covenant have landed and are setting up the Mega-Turret. However, if you're fast enough, you can reach this area and destroy the Turret (ideally with Scorpion bombardment or MAC Blasts) before the Covenant arrive to begin construction and activate it! Then remain at the forward cover near where a Spirit might have been hovering, and rake the enemy as they head down the ramped slope from the highway to the north.

CAUTION

The Mega-Turret fires a deadly barrage, but it has a long cooldown between shots. Take advantage of this to dash closely, and then order in a MAC Blast. This isn't likely to destroy the Turret in one shot, but sustained fire from your vehicles or air units can help you finally bring it down.

TIP

Make sure the Reactor at Waypoint 7 is garrisoned just before the Mega-Turret is destroyed, or it will hit the Reactor and usually take out the infantry inside with ease.

Once you've destroyed the Mega-Turret, begin building your second Firebase, upgrading it quickly (as you should have your first base completed and should be garrisoned at both Reactors) and holding off the Covenant forces while your Hornets fly from firefight to firefight. Pay particular attention to the number of Wraiths you're killing. Continue with this drawn-out defense, edging no closer than the highway, where you fled from at the beginning of this mission until Serina radios in, informing you reinforcements are arriving.

Fog

Once your fifth Wraith Tank has been mangled, send a unit (ideally a Warthog, although an infantry unit on the overpass, defending the destroyed Pelican cover area, is also an option) northwest along the overpass. Tread on the straight overpass, not the section that curves to the right. The Skull is located along here, near the buildings.

The wait for reinforcements has been worth it! Spartan Team Omega strides onto the battlefield and turns the tide in your favor thanks to their superhuman heroics! Cluster your forces, and group them all at Waypoint 2 (or head up the ramp from Waypoint 8 to Waypoint 1), and press forward, slowly culling the defending Covenant as you head back to the location where you first fled from these foes.

Black Box 5

Once the army is assembled, head north up the highway path past Waypoints 2 and 1. While the majority of your troops moves toward the final Waypoint, split off a Warthog or infantry unit down the short ramp to the northeast. The Black Box is lying in the semicircular walled area near cover. Grab it!

9 Move your Spartans and armored units north toward a base the Covenant has constructed. You could have attacked this previously, but you'd have faced heavy casualties, and a low Combat Bonus. With Team Omega leading, begin a methodical devastation of this base! Start with the Turrets and milling Covenant and then the shields, and finally the base itself. A MAC Blast as you arrive and another just before the base crumbles completes this mission in style.

Legendary Tactics

Ensure Spartan Team Omega attack the base with other units; Spartans are tough, but they aren't unstoppable.

Awards and Summary

GOLD	SILVER	BRONZE	TIN		Best Objective Score	Best Combat Bonus	Best Time Bonus
40,000+	25,000–39,999	15,000–24,999	0–14,999		3,500	x10 (35,000)	x5 (17,500)

		Theoretical Best Score	56,000 (3,500 + 35,000 + 17,500)

Mission 01 Mission 02 Mission 03 Mission 04 **Mission 05** Mission 06 Mission 07 Mission 08 Mission 09 Mission 10 Mission 11 Mission 12 Mission 13 Mission 14 Mission 15

Basics   Factions   Campaign   Multiplayer   Appendices   Art Gallery

97

06: DOME OF LIGHT

Forge and Anders move to a secret ONI base perched over a huge Covenant dome discovered on Arcadia. Request special Rhinos fitted with Plasma Cannons and maneuver them into position. Have them fire simultaneously and pierce a hole in the dome large enough to allow the Spirit of Fire's Mac Cannon through.

OBJECTIVES

Win Condition:
All primary objectives met.

Loss Condition:
All buildings and units destroyed, and heroes downed. Not enough supplies to recover.

Par Time:
15:00–30:00

PRIMARY OBJECTIVES

■ **Kill Approaching Covenant Infantry**
Completion Score: 300 Points
The Covenant are attacking in force. Fight off the assault.

■ **Request a Rhino at the Landing Pad**
Completion Score: 300 Points
Call on Anders to send down a Rhino to the pad adjacent to your base.

■ **Get the Rhino to the First Position**
Completion Score: 400 Points

■ **Place a Rhino at the Marked Second Position**
Completion Score: 550 Points

■ **Transport a Rhino to the Marked Third Position**
Completion Score: 500 Points
Positions for the Rhinos are marked. Protect each Rhino until it can safely deploy at the marked destination. The Spirit of Fire menu has an option that allows you to use Pelicans to transport Rhinos.

■ **Get Rhinos to the Last Two Marked Positions**
Completion Score: 600 Points
You will need to get several Rhinos in position to be able to bring enough firepower to bear on the dome. Rhinos will be dropped at the landing pad.

OPTIONAL OBJECTIVES

■ **Claim Two ONI Reactors**
Completion Score: 400 Points
Taking control of the nearby ONI Reactors will let you train advanced troops more quickly.

■ **Kill 50 Banshees [50]**
Completion Score: 600 Points
A fast-moving flying unit, the Banshee is highly maneuverable. Equipped with a plasma cannon, it provides deadly and effective air support for Covenant forces. Counter Banshees with Wolverines.

■ **Destroy the Dome Generators and Air Defenses**
Completion Score: 500 Points
The Rhinos are all in position. Wipe out the enemy structures and bring down the dome.

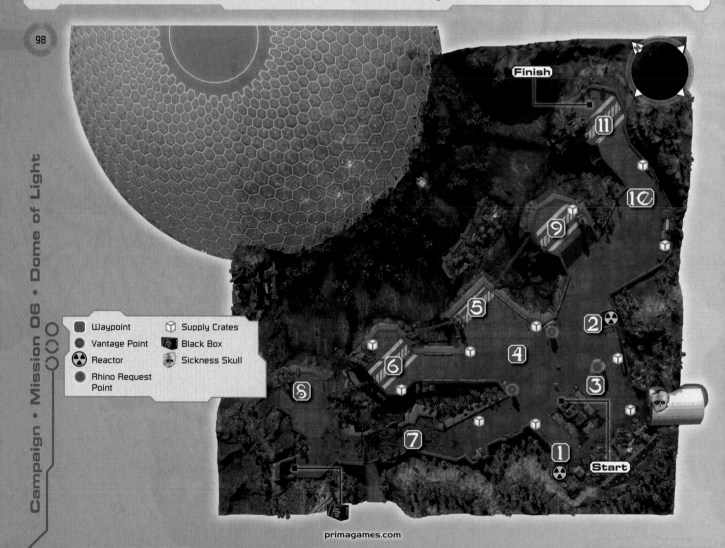

Legend:
- ■ Waypoint
- ● Vantage Point
- ☢ Reactor
- ● Rhino Request Point
- 🏠 Supply Crates
- ▨ Black Box
- ☠ Sickness Skull

Difficulty Modifications
(compared to Normal)

Easy: All enemy units have 50 percent less Health Points and inflict 50 percent less damage.

Heroic: There are extra Covenant turrets and bases. Hunters arrive earlier and are more upgraded.

Legendary: All enemy units have 25 percent more Health Points and inflict 25 percent more damage. There are extra Covenant turrets and bases. Hunters arrive earlier and are more upgraded.

MISSION COMMENCEMENT

NOTE

Before you begin, you should be extremely competent in building base structures and training or building a variety of troops, as a full lineup of UNSC forces is made available to you from your starting station.

Start

Punching through the energy dome is no easy task, but first there's a small but troublesome ground force of Covenant troops to wipe out, directly north of your station. Once you clear the immediate area of enemies, quickly begin a buildup, in a defensive posture, and a small expedition to the first four Waypoints. During this time, build two or three Supply Pads and upgrade them, affix two Turrets to the front of your base, and use your ragtag band of brothers to secure all the immediate supply crates surrounding the base, as shown on the map.

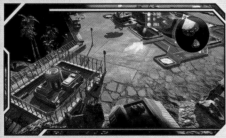

1 Before you call in a Rhino from the Spirit of Fire, it is cost-effective and strategic to send one of your Marine squads to the first ONI Reactor, located just to the southwest of your base. Send the Marine squad to collect supply crates around the back of the base; when they're done, situate them in the Reactor. Because the Reactor is behind your base, don't expect to receive heavy enemy attacks on it; immediately increase your Tech level without supply expenditure!

TIP

Picking up all the supplies gives you an early boost to your economy, allowing you to upgrade your units. Make sure Forge locates and grabs the supplies across the rest of the map, using his speedy Warthog to cover these distances.

2 To the northeast of your station is a second and equally important ONI Reactor to take and hold. Claim this as early into the mission as possible, as you can start building vehicles immediately. However, this Reactor is much more susceptible to Covenant attack, mainly from foes landing on the concrete roadway in front of it. For this reason, send in Marines but periodically check on them—or better yet, use a Spartan to take and hold this Reactor.

Legendary Tactics

Use Spartan "Alice" to garrison this Reactor, as she defends it proficiently for a long time while allowing you to keep the stronger Spartans with your main force.

99

[**3** and **4**] Waypoints 5, 6, 8, 9, and 11 are the locations for Rhino placement, but you must request Rhinos by clicking on the communications tower to the station's east. Dropped in seconds after you request them (Picture 1), Rhinos are reasonably

Picture 1

Picture 2

expensive, and you can have only one on the map at a time. However, they can fight alongside your regular army, so have one in your army at all times. As soon as you've built a few Scorpions, request a Rhino and send

Mission 01　Mission 02　Mission 03　Mission 04　Mission 05　**Mission 06**　Mission 07　Mission 08　Mission 09　Mission 10　Mission 11　Mission 12　Mission 13　Mission 14　Mission 15

Basics　　Factions　　Campaign　　Multiplayer　　Appendices　　Art Gallery

your small but heavily armored and armed force to the middle of the tarmac directly north of you (Picture 2). Bring the Scorpions' considerable firepower to bear on any Covenant troops on the ground or on Banshees in the air. Gradually creep forward.

TIP

On either side of Waypoint 4 is a lookout tower in which you can house troops, but this isn't usually necessary, as moving vehicles are much more adept and flexible at handling the Covenant threat. If you're looking for a place to put your remaining Spartans, have each drive a Scorpion Tank, adding additional combat effectiveness to that vehicle.

5 The first Rhino lockdown location is directly ahead—a vista point overlooking the giant Covenant dome below. Send your Rhino to this Waypoint, and make sure you clamp it down (using 🅨): Locking down a Rhino allows for an additional attack and greater firepower to defend against the increasingly hostile waves of Covenant forces.

Expect Banshees and Spirits to periodically fly up from the dome and swing around toward your station (which should now be at Fortress level). Spirits are also a problem, depositing enemy troops on the tarmac north of the base and to the northwest of Waypoint 4. Once you clamp down the first Rhino, immediately call for the next, as Cutter hot drops in a few ODST squads to help defend this initial location. You may place an additional Wolverine or Scorpion to patrol the area near Waypoint 5 before turning northwest.

TIP

By now, your Fortress should have four functioning Turrets. Add a mixture of add-ons to them, making sure at least the rear two Turrets have Missile Launchers to catch the Banshees flying in to bomb the base. This helps complete the Kill objective, and the earlier you raise Turrets at your base, the easier the objective becomes.

Legendary Tactics

If you can, upgrade your Turrets to Medium or Heavy versions; in addition, choose Flame Mortars to repel Hunters and choose Missile Launchers to drop Banshees from the skies.

TIP

This applies to each Rhino clamp-down location; keep your placed Rhinos protected and Heal & Repair them periodically; otherwise you'll have to replace them, ruining your Time Bonus. Prevent this by building and sending in a couple Wolverines at each Rhino location; their firepower helps a great deal.

Legendary Tactics

After you secure the first Rhino, be in position to destroy the Covenant buildings under construction, close to where you're about to place the second Rhino. Plan ahead and remove the Covenant's structures before they spawn their terrible troops.

6 The Covenant have been busy constructing a couple small buildings near the second Rhino deployment point, so take your lumbering Scorpion squad, along with at least a couple of Spartans; drop in a MAC Blast to soften up the targets; and rumble in, focusing on the Shade Turrets, Hunters, and buildings, clearing the area. Clamp down your second Rhino just as you call your third one in.

[7 and 8] As the second Rhino clamps down at Waypoint 6, you should have another Rhino dropped in and a couple of Wolverines waiting at the Rally Point near Waypoint 3. Previous bombardment (Picture 1) has reduced the road to the third vantage point to

Picture 1

Picture 2

impassable rubble, and the only way to reach Waypoint 8 is to call in the Pelican Transport from your Spirit of Fire menu (🅐, then 🅛). Group the Wolverines and Rhino close together so the Pelican swoops in and catches them all; then select Waypoint 8 as the deployment point (Picture 2). When they land, lay waste to the small Covenant detachment, and clamp the third Rhino into position.

NOTE

Wolverines aren't mandatory, but a couple of guarding units is usually handy to place near your Rhinos for protection. Alternatively, keep checking on each clamped Rhino for damage, and heal accordingly.

If you complete this mission without losing a Rhino, you're awarded the **Rhino Hugger** Achievement.

Black Box 6

Just after you position the third Rhino at Waypoint 8, search a blocked tunnel entrance behind you, to the west. **Black Box 6** is located here. You can quickly snag this without losing too much of your Time Bonus.

Cooperative Advice

With an additional teammate helping your progress, use the time-tested plan of separating responsibilities: Have the first player attack the Covenant and place Rhinos at their clamp-down locations. The second player should defend the Fortress, build units, call for Rhinos, and check the clamped Rhinos for signs of attack.

9 After Cutter's failed attempt to order the first three Rhinos to fire on the dome, which results in a few more airborne Covenant units but no punch-through, you're tasked with positioning two more Rhinos at the last two vantage points, both northeast of the main Fortress. This time, you may have to deal with an invasion of Hunters and some Locusts.

This can really hamper your progress, so time is of the essence. You need a strong force to charge past the second Reactor, from which you can disembark the Spartan and Jack enemy troops with your other two Spartans. Battle your way up onto the flat overlook, and position the fourth Rhino.

Legendary Tactics

If your army's Population rises above 15, the Covenant unleash a lot more troops, thus a light force of Scorpions is the best choice. Upgrade and repair Scorpions to maximize your combat bonus. It is wise to have troops positioned near Waypoint 11 to destroy any Covenant structures before the fourth Rhino is clamped down. The Covenant are easier to defeat if they cannot emerge from the Hall. At Waypoints 9 and 11, use transports to drop in Rhinos on already-cleared areas, saving you time (and your Bonus), as you don't have to worry about your Rhino being targeted within your vehicle squads.

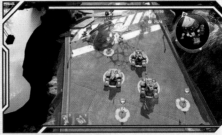

[10, 11, Finish] Continue to press on, with advance units already demolishing the buildings the Covenant are attempting to build at Waypoint 11. Transport in your final Rhino once this final route is cleared, and watch as all five Rhinos punch a hole in the dome big enough for Cutter to launch multiple MAC Blasts into the Covenant base beyond. You're tasked with aiming the MAC Cannon, so quickly aim and fire, making sure each shot lands squarely in the middle of a Covenant structure or vehicle cluster. Next stop: inside the dome!

Sickness

When you've shot your 50th Banshee from the skies (you may need Cobras in order to tag every one quickly enough so your Time Bonus doesn't suffer), have a Marine unit (like the one garrisoned at the Reactor at Waypoint 1) quickly dash across to the hangar in your base's southeast corner. Claim the **Sickness Skull** here!

Legendary Tactics

For a speedy resolution to this mission, it is recommended you complete all tasks as quickly as possible. With enough planning, you can have any Rhino clamp-down location cleared "one step ahead" of the Rhino being transported in. If you raise your Population above 15, only attempt this when you're aiming for the fourth and fifth clamp-down points. Let your Turrets defend your base, which you should essentially abandon in favor of a final push. You may lose your reinforced Turrets by mission completion. Also, don't leave troops behind to guard Rhinos, as a speedy completion finishes this mission without any Rhinos succumbing completely to enemy fire.

Awards and Summary

GOLD	SILVER	BRONZE	TIN	Best Objective Score	Best Combat Bonus	Best Time Bonus
45,000+	25,000–44,999	15,000–24,999	0–14,999	4,150	x10 (41,500)	x5 (20,750)

| | Theoretical Best Score | 66,400 (4,150 + 41,500 + 20,750) |

101

Mission 01 Mission 02 Mission 03 Mission 04 Mission 05 Mission 06 Mission 07 Mission 08 Mission 09 Mission 10 Mission 11 Mission 12 Mission 13 Mission 14 Mission 15

Basics   Factions   Campaign   Multiplayer   Appendices   Art Gallery

07: SCARAB

After insertion into the dome, a Covenant superunit is discovered: A Super Scarab is under construction but can track units, lock on to them, and deliver a devastating plasma payload. Destroy the Power Nodes to slow its tracking head cannon before defeating the mechanical beast itself.

OBJECTIVES

Win Condition:
All primary objectives met.

Loss Condition:
All buildings and units destroyed, and heroes downed. Not enough supplies to recover.

Par Time:
12:00–24:00

PRIMARY OBJECTIVES
■ **Destroy the Super Scarab**
Completion Score: 2,000 Points

The Scarab must be destroyed before it wipes out your base. Keep your forces out of the head's line of fire.

OPTIONAL OBJECTIVES
■ **Kill 10 Locusts [10]**
Completion Score: 750 Points

The spiderlike Locust is slow-moving but powerful. It is designed to destroy structures and is less effective against units. Counter the Locust with Marines or Scorpions.

■ **Destroy All Enemy Power Nodes [7]**
Completion Score: 750 Points

The nodes are secondary power sources for the Scarab. If they are destroyed, the Scarab will not be able to turn its head as quickly.

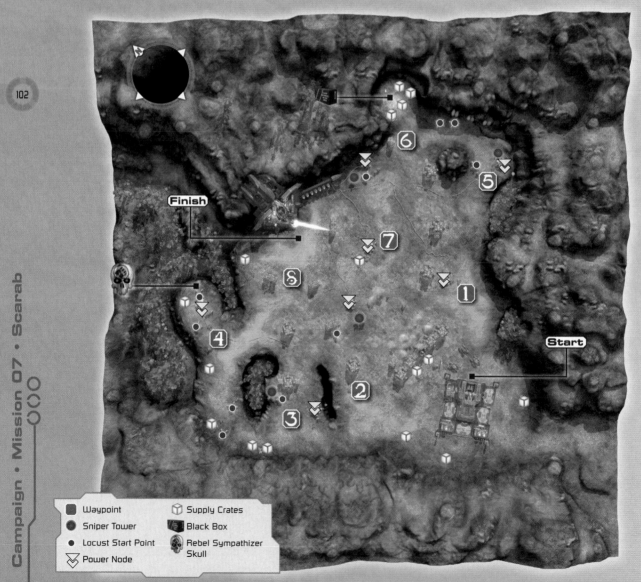

Finish

⑥

⑤

⑦

①

⑧

④

Start

②

③

	Waypoint		Supply Crates
	Sniper Tower		Black Box
	Locust Start Point		Rebel Sympathizer Skull
	Power Node		

Difficulty Modifications (compared to Normal)

Easy: All enemy units have 50 percent less Health Points and inflict 50 percent less damage. There are less enemies defending Power Nodes.

Heroic: There are Shade Turrets added to the Covenant forces. More attacks occur on your base.

Legendary: All enemy units have 25 percent more Health Points and inflict 25 percent more damage. Even more attacks occur on your base.

MISSION COMMENCEMENT

(Start) You begin with a Fortress to build. Concentrate on supplies and upgrades to your Warthogs and optionally your Scorpions, and at each corner, plant Turrets augmented with Flame Mortars and Rail Guns. As you gradually increase production, make sure your forces have reached and taken all the supply crates that are in the base's immediate vicinity. Use Warthogs to gather these supplies, and it may be wise to build four or five of these units in preparation for part one of a two-pronged tactical strike. Directly north of you is a gargantuan Super Scarab with a devastating mining laser. It's your job to destroy it before it cuts through the ancient Forerunner temple defenses and slices through your base!

TIP

You begin with a few units from the previous mission. Keep your Scorpion and Warthogs at the ready. Don't move your two Rhinos; instead, treat them like movable Turrets—clamp them down between two Turrets, facing into the grassy plateau but not at the temple wall. Rhinos can then guard against Covenant incursions.

NOTE

The following tactical plan can be attempted using only Scorpions, Warthogs, or a mixture of both. Warthogs are slightly more maneuverable and useful in the earlier stages, but even when fully upgraded, their weaponry takes time to inflict damage on the Super Scarab. The Scorpions are trickier to maneuver across the landscape, but once you remove the Power Nodes, the Super Scarab takedown is a little easier.

CAUTION

If you're determined to complete this mission without destroying any Power Nodes, the only bonus you receive is the **Micro Manager** Achievement. Don't attempt this and expect an impressive score!

[1] With your defenses building, you can opt to destroy one Power Node before moving your army to face the Super

Scarab. It is important to destroy at least one Power Node before striking the Super Scarab, or the Scarab's laser beam moves too quickly to dodge. Also remember that destroying the first and seventh (and final) Power Nodes slows the Scarab's head down the most. If you're adamant about only blasting one Power Node, choose the seventh one labeled on the guide map, northeast of the Fortress, which is close by, poorly defended, and easily destroyed. You can now move to Waypoint 8 or locate the other six Power Nodes (the latter is recommended, as the Optional Objective worth 750 Points requires you remove all Nodes).

Legendary Tactics

[With the increased Covenant attacks on your base, you still need to leave your base and concentrate on surviving the Power Node takedowns. Therefore, it is wise to build a few additional units to help nullify this additional Covenant threat. First, add Flame Mortars and Railguns to all four of your base Turrets to weaken incoming enemy ground forces. Then trundle out some Cobras to damage incoming Covenant vehicles at long range. A few Flamethrowers can help too.

[2] After your forces have darted out to destroy the Power Node at Waypoint 1, take Forge and a few Warthogs and drive west to the lone temple cover section, where you should destroy an Elite. You're making a looping route along the western perimeter of this grassy plateau, destroying all Covenant you see and leaving a Warthog to collect supply crates (such as those scattered between Waypoints 3 and 4) before rejoining the group.

103

Mission 01   Mission 02   Mission 03   Mission 04   Mission 05   Mission 06   **Mission 07**   Mission 08   Mission 09   Mission 10   Mission 11   Mission 12   Mission 13   Mission 14   Mission 15

Basics   Factions   Campaign   Multiplayer   Appendices   Art Gallery

Cooperative Advice

With two players, have one completely manage the Fortress and incoming foes, while the other takes down Nodes. Or, split forces with each player covering different groups of Power Nodes.

3 Using Forge to scout around the plateau for all the Power Nodes, you should now employ a "MAC, then attack" strategy for every Power Node you spot. This tactic begins at Waypoint 3, where you'll encounter a few Covenant troops, including Locusts. Remember to destroy each one to complete the Kill objective. As your troops first spot the Power Node, call in a MAC Blast (you have two free ones to use up) to decimate the Power Node and any nearby enemies, then lay into the nearby remaining foes.

> **TIP**
>
> Another great technique to try is blasting each Power Node with a group of Scorpions' Canister Shell upgrade attack; it takes out Nodes almost instantly!

4 Continue along the perimeter, ideally sending Forge to Waypoint 4 to reveal the Power Node and small Covenant defense force in this small peninsula overlooking the inaccessible canyon below. Call in your next MAC Blast to destroy the Power Node, perhaps damaging the Covenant forces milling around this location in the process. Then, once your Warthogs (or Scorpions) have laid waste to the two Locusts along the western perimeter, drive your force into the peninsula and remove all enemy threats.

Rebel Sympathizer

Although you won't be collecting this Skull yet, you must return to this peninsula later into this mission, once you defeat ten Locusts but before dispatching the Super Scarab. Claim the **Rebel Sympathizer Skull** floating in this area. Peel off a Warthog to claim it while the rest deal with the Super Scarab.

> **TIP**
>
> The guide map reveals the starting locations of all ten Locusts; head to these locations for the best chance of finding them.

5 The "MAC, then attack" technique continues as you bring your forces in a straight, southeasterly path; or retrace your steps if your vehicles are slower and likely to be struck by the Super Scarab's beam, and you want to ensure a sizable Combat Bonus. Pass Waypoint 1 (and the Power Node, which you may already have destroyed), and venture northeast to the corner of the plateau. As you reach the Power Node by Waypoint 5, execute a MAC Blast if you have one ready. Otherwise, push your forces between the large rock and the perimeter wall so you aren't blasted by the Scarab, and clean up the Covenant scum in this area.

> **TIP**
>
> The Super Scarab moves its head from left to right; by now, you should be able to spot where its head is pointing. So, for example, time your moves so you drive east just as the Scarab is shooting its beam from east to west; this gives you the most amount of time before the Scarab blasts the area you're in. Keep moving!

> **CAUTION**
>
> Don't keep a large number of troops behind the large temple wall north of your base; you don't want the Super Scarab focusing its power here, as it soon blasts through, then decimates your base in moments! Make sure the Scarab is occupied with your fast ground forces well away from the base.

6 Round the pathway curve, focusing on tearing the remaining assembled Locusts apart. Be very cautious, as there's little protection except for the large alcove to the north and a small temple structure by Waypoint 6. Tear through the perimeter Covenant Power Node; this should leave you with the final two Nodes in the map's center, near Waypoint 7. Time your maneuvering, and when the Super Scarab is looking and moving east to west, drive out into the middle of the plateau.

Legendary Tactics

If you're having trouble with the Hunters clustered around a couple Power Nodes, soften them up with your two free MAC Blasts before engaging them.

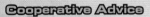

TIP

It is possible to play a game of cat and mouse with the Scarab, providing you're in a Warthog or other fast vehicle. Drive and coax the Scarab's head into following your Warthog, and it will track you for a few seconds. Do this while the majority of your army is driving in an otherwise dangerous location, moving the Scarab's focus away from your main troop groups. This is another possibility during Cooperative play.

Black Box 7

As you round the curve, the alcove to the north offers more than simple Scarab protection; it has a sizable stash of supply crates; leave a Warthog behind to collect these. In the middle of the alcove rests **Black Box 7**. Take this easily without detriment to your Time or Combat Bonuses.

Cooperative Advice

In Cooperative play, you can peel off a few of your troops to tackle and soften up the Super Scarab while you destroy all the Power Nodes. This eases the final battle against the Super Scarab considerably.

TIP

Be sure you destroy most (and ideally all) the Power Nodes before attacking the Super Scarab with your entire army.

7 The sixth and seventh (and final) Power Nodes are located in the middle of the plateau, as shown on the guide map. Drive to Waypoint 7 and destroy both Nodes. The reason you should tackle these Power Nodes last is that they are in the open, and your forces are most susceptible to the Super Scarab attack. However, if the five previous Nodes are knocked out, the Scarab's beam is much easier to dodge now. You may also wish to use the MAC Blast on one of the Nodes to quicken the Node takedowns.

8 Your assault on the Super Scarab begins now! Continue to train your army up to its maximum population, and create a Global Rally Point in the vicinity of Waypoint 8 so new units are easily accessible. A good place for the Rally Point is behind either of the temple blocks, but be wary of them being struck by the Scarab and demolished. The only remaining Covenant forces to face are the Super Scarab and a few Banshees flying around from the Scarab's left. Then attempt the following tactics for demolishing this behemoth once and for all!

Upgrade your Warthogs' main armament to the Gauss Cannon (the final upgrade), and it becomes effective against both the Banshees and the Super Scarab.

Trundle your forces in a large mass to one side of the Super Scarab. You should attack the Scarab from the left side, then the right, before moving back and forth (as shown in the picture). Do not engage the Scarab with frontal assaults, as this can cause the Scarab's beam to erode the temple wall shielding your base, whether or not the Scarab strikes your forces.

TIP

Scorpions are excellent during the latter stages of combat providing you've upgraded this tank as it is hardy and the Canister Shell ability whittles down a Scarab. Don't forget to fire off as many MAC Blasts during the fight!

Movement is extremely important when demolishing the Super Scarab. Begin with your entire force on either side of the Scarab. Then send one unit to the Scarab's other side. The Scarab's head tracks that unit. Then send over the next unit, triggering the Scarab. Continue until all units are on the opposite side, and then start over. This gives the rest of your army more time to inflict damage before fleeing from its beam (which is still necessary), until the Super Scarab yields to your inferior firepower but superior tactics!

Cooperative Advice

Leave one player to dodge the Scarab's beam and launch the all-out vehicular attack, while the other fires the MAC Blasts.

Awards and Summary

GOLD	SILVER	BRONZE	TIN		Best Objective Score	Best Combat Bonus	Best Time Bonus
32,000+	20,000–31,999	12,000–19,999	0–11,999		3,500	x10 (35,000)	x5 (17,500)

Theoretical Best Score	56,000 (3,500 + 35,000 + 17,500)

Mission 01 Mission 02 Mission 03 Mission 04 Mission 05 Mission 06 **Mission 07** Mission 08 Mission 09 Mission 10 Mission 11 Mission 12 Mission 13 Mission 14 Mission 15

Basics   Factions   Campaign   Multiplayer   Appendices   Art Gallery

105

CAMPAIGN • ACT 3

MISSION II

pg. 122

The Spirit of Fire enters a strange world, inhabited by odd and twisted entities. Only after two recon teams are swamped and infected is the true horror of the Flood revealed. Once the UNSC's forces regroup, Anders' signal is detected, and a group of Spartans are sent to investigate. Revealing monstrosities are torn apart, and a Shield World is discovered. Despite valiant attempts to prevent it, the Spirit of Fire is dragged by tractor beam into a tunnel, deep in the shell of the Shield World, where the true majesty of Forerunner science is unveiled.

08: ANDERS'S SIGNAL

Anders's signal has been traced to an unknown and inhospitable world. Advance recon units have reported being swamped by floods of unknown alien life-forms, and two mobile barracks vehicles known as Elephants have been lost. Investigate the area and retrieve all Elephants, bringing them back to your base.

OBJECTIVES

Win Condition:
All primary objectives met.

Loss Condition:
Loss of an Elephant vehicle.

Par Time:
18:00–30:00

PRIMARY OBJECTIVES

Get to Base Drop Beacon
Completion Score: 250 Points

Spirit's forces must secure the marked location for a base. This planet's atmosphere is highly unusual; use caution and stay alert for signs of trouble.

Investigate Echo Team
Completion Score: 500 Points

Contact with Echo Team has been lost. It is vital to learn what became of them and their Elephant.

Find and Recover Lost Elephants [2]
Completion Score: 500 Points

The vehicles were taken by the strange life-forms. The Elephants are an expansive and important weapon in Spirit of Fire's arsenal; they must be found and recovered.

Bring All Three Elephants Back to Base
Completion Score: 500 Points

The Elephants are extremely valuable military hardware and must be retrieved at all costs. Send your forces out to recover them.

OPTIONAL OBJECTIVES

Train Squads out of an Elephant
Completion Score: 250 Points

The Elephant is a fully equipped mobile training center. Once deployed, it can mobilize and serve as a forward base.

Find Lost ODST Squads [4]
Completion Score: 500 Points

Several squads of ODSTs are missing. Locate and rescue them.

Kill 750 Infection Forms [750]
Completion Score: 750 Points

The first stage of a mysterious alien life-form, it is highly aggressive and dangerous. The Infection Forms attempt to penetrate the spinal cords of their victims. They can be countered by massed fire from virtually any military unit.

■ Waypoint	🦠 Flood Den	
● Pinned Elephant	📦 Black Box	
01 Pinned ODST Position	💀 Rebel Supporter Skull	

Difficulty Modifications (compared to Normal)

Easy: All enemy units have 50 percent less Health Points and inflict 50 percent less damage.

Heroic: There is extra Flood artillery forces.

Legendary: All enemy units have 25 percent more Health Points and inflict 25 percent more damage.

MISSION COMMENCEMENT

(Start) After disembarking and listening to Echo's and India's recon groups begin the search for Anders, you have a group of Covenant forces to repel. These are more vicious infantry than you've encountered before, aside from Hunters. These Brutes live up to their name, and a savage mixture of Brute infantry and Brute Choppers have the fire-line gully in front of you well defended. Immediately select only your Elephant, and lock it down into the ground (❤).

CAUTION

Do not advance forward from your starting location! If you lose any of the three Elephants available during this mission, you fail!

NOTE

Although you can assign one of your Spartans (ideally Alice, as she has a less potent weapon than her colleagues) to drive the Elephant, it isn't necessary or needed; keep your Spartans on foot and ready to dish out pain from their enhanced weaponry.

Select the Elephant as quickly as possible after you lock it into the ground. Move its Rally Point to the near side

of the rocky clump in front of you, with the two paths on either side. Ahead, the Brutes are getting restless. After training your initial squad of Marines, spend your remaining Supply Points (which constantly increase a small amount prior to you acquiring a Firebase) training a good half dozen or so squads of Flamethrowers. Then send Forge forward as your sixth or seventh Flamethrower squad appears.

Next, spend the rest of your points training around four or five additional groups of Marines. The Flamethrowers are adept at scorching all the Brute infantry with minimal problems, while the Marines should have their weapons trained on the Brute Choppers—the bipedal vehicles maneuvering around this area. As Forge moves ahead, wait until he's fired on, then retreat him back to the Elephant. Lure the Brutes back to your locked-down Elephant, and massacre them at this point (if you're concerned about your Combat Bonus). This way, none of your infantry succumb to the Brutes' fearsome combat prowess.

TIP

Show the Covenant you mean business, and call in a Carpet Bomb strike via your Spirit of Fire menu. Lay waste to the front line of Brutes; aim at the longest line of them you can see. Do this prior to the attack so Forge isn't caught in the explosions. This will weaken the Brutes and make them easier to finish off.

2 As combat continues, utilize the Marines' grenades to defeat the Brute Choppers. Remember to lure the Brutes all the way back to the Elephant so its guns can also cut down these foes. When you've defeated about one-third of the Brute forces in this manner (or, you could just charge in, lose some units, and risk a lower

109

Mission 01 Mission 02 Mission 03 Mission 04 Mission 05 Mission 06 Mission 07 **Mission 08** Mission 09 Mission 10 Mission 11 Mission 12 Mission 13 Mission 14 Mission 15

Basics   Factions   Campaign   Multiplayer   Appendices   Art Gallery

Combat Bonus), Spartan Red Team—a familiar trio of uber-soldiers—enters the fray and immediately lays waste to the remaining Brutes and Choppers. Fall back and let them handle the enemy if you are low on troops. You can control these Spartans after the Brutes are defeated; they later prove to be the key to an effective victory. When combat has ended, head toward Waypoint 2, a beacon showing that Echo and India teams were in this vicinity.

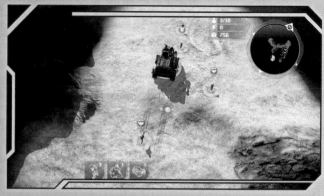

Black Box 8

Before you reach Waypoint 2, check the semicircular plateau on the fire line's right side, near a Flood Den. Grab **Black Box 8** here.

3 Once the distress signal has sounded and the rescue for Echo's and India team's Elephants is under way, move from Waypoint 2 along the main gully toward the slight slope. Signal Flare that Echo Team left just before they were overrun. Keep your Elephant and infantry at the Signal Flare; this is a job for Spartan Red Team!

Know Your Alien Parasite Menace!

Throughout this and subsequent missions, it is important to know the disgusting alien entities that are threatening your existence and the Covenant's. These enemies are collectively known as "the Flood," and there are two different types to worry about: mobile forms and stationary podlike entities.

MOBILE FLOOD FORMS

These are either small, vicious little critters, carriers that easily infect infantry, or already-infected UNSC or Covenant forces. Simply use vehicles to mow these atrocities down, and do not train any infantry!

Infection Forms   *Thrasher Form*   *Infected Brutes*   *Infected ODST*   *Flood Cloud*   *Flood Carrier*

STATIONARY FLOOD FORMS

Larger and stationary, these flappy, tendrilled sacks of ooze are the ultimate in parasitical combat! The Launcher is of particular alarm, as it can easily down a vehicle or aircraft. Concentrate on these first. The Flood Dens† (marked on the guide map) expel Infection Forms. These are shown so you can locate areas where you can defeat mobile Flood if you're attempting the Kill objective. Flood Eggs‡ sometimes have Infection Forms or supplies inside. Flood Tentacles are always surrounding trapped Elephants and must be nullified at range. Stalks and Nests are simply disgusting, sometimes expelling critters. All should be culled!

Flood Launcher   *Flood Den*   *Flood Nest*   *Flood Eggs & Stalk*   *Flood Tentacle*

NOTE

†Flood Dens are shown on the guide map, allowing you to locate the source of the Infection Forms and send units there if you're concerned with completing the Kill objective.

‡Flood Eggs sometimes contain nasty infectious surprises, but sometimes they contain supply crates. However, you don't really need the supplies, as your Firebase's Supply Pads are an easier source of economy!

Legendary Tactics

■ From the moment you reach the first beacon, let the three Spartans complete the remaining mission objectives. Do not bring infantry and the Elephant to search for the Echo Team Elephant, as the infantry are easily infected and must then be fought, wreaking havoc with your Combat Bonus. Instead, leave the Elephant locked down with the Marines and Flamethrowers at Waypoint 2.

④ Descend the shallow slope with all three Spartans (and optionally Forge, but watch his health, as he doesn't have the shielded armor the Spartans possess) until you encounter a strange and disgusting vision: Odd, tendrilled aliens are scattering, and some have enveloped Echo Team's Elephant completely! Move gingerly toward the Elephant, ideally remaining close to the shadow of the rocky plateau above the Spartans. You're looking for a Flood Launcher, a despicable device that spits out harmful projectiles. Train all three Spartans' weapons on this first, and blast it until it bursts.

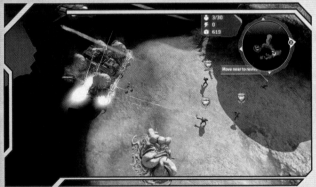

Back off if any of your Spartans begin to suffer damage through their shields, then reconvene and begin to demolish the Infection Forms and the Flood Den that is spewing them forth. Stay at range so you can mow down the Flood before they reach you. Focus your firepower on the Flood Eggs and Tentacles surrounding the Elephant. These can't move, so as long as you stay at range to unleash Spartan weaponry, you can defeat any straggling forms that appear from the exploding eggs. Continue this Flood massacre until the Elephant is freed.

② [Return] Move the Elephant back the way you came, as the Spirit of Fire tells you there's a Firebase incoming. Return the Elephants and any infantry you trained to tackle the Brutes back to the Firebase. You now need to make a stand against the waves of Flood, their Infection Forms, and the occasional Brute Jet Pack and infantry troops that attempt to attack your base. A well-defended base is of paramount importance, so try some or all of the following plans:

CAUTION

■ Remember to keep all Elephants away from reckless combat; if any are destroyed, this mission is over!

Bring the two Elephants around and lock them down at the base's rear. Their Turrets (which you can further upgrade inside your Firebase) can now help fend off waves of enemies approaching from all three directions. Place any infantry between the Elephants so the Flood doesn't reach and infect them. Upgrade them fully if you're playing on Heroic difficulty or harder.

Immediately construct Turrets if your base doesn't appear with them, and augment them with Flame Mortars for all four corners. This helps immensely as the Flood swarm in from the gully and the flat areas on either side of your base.

With Turrets augmented, create three Heavy Supply Pads, two Reactors, an Air Pad, and a Field Armory. This is only necessary if you wish to complete the Kill objective. For a quick completion, follow the Legendary difficulty advice later in this chapter.

111

Mission 01 Mission 02 Mission 03 Mission 04 Mission 05 Mission 06 Mission 07 **Mission 08** Mission 09 Mission 10 Mission 11 Mission 12 Mission 13 Mission 14 Mission 15

Basics   Factions   Campaign   Multiplayer   Appendices   Art Gallery

Use your Field Armory to increase the toughness of your Turrets; you must make your base impenetrable to the Flood. Periodically Heal & Repair the Turrets—especially those at the front—that bear the brunt of the Flood onslaught.

Construct and upgrade Hornets or Vultures, as they can easily cover the scenery compared to ground vehicles. Your first few Hornets, with only one or two upgrades, should be positioned to help defend the base, helping the Turrets cut down infectious foes.

Cooperative Advice

With an additional player to help you, perform the now-mandatory task of having one player build and guard the base while the other searches for the ODST and Elephants.

Picture 1

Picture 2

Picture 3

Picture 4

Once your base is as secure as possible, send in your preferred units (Hornets or your three Spartans) toward Waypoint 3 and then to the rocky plateau with the Flood Eggs on it. Nearby are the remains of an ODST squad (Marker 01; Picture 1). Explode the Eggs into greasy chunks, then send the first squad (once you rendezvous with them) back to the base. Position them between the Elephants so they aren't infected.

Continue your sweep for ODST troops by crossing the gully to the plateau on the opposite side. Clear the Eggs away from another squad of ODST (Marker 02; Picture 2), then head between the two plateaus to another group of ODST trapped between two disgusting Flood Stalks (Marker 03; Picture 3). Watch out! One of these units is infected, so dispatch it before it claims the other. Finally, trek back near Waypoint 3, then up to a final Egg plateau. Free the final ODST at Marker 04 (Picture 4). Send all units back to your base, ensuring they aren't attacked on the way there.

CAUTION

If you're after a Gold rating upon mission completion, you won't be able to kill 750 Infection Forms and expect a Time Bonus.

There's a similar problem if you want to obtain the **Ramblin' Man** Achievement. This involves training 100 infantry. Unfortunately, infantry are poor fighters against the Flood and become infected. This means you must churn out infantry from the two Elephants at your base, send them to a certain death, and keep up this Marine and Flamethrower massacre until you earn this Achievement.

⑤ As soon as you wish to end this mission (which can be drawn out if you require the Kill objective and Skull, as detailed below), move your favored attack squad (Hornets or Spartans are recommended) to Waypoint 5, where the other USNC

Elephant is entombed in tendrils. Blast the Flood Launcher first; then the Den where the Infection Forms are scuttling out from; and, finally, destroy the Eggs and tentacles surrounding the Elephant. Once it is freed, retreat back to the base and complete the mission.

TIP

The Spirit of Fire's Carpet Bomb attack and Heal & Repair are both useful, as you can Carpet Bomb the Flood during a hard-fought attack, easily ridding the Elephant of its bonds. Have a Heal & Repair on hand to administer to any Elephants damaged during the attack; however, for the power to be effective, administer the Repair only after combat is over.

Legendary Tactics

Upgrading Hornets and wasting time amassing troops is never a good idea if you're planning on being Legendary! Instead, once the Firebase is under construction, beef up the defenses properly, as advised previously, and take your Spartan trio to each of the ODST locations. Free them, send them back to the base, and then attack the Flood at Waypoint 5, bringing the vehicle back for a quick victory. You won't achieve the optional Kill objective, but your Time Bonus makes up for it and still allows you to claim Gold.

TIP

If you want to kill 750 Infection Forms, the trick is to prepare for a long battle, and try the following plan:

Ignore rescuing the third Elephant until you reach around 700 kills, as freeing it from the Flood means you need to defend it (forcing troops from other activities) or move it to the Firebase (finishing the mission).

Position Spartan Alice near a Den, far enough away so she doesn't destroy it but close enough so she rakes the Infection Forms coming out. Repeat this until you reach your target.

Or, build a squadron of Hornets to easily maneuver over the terrain, and search out Eggs and moving Infection Forms. Kill everything except Dens, which you need to remain alive and pump out more Infection Forms for you to destroy, upping your kill count.

Follow the trails until every Egg, Nest, and other Flood unit is down, then return to three or four Den locations and shoot Infection Forms as they spill out. Repeat this until you near your Kill total, and then rescue the Elephant.

Rebel Supporter

After you massacre 750 Flood Forms, the **Rebel Supporter Skull** appears on a narrow ridge close to Marker 04, farther up the gully from Waypoint 5. This prize is difficult to spot, so try for it only if you're not interested in a Time Bonus.

Awards and Summary

	GOLD	SILVER	BRONZE	TIN		Best Objective Score	Best Combat Bonus	Best Time Bonus
	30,000+	20,000–29,999	12,000–19,999	0–11,999		3,250	x10 (32,500)	x5 (16,250)†

† *Destroying 750 Flood Infection Forms while maintaining a maximum Time Bonus isn't feasible, so don't expect to reach this theoretical maximum score.*

Theoretical Best Score 52,000 (3,250 + 32,500 + 16,250)†

Mission 01 Mission 02 Mission 03 Mission 04 Mission 05 Mission 06 Mission 07 **Mission 08** Mission 09 Mission 10 Mission 11 Mission 12 Mission 13 Mission 14 Mission 15

Basics   Factions   Campaign   Multiplayer   Appendices   Art Gallery

09: THE FLOOD

The transponder source for Anders has been traced to this general location, and a Spartan team is valiantly attempting to defeat the numerous oddities and alien threats in the area. Fight through the Flooded areas, optionally defeating Flood colonies before facing and destroying the Hive Mind boss.

OBJECTIVES

Win Condition:
All primary objectives met.

Loss Condition:
All buildings and units destroyed, and heroes downed. Not enough supplies to recover.

Par Time:
18:00–30:00

PRIMARY OBJECTIVES

■ **Reinforce Spartan Red Team**
Completion Score: 400 Points

The Spartans have gone ahead, following Anders's signal. Link up with them and reinforce their position before it's too late.

■ **Destroy Flood Boss**
Completion Score: 1,000 Points

Once enough of the pods are destroyed, the primary infection should be engaged. Use caution—even after it has been weakened, it is still an extremely dangerous opponent.

OPTIONAL OBJECTIVES

■ **Kill 20 Flood Stalks [20]**
Completion Score: 600 Points

These alien life-forms are possibly providing nutrients to the smaller Infection variants. They are easily destroyed by any unit.

■ **Have All Five Flood Colonies Dormant at Once**
Completion Score: 1,700 Points

Forcing all five colonies into a dormant state at the same time will make the Hive Mind much easier to destroy. Stay alert: UNSC weaponry cannot completely destroy the dormant colonies, and they will regenerate over time.

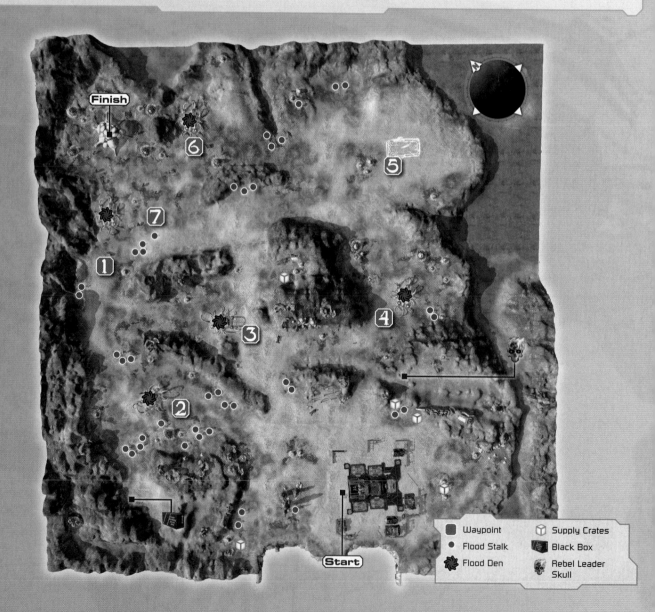

Legend:
- ■ Waypoint
- Flood Stalk
- Flood Den
- Supply Crates
- Black Box
- Rebel Leader Skull

Difficulty Modifications (compared to Normal)

Easy: All enemy units have 50 percent less Health Points and inflict 50 percent less damage.

Heroic: There is extra Flood artillery.

Legendary: All enemy units have 25 percent more Health Points and inflict 25 percent more damage.

MISSION COMMENCEMENT

(Start) After Spartan Red Team's tumble, it is up to you to retrieve them from this rocky and Flood-filled terrain. Before you head for the Spartans' location (Waypoint 1, which Serina also marks with a gold star on your in-game minimap), be sure to inspect your own station—an improved Firebase with two additional Base Pads already working as Supply Pads. Consider building a Warthog or two and gather the supply crates from the immediate area around your base, but only after you upgrade them with enough firepower to destroy the Flood Eggs and Stalks that lurk around your base.

This example of a completed base is simply one way of augmenting your force's survivability in this forsaken zone. Upgrade the two Supply Pads in the southern corner, outside the main base, to make them Heavy. Next, plug in two more Supply Pads; two or three Reactors; a Field Armory; and an Air Pad, as airborne units are much less susceptible to Flood attacks (they can only be harmed by the Flood Launcher and Swarms). If you want a methodical approach, train Hornets to help you in your struggle. Also note the upgraded Turrets with a mixture of air and infantry add-ons.

TIP

You have three parked Elephants at your base. Move them into a defensive position to back up your Turrets, and lock them down so the additional Turret guns on the Elephants are used. You'll move them later, but use them as extra Turrets initially.

CAUTION

Be extremely careful if you wish to Recycle at this base; the two Supply Pads outside the base structure simply explode if you Recycle them (or the Flood attack and destroy either of them), and nothing can be rebuilt on top of them.

Know Your Alien Parasite Menace: Part 2

Aside from several foes you've already encountered (and should be able to dispatch in the same manner as you did in the previous mission), there are a few new bulging and unspeakable forms to worry about this time:

Flood Stalk: You've encountered these dastardly entities before, but this time, the Kill objective requires you to burst 20 of these open. Watch out for spewing Infection Forms as you go!

Flood Swarm: Flapping sinewy skin horrifies and damages in equal measure. These airborne attackers usually swarm the base, so ensure your north and east Turrets are upgraded with additional armor (thanks to your Field Armory) and have the Rail Gun add-on.

Flood Colony: These seething tendrils spit out various Infection forms and cannot be killed by your usual weaponry; you can only shoot them into a dormant state before they reactivate. The trick is to have all five of these colonies dormant before you kill the Proto Hive Mind.

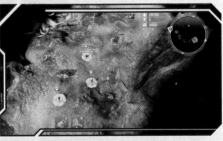

1 Before you even build your first base structure, you should be driving at break-neck speed to reach Spartan Red Team. Sergeant Forge is the finest candidate for this job, as his Warthog is upgraded. Rendezvous with the Spartans as rapidly as possible, taking the narrow path from your base [Start], through Waypoint 3, and to Waypoint 1 and the Spartans. When you meet up, you don't need to return to the base just yet; let the killing spree begin!

115

Mission 01 | Mission 02 | Mission 03 | Mission 04 | Mission 05 | Mission 06 | Mission 07 | Mission 08 | **Mission 09** | Mission 10 | Mission 11 | Mission 12 | Mission 13 | Mission 14 | Mission 15

Basics | Factions | Campaign | Multiplayer | Appendices | Art Gallery

TIP

Back at the base, you should be constantly upgrading and building Hornets as quickly as possible and then sending them to support the Spartans and Forge.

2 From Waypoint 1, you may be tempted to start firing at the two Flood Colonies near Waypoints 6 and 7. This is unwise, as you need slightly more backup from Hornets than you can currently manage. Instead, blast the nearby Flood Stalks around Waypoint 1, and then head southwest, down the main path, and blast away at three more Stalks. You're making a slow and steady path toward your first Flood Colony at Waypoint 2. Kill Flood along the way from range so you aren't swamped.

When you reach the Colony, let rip from the north side so you're out of range of the Flood Launcher. Send in as many Hornets as you've constructed to back up the trio. Tear into the first Flood Colony, and whittle it down so it becomes dormant. Then defeat the Launcher, and blast the copious amounts of Flood Stalks dotted around this lumpy plateau. If you've destroyed all the Flood Stalks from Waypoint 1 to this point, you should have obtained your Kill objective.

Rebel Leader

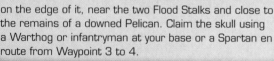

This means you can obtain the **Rebel Leader Skull**, which is very easy to spot. From your base, look to the plateau to the east. The Skull is on the edge of it, near the two Flood Stalks and close to the remains of a downed Pelican. Claim the skull using a Warthog or infantryman at your base or a Spartan en route from Waypoint 3 to 4.

Black Box 9

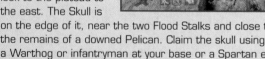

Forge, in his Warthog, is the best unit to fetch this Black Box. West of Waypoint 2, in the map's western corner, is a small, empty rocky clearing where **Black Box 9** resides. Take this easily before you return to the action.

3 With most of Waypoint 2's plateau cleared of alien scum, leave a small squadron of Hornets hovering above the Flood Colony so that the moment the Colony wakes up, it receives Hornet gunfire to put it back to sleep. Take Spartan Red Team around the rocky outcrop and northeast to Waypoint 3. If you're low on Hornets, bring the ones you used to tackle Waypoint 2's Colony, and send more Hornets to strike the Colony later. When you reach Waypoint 3, optionally use the barricade to the south for extra protection, then blast away at the Colony and any Infection Forms in the area.

NOTE

If you're determined to complete the **Sweet Naptime** Achievement, follow the advice for slaying the five Colonies, but move the Hornets out of range until you wish to massacre the Colonies at the same time. Then attack everything at once; this requires quick selections and map movement!

TIP

Not building Hornets fast enough? Then construct a second Air Pad: one to churn out Hornets and the other to upgrade them. Then double the Hornet output! Don't forget to increase your Population at the Field Armory too.

CAUTION

Watch your Combat Bonus! Hornets are easily damaged by Flood Launchers and Flood Swarms, so concentrate on blasting them first or avoiding Swarms altogether.

Cooperative Advice

The usual multiplayer tactics are advisable, but with a few tweaks. Ensure one of the players is completely responsible for the base, upgrades, and defenses and for churning out as many Hornets as possible. The other should be controlling Spartan Red Team and some Hornets. The base commander can also help out by covering ground and taking two of the three Colonies, quickening the completion time considerably as multiple Colonies are laid dormant at once.

[6] and **[7]**] Trek to the map's far north and engage the final two Colonies, ideally both at the same time. Although there are four Flood Launchers in the vicinity of the disgusting Proto Hive Mind, two are behind the target, so you can keep your troops out of their range. Execute a joint barrage, and if you're worried about previous Colonies awakening, execute a precisely placed Carpet Bomb on one Colony while focusing all your other firepower on the second one. When all five are dispatched, you can begin the assault on the Proto Hive Mind.

[4] Head down the trench that runs northwest to southeast, from Waypoint 3 to 4. At the same time, continue your Hornet-build program and upgrade path. Build two Air Pads as soon as possible to churn out these aircraft while simultaneously unlocking your Elephants from the base, which should now be upgraded with Heavy Turrets and perhaps a couple Hornets; move them northeast, toward Waypoint 4. When you reach the third Flood Colony, fly your Hornets over and concentrate on defeating the two Flood Launchers immediately. After you destroy the Colony, clamp down two of the Elephants and continue northeast.

> **TIP**
>
> One the in-game minimap, the red icons show you which Colonies are dormant and which are active. If you want to know precisely how long Colonies stay dormant, start this mission, destroy a Colony, and time how long it takes to regenerate.

Legendary Tactics

> Time is definitely a factor here: If your Colonies awaken again, you may wish to attempt defeating two Colonies at once or keep troops behind to blast them again. This is an absolute necessity if you're attempting a Gold ranking.

Legendary Tactics

> The trio of Spartans should be your main focus for completing this mission; use them to finish most of the objectives, with Hornets as backup, for the quickest times and easiest finish on Legendary.

[5] Take an Elephant or two and place them near the Flood Stalks near this Firebase construction point. Although building another base may seem like an excellent plan, it ruins your Time Bonus. Building Hornets that can cover large expanses of this huge map in seconds is a much better idea. Allow the Elephant to strafe the remaining Flood Stalks to claim the Kill objective; this allows the Spartan Red Team to ignore a large portion of them earlier, between Waypoints 1 and 2. Once the Stalks are squelched, move an Elephant near a dormant Colony to keep it from regenerating.

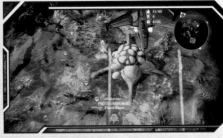

With all the Colonies dormant, attack the Proto Hive Mind. Do not attack it before the Colonies are dormant, or it'll be too tough to dispatch. If you've built the Field Armory in your base, upgrade the Carpet Bomb, as one of the fully upgraded Bombs can defeat the Hive Mind without you firing a regular shot! Otherwise, bombard it with all your forces, collecting any Hornets guarding the other Colonies and focusing all firepower on bursting open this abomination!

Awards and Summary

GOLD	SILVER	BRONZE	TIN		Best Objective Score	Best Combat Bonus	Best Time Bonus
⬥	⬥	⬥	⬥		✔	✊	⏱
35,000+	20,000-34,999	15,000-19,999	Tin: 0-14,999		3,700	x10 (37,000)	x5 (18,500)

Theoretical Best Score	**59,200**	(3,700 + 37,000 + 18,500)

Mission 01 Mission 02 Mission 03 Mission 04 Mission 05 Mission 06 Mission 07 Mission 08 **Mission 09** Mission 10 Mission 11 Mission 12 Mission 13 Mission 14 Mission 15

Basics   Factions   Campaign   Multiplayer   Appendices   Art Gallery

10: SHIELD WORLD

The Spirit of Fire is being pulled inside the Shield World by an incredibly large and powerful tractor beam. Before the ship disappears entirely into the Shield World, you must remove all essential units trapped and fighting on the planet's surface and evacuate them to a Landing Zone. Optionally slow this eventuality down by placing Gremlins near Tractor Beam Towers.

OBJECTIVES

Win Condition:
All primary objectives met.

Loss Condition:
All buildings and units destroyed, and heroes downed. Not enough supplies to recover.

Par Time:
20:00–32:00

PRIMARY OBJECTIVES

■ **Clear Evacuation Flight Paths**
Completion Score: 2,250 Points

Alpha, Bravo, and Charlie platoons have been cut off beyond the areas overrun by the Flood. Your soldiers will have to clear a path through the Flood and bring them back to the Landing Zone (LZ).

■ **Get the Last Platoon to the Landing Zone**
Completion Score: 500 Points

Escort the platoon back through the Flood-infested areas. Watch out for any Infection forms and keep them away from your infantry.

OPTIONAL OBJECTIVES

■ **Kill 350 Swarms [350]**
Completion Score: 250 Points

The Swarms pose a serious threat to the evacuation. Counter them with Wolverines.

■ **Place Gremlins at a Pylon [4]**
Completion Score: 1,000 Points

A Gremlin may be able to temporarily disrupt the pylons and delay the automatic docking procedure. In theory, this should buy Spirit of Fire more time.

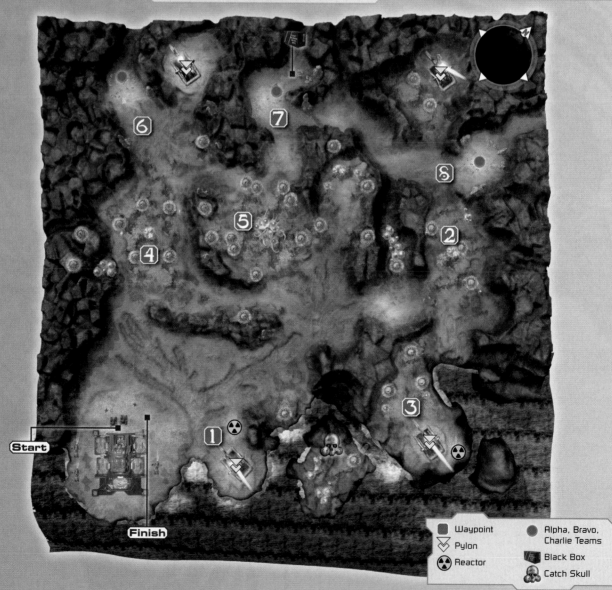

	Waypoint		Alpha, Bravo, Charlie Teams
	Pylon		Black Box
	Reactor		Catch Skull

Difficulty Modifications (compared to Normal)

Easy: All enemy units have 40 percent less Health Points and inflict 40 percent less damage. UNSC Platoons are 100 percent tougher.

Heroic: Flood population is greater.

Legendary: All enemy units have 50 percent more Health Points and inflict 50 percent more damage. UNSC Platoons are 50 percent weaker. Flood population is greater.

MISSION COMMENCEMENT

NOTE

For this mission it is especially important that you study the guide map closely, as the rocky pathways of this terrain are tricky to negotiate in the dark.

(Start) Your station is ready, and Pelicans are prepped for dust-off, but they require the remaining troops from Alpha, Bravo, and Charlie companies. With this in mind, it is time to bolster the existing base while purging the area of hated Flood Forms. Begin by building up your base with the obligatory Supply Pads and Reactors; you need only two Reactors, as there are two Forerunner Reactor structures on the map that can be Commandeered if you're adept at multitasking. Investigate those locations in a moment.

Once upgraded to a Fortress with three or more Heavy Supply Pads, your base churns out supplies and you have two Reactors online, along with the Reactor-based advantages associated with heading to Waypoint 1. You should also have Turrets at every corner and a few troops guarding the base so it is never overrun. Refrain from training infantry, or they're likely to be overrun and turned into Infected Marines. Usually, airborne units would be a sound strategic plan, but the huge number of Flood Launchers on this map makes Hornets and Vultures extremely vulnerable. Instead, place one or two Vehicle Depots inside your base, and crank out upgraded Scorpions, Wolverines, and perhaps some Cobras.

TIP

Once you have a force of eight or more upgraded vehicles, you should be building an Air Pad and a few Hornets with the express intent of leaving them at the base to guard against the incoming Flood Swarms.

Flood Swarms periodically flap toward your base and spawn from the two Flood Dens and Flood Colony in the center and sides of the map. For this reason, arm your Turrets with Missile Launchers to cut down the Swarms before they envelope your station. Position your Hornets over your base, hovering far enough away to be able to fire on the Swarms but not be cut down by them.

Your first two trained vehicles should be Wolverines, as these antiair vehicles are the perfect plan for culling the Swarms and completing the Kill objective. Park them between the Turrets and watch them tear apart the Swarms.

CAUTION

You can also train infantry to defeat the Flood on the ground. Be warned, however, that the Flood Clouds infect your foot soldiers with alarming frequency, and you don't want to be fighting the remains of your own team! For this reason, it is usually recommended to ignore a Barracks, especially if you're requiring a quick Time Bonus.

1 While your base is under construction and the first Scorpion tanks are wheeling out, investigate Waypoint 1, adjacent to your base. On a small plateau is a Forerunner Pylon emitting a tractor beam that is slowly sucking the Spirit of Fire toward the Shield World. When you discover this area, you are sent down a Gremlin from the Spirit of Fire and given instructions on disrupting this tower and the three other Pylons dotted at each of this map's corners. Each time a Pylon is discovered, another Gremlin is dropped, or you can construct them in your Base.

Once the Gremlin appears at the front of your base, trundle it toward the Pylon and move it into the position indicated. After a massive power rupture, the Pylon's tractor beam is disrupted. This delays the inevitable

119

Mission 01   Mission 02   Mission 03   Mission 04   Mission 05   Mission 06   Mission 07   Mission 08   Mission 09   **Mission 10**   Mission 11   Mission 12   Mission 13   Mission 14   Mission 15

Basics   Factions   Campaign   Multiplayer   Appendices   Art Gallery

incoming Spirit of Fire, and it allows additional time to save the three UNSC teams. In addition, it is extremely important to take one of the two infantry squads that you began the mission with and garrison them inside the Reactor adjacent to the Pylon. Do so as soon as possible so you can begin upgrading your vehicles quickly.

Legendary Tactics

Even if you're aiming for a Time Bonus, it is imperative you disrupt all four Pylons. This adds an additional 20 minutes to the countdown timer (each Pylon grants a five-minute extension). Fortunately, the mission can also be beaten without Pylons, and you can still claim a good Time Bonus even if you peel off to disrupt the Pylons; you simply have to be very fast in your Flood takedowns.

TIP

If you intend on completing **The Procrastinator Achievement**, this is straightforward, as you should be disrupting all four Pylons anyway. Do this to gain both the Optional objective and this Achievement.

2 With a small convoy of Scorpions chaperoning the squad, send your Flamethrower infantrymen along the pockmarked pathway, pushing the Scorpions forward first to destroy the Flood Launchers and their disgusting projectiles, taking care not to let any land on your infantry. Avoid the main Flood plateau (Waypoint 5) as your convoy continues along the path to Waypoint 2. Bring four or five upgraded Scorpions, two Wolverines, the Gremlin, and the Flamethrower troops at the rear.

Stop at the small cluster of despicable Flood Launchers and the Flood Den in the center of the rocky plateau at Waypoint 2. Begin a massive, Canister Shell–infused cluster-bombing of the area, with an optional Cryo Bomb from the Spirit of Fire to nullify the Swarms in the area. Continue this hellfire battering until the Flood nodules recede, and you defeat the clusters on the nearby ridges.

3 With the coast relatively clear in this general vicinity, take your lead Scorpions and pick off the Flood pods between

Waypoints 2 and 3, following the narrow, slightly U-shaped route to the second Pylon. Immediately bring the Gremlin and the Flamethrowers forward, and garrison the infantry in the Reactor (which is almost never attacked and now allows you to reach Tech Level 4 at your base). Position your Gremlin correctly to disrupt the second Pylon. Another five minutes are added to your time. Now for the final push!

4 Depending on whether you have troops at Waypoint 2, your assault on Waypoint 4 should involve taking across at least six

Scorpions from your Fortress and scanning the edges of the blackness for Flood Launchers, battering them with barrages of Canister Shells while edging toward the Flood Den. From your Spirit of Fire menu, drop a Cryo Bomb to hinder the Flood Swarms so your vehicles can concentrate on the Launchers before ripping through the Den. Stay on the map's outer edge so you don't encroach on the main lumpy plateau where the main Flood Colony resides.

Legendary Tactics

If you're intending to complete this mission quickly, you might try splitting your forces and attacking Waypoints 2 and 4 simultaneously.

5 As teams strike the Flood, make additional vehicles and attack the remaining plateau with overwhelming

odds. Set a Global Rally Point just beyond the reach of the Flood Launchers. Then attack the main plateau. Note the guide map showing three entrance points.

TIP

When you build the Field Armory, you can upgrade the Cryo Bomb power. The improved attack is much more effective at neutralizing the clouds of Flood Swarms, which also helps complete your Kill objective. When the Cryo Bomb is fully upgraded, Swarms simply break up and fall to the ground, nullifying the threat to your vehicles.

Use the entrance on the side closest to your Fortress base, as it is wider; the ones close to Waypoints 6 and 7 are much more narrow and steep, making vehicles susceptible to Flood ordnance. Use your Leader Powers from Spirit of Fire. Continue the incessant barrage!

Cooperative Advice

With another tactician at the ready, you can employ one as a base constructor and have them maneuver any arriving Gremlins (plus the two initial infantry units) to the Reactors and Pylons on the map's near side. The other player should concentrate on eradicating the Flood. Later into this mission, the base builder should be in charge of sending Gremlins to the last two Pylons.

6 With most, of the Flood's forms reduced to goo, trundle to Waypoint 6, where Alpha Team is waiting. If you require more troops, think about utilizing Alpha Team, as long as none of them become infected. At the same time, maneuver the third Gremlin over the already-cleared plateau at Waypoint 4, and across to disrupt the third Pylon.

7 Assuming you've dealt with all the Launchers in the area, and there are no more Swarms flapping about (or you're containing them with Wolverines), head along the narrow gorge path to the location of Bravo Team. By now, you should have spotted some heavy armor among the rescued troops; the Grizzly tank that you rescue should be at the tip of your spear, fronting your formation when moving through this rocky pathway. It has a high damage rating that is excellent for absorbing any remaining Flood attacks.

CAUTION

Flood Launchers can sometimes release Flood Clouds from their projectiles. Demolish all Launchers before moving any of Alpha, Bravo, or Charlie Teams' infantry.

Black Box 10

Both Alpha and Bravo teams have a group of supply crates behind them. The company at Waypoint 7 is waiting with **Black Box 10**.

8 Construct a Gremlin as you continue along the gorge path. Blast the third Pylon with a previous Gremlin. Then move the new Gremlin all the way to the final Pylon. A couple Scorpions should clear the Flood away from the Pylon's base. This completes the Pylon Disruption objective. Next, rendezvous with the final trapped UNSC company.

(Finish) Bring all Companies to the Finish spot, where Pelicans are waiting. With almost no Flood left, you should have little stopping you achieving the final objective.

Catch

Before this mission ends, all that remains is to locate the Skull once your Flood Swarm culling is over. The Skull is devilishly difficult to spot; it appears on the small island between the two Pylons and Waypoints 1 and 3. A flying unit, such as the Hornets you built to help guard the Fortress, should pick up the **Catch Skull** while your other forces chaperone the collected UNSC companies.

Awards and Summary

GOLD	SILVER	BRONZE	TIN	Best Objective Score	Best Combat Bonus	Best Time Bonus
55,000+	40,000-54,999	20,000-39,999	0-19,999	4,000	x10 (40,000)	x5 (20,000)

Theoretical Best Score	64,000 (4,000 + 40,000 + 20,000)

Mission 01   Mission 02   Mission 03   Mission 04   Mission 05   Mission 06   Mission 07   Mission 08   Mission 09   **Mission 10**   Mission 11   Mission 12   Mission 13   Mission 14   Mission 15

Basics   Factions   Campaign   Multiplayer   Appendices   Art Gallery

121

11: CLEANSING

Wrenched into a strange and gargantuan tunnel within the shell of the Shield World, the Spirit of Fire was followed by the Flood. It is being bombarded by various alien life-forms, and the appearance of Forerunner Sentinels further complicates matters. Remove all alien forms from the hull of the ship.

OBJECTIVES

Win Condition:
All primary objectives met.

Loss Condition:
All hatches destroyed.

Par Time:
20:00–30:00

PRIMARY OBJECTIVES

■ **Clean the Flood off the Hull**
Completion Score: 0 Points
Flood structures have attached themselves to the outside of Spirit of Fire's hull and are threatening to break through the air locks. Destroy them all before they infect the ship.

■ **Permanently Remove the Flood Structures**
Completion Score: 1,250 Points
UNSC weapons can damage but not completely destroy the alien structures. Only the tunnel's technology can permanently clear the forms off Spirt's hull.

■ **Garrison Your Squads into the Air Locks to Protect Them**
Completion Score: 0 Points
The air locks provide some cover for our infantry. Order them inside.

OPTIONAL OBJECTIVES

■ **Destroy 100 Sentinels [100]**
Completion Score: 750 Points
Controlled by some sort of AI, these small high-tech constructions appear to be designed to contain the infection forms. Counter them with any military unit.

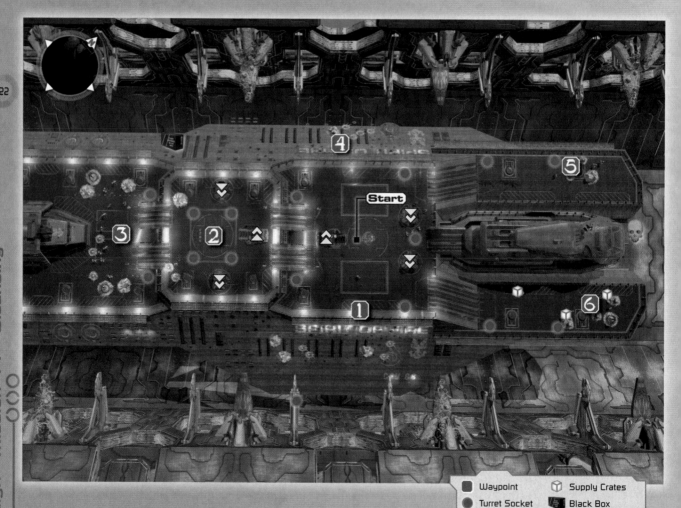

Legend	
■ Waypoint	⬡ Supply Crates
● Turret Socket	▣ Black Box
△ Vehicle Airlock	☠ Boomstick Skull
▽ Infantry Airlock	

Difficulty Modifications (compared to Normal)

Easy: All enemy units have 50 percent less Health Points and inflict 50 percent less damage. Lower number of Flood units on the hull, and free Turrets already constructed.

Heroic: All enemy units have 20 percent more Health Points and inflict 20 percent more damage. No free Turrets (Normal mode has one free Turret built).

Legendary: All enemy units have 35 percent more Health Points and inflict 35 percent more damage. No free Turrets. Maximum Flood population on ship.

Legendary Tactics

Flood waves arrive more quickly and move faster at higher difficulties. They are upgraded progressively for each difficulty too.

Spirit of Fire: Hull Structures

NOTE

Before you begin this mission, examine the Spirit of Fire's exterior shell for UNSC limpet structures designed to help your cause.

Infantry Air Lock

There are four of these air locks, two on the northeastern end of the lower deck and two on either side of the upper deck. Both types of air lock provide invaluable help and cover during this mission. The following actions are available inside the infantry air lock:

Base Rally Point

Utilize this as soon as you decide to train infantry units from this location. Place the Rally Point at a defendable location or where reinforcements are needed. As time is of the essence and infantry move slowly, position Rally Points on the same deck as the air lock or train troops from a nearer air lock.

Marines and Upgrades

Although these battle-hardened troops prove their worth time and time again, for Flood takedowns and cleansing, you should choose Flamethrowers or no infantry troops whatsoever; it is too risky to let Marines get infected, and it wreaks havoc with your Combat Bonus.

Flamethrower and Upgrades

Of the three types of infantry units readily available, these are the most proficient at dealing with the Flood enemies on the ground (but not the airborne Swarms). However, they are still susceptible to infection. Flamethrowers are also useless when dealing with the Forerunner Sentinels that buzz around the superstructure.

Cyclops (No Upgrades)

Impressive and skilled engineers clad in exoskeletons are great for mending damaged vehicles but are very slow-moving. You should be able to maneuver away from combat to keep your Combat Bonus high. There are better ways to spend your supplies, so ignore training Cyclopes for this mission.

Eject

It is vitally important that you send your troops scurrying back to the nearest infantry air lock once the cleansing ring passes over the ship. It is equally important to eject the troops to continue fighting the two-species threat afterward. This is the command that sends the troops inside a particular air lock back on deck.

Vehicle Air Lock

Adjacent to each other but on different decks, the vehicle air lock is easily distinguished from the infantry air lock due to the Firebase ramp, allowing wheeled and airborne vehicles to be created and returned during the cleansing ring sweep.

Base Rally Point

As vehicles usually move faster than troops, you can position Rally Points anywhere on the Spirit of Fire's super-structure.

123

Mission 01　Mission 02　Mission 03　Mission 04　Mission 05　Mission 06　Mission 07　Mission 08　Mission 09　Mission 10　**Mission 11**　Mission 12　Mission 13　Mission 14　Mission 15

Basics　　　Factions　　　Campaign　　　Multiplayer　　　Appendices　　　Art Gallery

Hornets and Upgrades

The superior maneuvering and extremely competent takedowns of every Flood Form make the UNSC Hornet and its available upgrades the best choice in superstructure tactical takedowns. As they can fly over the side of the decks, Hornets are invaluable and must be built as quickly as possible—ideally from both vehicle air locks at once, as supplies allow.

Wolverine and Upgrades

Designed to primarily tackle airborne foes, Wolverines are an option if you're determined to rid the Spirit of Fire of every Forerunner Sentinel. However, the wheeled nature of this vehicle means its maneuverability is compromised, especially when it has to rely on the Spirit of Fire's ramps. In addition, it cannot quickly counter the more mobile Sentinels. Not recommended.

Gremlin and Upgrades

Damaging to the Sentinels but not proficient at Flood takedowns, the Gremlin is another unit that is useful if you have limitless supplies but pales in effectiveness when compared to the UNSC Hornet. Mothball these EMP vehicles while you have the Hornet in your airborne arsenal.

Eject

There are only two air-lock locations on board the Spirit of Fire where vehicles can go to avoid the cleansing ring; therefore, it is vitally important you send them to either air lock and Eject them immediately afterward.

> **TIP**
>
> You can have one of your Spartans Commandeer a vehicle, enhancing its combat capabilities, but this is not recommended, as the weapons they carry are more potent.

Turret (Socket): There are 15 Turret Sockets on the Spirit of Fire's hull. When built, the Turrets provide an exceptionally helpful (and automated) method of tackling foes both on and off the ship. Remember to augment the Turrets with Mortars and Missiles.

Deck Gun: The gargantuan Deck Guns planted on the superstructure are not designed to blast entities as small as the ones on the ship's hull. Try to save the Deck Guns if they come under attack, but otherwise ignore them.

124

MISSION COMMENCEMENT

(Start) As you begin, your infantry units are embroiled in a fierce on-deck battle against a variety of disgusting Flood Forms. When this initial wave of goo-filled atrocities are gibbering in pools of their own filth, quickly check your vehicle air locks. You'll see a Hornet is already being trained in one of them. Continue with this sound strategy and build Hornets in one air lock and upgrade them in the other, as quickly as your supplies allow.

> **NOTE**
>
> In this mission, supplies are automatically generated without the need for Supply Pads. However, if you need a boost of supplies, the only place to find some is the low aft deck (Waypoint 6), near some Flood remnants.

> **TIP**
>
> To preserve your Combat Bonus, one option is to send all none-essential infantry (basically anyone who isn't wearing Spartan armor) to an infantry air lock to sit out this mission. They won't be infected, and they won't be destroyed by the cleansing ring. The only problem is if the air lock explodes, but you're tasked with preventing this from happening!

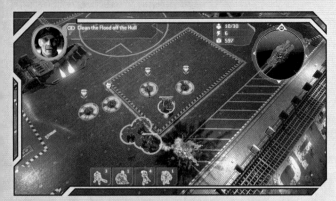

1 As soon as the battle is over, you can optionally check the edge of the hull. There are a few disgusting limpets on the side of the ship, but ignore them with your current infantry, as the Flood Infection Forms are much more problematic to your south. With this in mind, remember the Flood's side locations, as you'll need to purge them later in this mission. For now, begin to split your forces, with your Hornets (which you should be building from both vehicle air locks like crazy) heading up to the top deck (Waypoint 2) while your initial infantry head northeast, toward Waypoint 6.

Although you may need a Spartan to help tackle this upper deck area, there's another incredible asset you should use: Turrets. Build at least two of the Turrets available on the upper deck, and outfit them with Flame Mortars, leaving them to deal with the scurrying Infection Forms and other Flood infantry so you can concentrate on the major building threats. Continue to tear through the two Nests so that the upper deck is completely cleared.

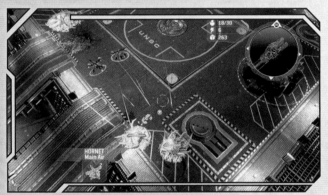

2 Immediately and quickly ascertain the threats in this area. By far the biggest problems are the Flood Launchers and Dens at the edge of the top deck. The Dens in particular are incredibly proficient at spawning beasts that can viciously tear through your air locks. Counteract this ominous threat by heading up to Waypoint 2 as early as possible, ideally with two or more Hornets, and lay waste to the Flood Den on the top deck to the south, in the corner. Don't get bogged down tackling the Flood Infection Forms and smaller Flood units; your main threats are the Dens that spawn them.

3 Now for the main Flood infestation! With as many Hornets as you're capable of building as quickly as possible, head toward Waypoint 3; however, don't charge right in, as there are Flood Launchers on either edge of the deck, which can thoroughly damage your Hornets. Instead, swing out, flying over the side of the Spirit of Fire, and then double back so you're attacking from the deck's side. As you near the cluster of Flood structures, take out the Launcher so the Flood have no offense against you.

TIP

At the same time, drop in a Carpet Bomb that severely softens up your Flood targets; see if you can hit the Launcher, Den, and a few nests with the bombing run.

125

Mission 01　Mission 02　Mission 03　Mission 04　Mission 05　Mission 06　Mission 07　Mission 08　Mission 09　Mission 10　**Mission 11**　Mission 12　Mission 13　Mission 14　Mission 15

Basics　　　　　　Factions　　　　　　Campaign　　　　　　Multiplayer　　　　　　Appendices　　　　　　Art Gallery

With one side of the deck at Waypoint 3 cleansed of Flood monstrosities, concentrate on the one remaining Flood Launcher in this area and destroy it quickly. Then launch all your weaponry at the final Den, which effectively halts the Flood intrusion on this ship. Spend the next few moments clearing the remaining Flood off this area before congratulating yourself. However, you're not done yet!

Black Box 11

Waypoint 3 is close to the location of **Black Box 11**, clamped to the side of the ship to the west, over the side. Take a Hornet to this location; it's the only way to reach it and gather it before continuing the mission.

By now, you should have seen the Forerunner technology at work, as a cleansing ring strafes the Spirit of Fire from north to south. Check the timer, being especially careful with infantry troops, as they require extra time to return to their air locks. Take all your vehicles and send them back inside either vehicle air lock. Do the same for your infantry, ensuring they reach the nearest air lock. Aim to have no troops on deck (with the exception of your Spartans if they are fully shielded) for each pass. This is better than the alternative, which are damaged forces that impede your Combat Bonus.

Legendary Tactics

When you're playing on harder difficulties, you should employ some mental calculations; for example, you should know how many seconds it takes to reach each air lock from the different decks, for each unit you have on board. Similarly, you should understand how much damage a cleansing ring causes. For example, you can keep your Hornets on deck and survive a cleansing before using the Heal & Repair power to nullify the damage, but this takes time away from your Time Bonus.

4 With your Hornets at the ready, fly from the Black Box toward the remaining Flood Nests that still spill Infection Forms that scurry onto the lower deck. Retaliate by building Turrets everywhere, upgrading and building Hornets, and clearing all Flood barnacles off the craft's sides, at both Waypoints 4 and 1. By this time, the Forerunner Sentinels (which appear in two forms) have deemed you a threat, and your main combat switches to tackling them, if you're determined to finish the Kill objective.

Legendary Tactics

A maximum Time and Combat Bonus is much more important than the points you gain from attacking 100 Sentinels. Ignore this Optional objective in favor of completing this mission as soon as possible; the Time Bonus helps you obtain the Gold ranking.

Cooperative Advice

With a friend helping you out, have one of you train, build, upgrade, and provide Carpet Bombs (but only if supplies allow) while the other tackles all combat duties. Alternatively, one of you could be responsible for airborne attacking, while the other focuses on the Spartans and infantry. Each is responsible for hiding their forces prior to the cleansing ring.

Legendary Tactics

Have your Hornets "camp" over the Flood structures located on the outer potions of the ship's hull so when the Nests attempt to regenerate, they are quickly nullified.

Toward the end of this mission, the Forerunner Sentinels consider you a threat, and you must attack them. First, augment the Turrets you've built and construct more, making sure to add Missile Launchers. This quickens the kill count. Second, leave a Flood alive on the outer deck side, so you don't complete the mission without defeating the Sentinels. Then simply crush the Sentinels in air combat, scanning the air above the Spirit of Fire for their flying formations, and then dropping them out of the sky. You may wish to build and place Wolverines near your turrets to help with this task. Mill around the Start position and Waypoint 2 to maximize the chances of catching a Sentinel squad. Ignore this plan if you're after a Gold ranking.

5 and 6 Concurrent to the Hornet tactics, for a proficient mission completion, take your infantry unit from Waypoint 1 and send them down to the front of the Spirit of Fire. Build a Turret near a small group of Flood to help provide support fire as you destroy a Flood Launcher and other small entities at Waypoints 5 and 6. Although it takes longer for the infantry to reach both these locations, the time saved is enormous, and you may wish to provide either Hornets, Turrets, or Carpet Bombs at Waypoint 6 to finally finish off the Flood. Collect the supply crates here afterward.

TIP

You should now continue to eradicate the Flood from the ship until mission completion. Flood locations pulse on your minimap and are colored red, so you can quickly see the Flood entities you've missed.

TIP

With the tactics presented, you should be easily able to unlock the **Battened Down the Hatches** Achievement, awarded if all air locks survive.

Sugar Cookies

When your 100th Sentinel crashes and burns, quickly locate the **Sugar Cookies Skull**, floating in front of the Spirit of Fire. This is accessible only by Hornet.

Awards and Summary

GOLD	SILVER	BRONZE	TIN	Best Objective Score	Best Combat Bonus	Best Time Bonus
30,000+	15,000-29,999	10,000-14,999	Tin: 0-9,999	✓ 2,750	✊ x10 (27,500)	⏱ x5 (13,750)

| | | | | Theoretical Best Score | 44,000 (2,750 + 27,500 + 13,750) |

Mission 01 Mission 02 Mission 03 Mission 04 Mission 05 Mission 06 Mission 07 Mission 08 Mission 09 Mission 10 **Mission 11** Mission 12 Mission 13 Mission 14 Mission 15

Basics   Factions   Campaign   Multiplayer   Appendices   Art Gallery

127

CAMPAIGN · ACT 4

MISSION 15

pg. 142

Careening up into the Shield World, the Spirit of Fire grazes a Covenant Destroyer, damaging its Power Core. After a vicious retaliation and a quick fix, Anders is discovered, and attempts are made to rescue her from the planet's surface. Once a major Covenant threat is nullified, an FTL Reactor Core is moved into position, and inserted deep into the Apex Site Base. Forge faces his ultimate threat, as he battles the Arbiter to activate the Core, as an all-out evacuation and Shield World detonation is attempted.

12: REPAIRS

Having escaped the tunnel through the shell of the Shield World, the Spirit of Fire collides with a Covenant Destroyer. Head back onto the hull with the units you utilized previously and repair the Spirit of Fire's damaged Power Core, while fending off attacks the Destroyer is jettisoning.

OBJECTIVES

Win Condition:
Power Core reaches 100 percent Health Points.

Loss Condition:
Power Core reaches 0 percent Health Points.

Par Time:
10:00–20:00

PRIMARY OBJECTIVES

Repair the Power Core
Completion Score: 1,500 Points

Spirit of Fire was heavily damaged in the collision. The power center must be repaired and brought back online before the ship can disengage.

OPTIONAL OBJECTIVES

Keep at Least One Deck Gun Alive
Completion Score: 500 Points

The Deck Guns are helping to hold back the Covenant assault. Keep as many as possible intact.

Kill 12 Spirit Transports [12]
Completion Score: 1,000 Points

A Spirit is the Covenant dropship, used for transporting infantry and support troops. Spirits carry groups of Covenant units to battle.

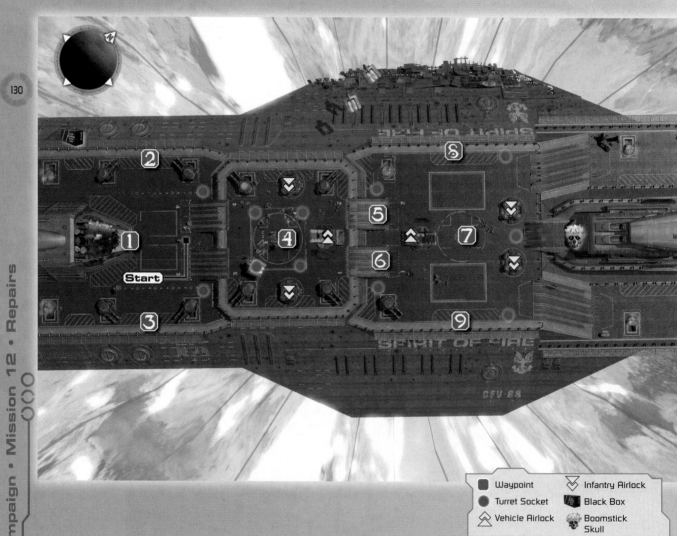

Legend:
- ■ Waypoint
- ● Turret Socket
- ⌂ Vehicle Airlock
- ⬇ Infantry Airlock
- ▮ Black Box
- ☠ Boomstick Skull

Difficulty Modifications (compared to Normal)

Easy: All enemy units have 50 percent less Health Points and inflict 50 percent less damage.

Heroic: More Covenant attacks on the Power Core. Jackals are enhanced, and more Deck Guns are initially damaged.

Legendary: All enemy units have 20 percent more Health Points and inflict 20 percent more damage. More Covenant attacks on the Power Core. You begin with fewer units.

Spirit of Fire: Hull Structures, Part 2

Like your previous Mission, there are the same number of Infantry and Vehicle Airlocks on the Spirit of Fire's super-structure. Below are the recommended units to use from each. All troops come already upgraded.

Infantry Airlock

Firstly, use the Rally Point to send Cyclopes to the Power Core. Cyclopes play a vital role in this Mission, so train at least three additional ones   to Repair the Core. Marines aren't needed, and although Flamethrowers are excellent at blazing through Hunters, they are lightly-armored and slow. Place them atop ramps, near Turrets that give supporting fire.

Vehicle Airlock

Thanks to Anders, you have the incredible Hawk aircraft; these are recommended and should make up at least half of your   forces. They have a devastating attack and move quickly across the hull. As the vast majority of Covenant troops are dropped in by Spirits, build a number of Wolverines to patrol the western decks. Don't overly rely on Wolverines as some Covenant must be faced on the hull itself.

TIP

Although not recommended, as the weapons they carry are more potent, you can have one of your Spartans commandeer a Vehicle, enhancing its combat capabilities. However, Spartans Jacking enemy vehicles (particularly Wraiths) is thoroughly recommended!

Spirit of Fire Hull

There are 15 **Turret Sockets** on the Spirit of Fire's hull locale. When built, the Turrets provide an exceptionally helpful (and automated) method of tackling foes both on and off the ship. Remember to augment the Turrets with add-ons (Mortar, Rail Guns and Missiles).

The gargantuan **Deck Guns** planted on the superstructure are not designed to blast entities so small as the ones on the ship's hull. However, it is worth Repairing the ones close to the Power Core, so they can help defend against Banshee attack.

Located at the southwest end of the Spirit of Fire, the ship is crippled until the **Power Core** is repaired. For this reason, send all available Cyclopes engineers to this location to mend this structure, and don't forget to protect it, and them!

131

MISSION COMMENCEMENT

(Start) You begin with a Covenant attack under way and your Power Core approaching critical. React swiftly and deftly to this problem by immediately selecting all your troops and subselecting all your Cyclopes before ordering them to the Power Core (Waypoint 1). While your troops mill about in the initial starting area, construct both Turrets close by, and build the Missile Launcher add-on to help repel the annoying Banshees flying about this area.

1 As you continue into this mission, train a few more Cyclopes and send them over to the Power Core. The more you have here, the quicker you complete the mission. Remember you can also utilize your Heal & Repair Leader Power at the Power Core, repairing it at an even faster rate. This is excellent when attempting a proficient Time Bonus but is not recommended if you want to finish the Kill objective and find the Skull. While your Cyclopes are in training, construct three or four

Mission 01   Mission 02   Mission 03   Mission 04   Mission 05   Mission 06   Mission 07   Mission 08   Mission 09   Mission 10   Mission 11   **Mission 12**   Mission 13   Mission 14   Mission 15

Basics   Factions   Campaign   Multiplayer   Appendices   Art Gallery

Wolverines at the upper deck's Vehicle Air Lock, and place the Base Rally Flag near the Power Core. Once the Wolverines are established near the Core, they usually eliminate your Banshee problem.

Legendary Tactics

Legendary tacticians know how long it takes to heal the Power Core based on the number of Cyclopes and available Heal & Repair powers. A quick Par Time is 10 minutes for this mission, so you can then figure out how long you have to take down the 12 Spirits for the Kill objective, and build Wolverines and Hawks accordingly.

Legendary Tactics

Turrets are also important, as they can absorb a lot of the Covenant's firepower, keeping your troops alive longer.

CAUTION

Don't go crazy with your Cyclopes training; around four or five is a good number to train, as you also desperately need defensive vehicles out on deck to neutralize the advancing Covenant hordes!

TIP

If you're aiming for the Handy with Tools Achievement, the Power Core can be repaired in under four minutes if you use Heal & Repair immediately. Again, send all Cyclopes to immediately repair the Core and ignore your air locks, pulling back to hold your starting position.

[**2** and **3**] As the battle begins, you should shift your attention to the upper deck [Waypoint 4], as the sides of the lower deck near the Power Core are relatively quiet. As the battle progresses, expect a few Hunters and dropped-in Covenant troops from Spirits to appear between Waypoints 2 and 3. Counteract these problems by constructing both Turrets and adding Missile Launchers to them both, and then packing a few Wolverines in to demolish Spirits before they can land. Patrol this area using Hawks when you're not embroiled in the more ferocious combat around Waypoint 7.

Black Box 12

The Black Box located on this mission is pinned to the superstructure of the Spirit of Fire, over the side of the railings south of Waypoint 2. As soon as you construct a Hawk unit, you can retrieve **Black Box 12**. Attempt this during a lull in the fighting.

4 You encounter Covenant forces en masse at this location, and it is a favored spot for single Spirit dropships and their Covenant landing troops. React accordingly by immediately building several Hawks. These aircraft are spectacularly powerful and can move quickly from Waypoints 4 to 7, blasting the foes that attempt to head toward the Power Core to destroy your air locks. As these two building types are under constant threat, build Turrets near them.

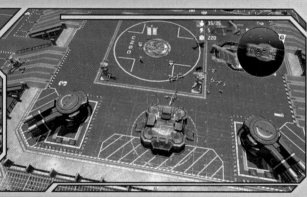

As the battle rages on, make sure all four Turrets are built. Arm the southern two (nearest the Start position) with Missile Launchers, and arm the front two, pointing at the ramps (Waypoints 5 and 6), with Flame Mortars to strike the infantry, especially the Hunters. With two Infantry Air Locks and a Vehicle Air Lock, you can pull back and hold this location if the battle is going badly for you. This isn't recommended, though; you need to push north and contain both decks!

[5] and [6]]
The main ramps between the upper and lower decks are between the two main Covenant drop points, and it is easy to get swamped from both angles if you don't have Waypoint 4 contained. Bolster your defenses here, and then move your Spartans to Waypoints 5 and 6. Have each of them run down toward Waypoint 7 as soon as you see a Wraith or Locust appear. Locusts are particularly problematic, as they easily wipe out your air locks, so Jack them quickly, retreat to the ramps, and use the Covenant vehicles to block the advancing enemies. Wraiths are good to keep and repair, while Spartan-controlled Locusts can be left prone so your Spartan can exit and find another machine to take over.

[7] This is the one area where the Covenant can get a good hold. You must prevent this from occurring by sending in your Hawks to devastate the area, backing them up with additional troops at the ramps and constructing Turrets in this area (first to the west, in order to damage the incoming Spirits). Of particular concern are the two Infantry Air Locks, which are easily destroyed by Covenant forces landing from Spirits. Prevent this by sending in Hawks to try and take down the Spirits.

NOTE

Although the Carpet Bomb is an option, you can better use your resources to construct two or more vehicles for the supply cost (600 points).

[8] The battle is only stopped by the completion of the Power Core repair, so send in Cyclopes accordingly (and Heal & Repair the Core). However, to safely contain the Covenant, position Wolverines along the side of the deck at Waypoint 8, so they completely demolish any Spirits that try to land. Help out the Wolverines using Hawks and Missile Launcher Turrets. Keep this up, and you'll receive a quick Time Bonus and finish the Kill objective without delay. Continue the fight until the Power Core is back online, and the mission is over.

Legendary Tactics

Don't expect to ever receive a x10 Combat Bonus at Legendary difficulty; you simply lose more troops than you can save during the initial stages of the attack.

133

Cooperative Advice

With another pair of hands at the controls, you can slice the Spirit of Fire up and have one player focus on the repair of the Power Core while the other tries to contain the Covenant landing forces to the north.

Boomstick

With Wolverines and Turrets bombarding Spirits as they land, the **Boomstick Skull** is easily accessed once you down 12 Spirits. Once the Spirits deposit their forces, you can't finish them off, so be sure they explode prior to delivering their troop payload. Then head north to the sloping ramps where the Skull appears on an upper structure, and use Hawks to obtain it.

Awards and Summary

GOLD	SILVER	BRONZE	TIN	Best Objective Score	Best Combat Bonus	Best Time Bonus
32,000+	22,000-31,999	12,000-21,999	0-11,999	3,000	x10 (30,000)	x5 (15,000)

	Theoretical Best Score	48,000 (3,000 + 30,000 + 15,000)

Mission 01 Mission 02 Mission 03 Mission 04 Mission 05 Mission 06 Mission 07 Mission 08 Mission 09 Mission 10 Mission 11 **Mission 12** Mission 13 Mission 14 Mission 15

Basics   Factions   Campaign   Multiplayer   Appendices   Art Gallery

13: BEACHHEAD

Temporarily marooned on the planet, Anders must be evacuated off immediately and sent back up to the Spirit of Fire. Once a Pelican has survived both Covenant and Flood forces and transported her away, you must battle to control four bases in order for Anders's plan to succeed.

OBJECTIVES

Win Condition:
All Primary Objectives met.

Loss Condition:
Forge or Anders dies before she is evacuated. All forces defeated and unable to rebuild bases afterward.

Par Time:
20:00–01:00:00

PRIMARY OBJECTIVES

■ Get Anders to the LZ
Completion Score: 250 Points
Professor Anders must be rescued. Push forward and secure the Landing Zone.

■ Find a New LZ
Completion Score: 250 Points
The initial LZ is not secure. A safer, alternative LZ might be found beyond the teleporter.

■ Hold the LZ
Completion Score: 500 Points
Hold the Landing Zone at all costs. If your forces are overrun, all hope is lost.

■ Capture and Hold Four Bases [4]
Completion Score: 1,500 Points
If Professor Anders is correct, you must control all four bases for the plan to succeed.

OPTIONAL OBJECTIVES

■ Take Control of the Scarab
Completion Score: 250 Points
The Scarab is a powerful Covenant superweapon. If captured, it would provide much-needed support for our forces. Only Spartans are capable of capturing the Scarab.

■ Kill 10 Bomber Forms [10]
Completion Score: 750 Points
The alien Bomber Forms are a threat to our ground forces. Counter them with Wolverines.

Legend:
- Waypoint
- Forerunner Supply Pad
- Two-Way Teleport
- Supply Crates
- Black Box
- Pain Train Skull

Difficulty Modifications
(compared to Normal)

Easy: All enemy units have 50 percent less Health Points and inflict 50 percent less damage. The small Covenant base sending Banshees to attack your southern base is gone.

Heroic: Larger flights of Banshees attack your base. Covenant base defenders that land as you attack are tougher.

Legendary: All enemy units have 25 percent more Health Points and inflict 25 percent more damage. Covenant base defenders that land as you attack are tougher.

MISSION COMMENCEMENT

[Start) and 1] With security for Forge and Anders woefully inadequate, you must immediately flee the encroaching Flood parasites and proceed to the LZ at Waypoint 1. The Pelican hovering at the Landing Zone is demolished by Flood Swarms. A moment later, ODST troops are hot-dropped into the earth. With them and three Spartans, you must head south, away from the Flood menace, and begin to secure four Covenant bases in order for Anders's plan to work. Head through the nearby teleport.

NOTE

There are Flood production Dens to the west of Waypoint 1. Ignore them initially, as they send out Flood Bomber forms that tangle with the Covenant, diverting both enemies from you. Return here later to complete your Kill objective.

2 The first test for your troops is the small Covenant stragglers to the southwest, at Waypoint 2. Defeat

them all so they don't follow you to either of the nearby bases (Waypoints 3 and 5), then wait for a second Pelican to arrive and whisk Anders back to the Spirit of Fire. You now have a choice of bases to overrun, the most important of which is the base to the south. Head there, as it is less susceptible to attack than the base at Waypoint 5.

TIP

The Flood infects anything it comes into contact with, including Covenant forces. Wherever possible, allow these two factions to fight, then mop up the survivors.

3 Take your troops along the grassy path, ignoring the light bridge with the Wraith guarding it for the moment (you can Jack the Wraith and add it to your ragtag collection of troops, but this is unwise, as there are specific units you should intend to Jack). Instead, approach the southern Covenant base and begin a precision attack. Start by sending a Spartan (not the one carrying the Rocket Launcher) to Jack the Locust guarding this base. Back the Locust up, and begin taking out the ground infantry units and the Wraith before ripping through the base's defenses. Attempt this as soon as possible, and the threat posed is minimal.

135

Mission 01 | Mission 02 | Mission 03 | Mission 04 | Mission 05 | Mission 06 | Mission 07 | Mission 08 | Mission 09 | Mission 10 | Mission 11 | Mission 12 | **Mission 13** | Mission 14 | Mission 15

Basics | Factions | Campaign | Multiplayer | Appendices | Art Gallery

Once the base has exploded, immediately send a squad of ODST north, to the Forerunner Supply Elevator on the edge of the stone chasm. Begin supply production there at once. When the Firebase is installed, quickly upgrade it to a Station, and then add Turrets in all four corners. Pause in your Turret manufacturing only to slot in three Heavy Supply Pads; your economy must be as strong as your defenses. Upgrade the Station to a Fortress, adding enough Reactors to reach Tech Level 4. This may take some time but shortens the mission in the long run, once you build Vultures. For this to happen, build an Air Pad and begin Vulture construction.

Throughout the base build, Banshees attack you incessantly. These can cause significant damage to your base and reduce your Combat Bonus. This is why you should build Turrets as quickly as possible, and then augment them with Missile Launchers. Keep careful watch of the Turrets, and Heal & Repair any that become critically damaged. Continue with your Vulture production, keeping the aircraft close until you have two or three upgraded Vultures.

CAUTION

Covenant Spirits will drop off extra defenders at the bases as you attack them. Make sure you're ready to fight them before taking out the base. Airborne troops are excellent, as there's less chance of the Covenant being able to strike them.

Legendary Tactics

The Banshees head in from one of three Summits (all shown on the guide map). Take an airborne unit (such as a Jacked Banshee or a couple of Vultures) and fly to the Summits one at a time and destroy them, optionally using a Carpet Bomb to help you. This curtails the Banshee bombing runs and improves your Combat Bonus.

[4] While you're building up your first base, manufacture and send out two or three Warthogs for a recon operation. Drive them over the light bridge, ignoring the Wraith and any assembled Covenant at Waypoint 5's base. Cross the bridge to the southeast, stopping in the

vicinity of Waypoint 4. You'll discover a Scarab, abandoned due to the Flood Tentacles wrapped around it. Back off to the grassy area near the light bridge, and call on a Pelican to transport one of your Spartans across to the Warthogs. As your base build continues, have your Spartan tackle the tentacles single-handedly, and then Jack the Scarab!

TIP

An even easier way is to Jack a Banshee and fly to this point, as you don't have to waste resources building a Warthog. Remember to utilize the Scarab by cutting down 25 or more enemies, as this massacring results in the **Beaming with Pride** Achievement.

Cooperative Advice

Your teammate should be building up and defending the bases you overrun, but without overpopulating the map; the more units you produce, the more you have to worry about dying and ruining your Combat Bonus. The other player should try tackling the bases in the order shown or sending in Vultures to rake the base and Summits around the map.

[5] As you're building up your refineries and hopefully building your first Vulture, you can send your Scarab northwest toward Waypoint 5 and the central Covenant base. Stay on the light bridge, and the Scarab can single-handedly demolish the entire base! If any Elite Honor Guards sprint toward the Scarab, back away to Waypoint 4, as they don't follow you. Then return and rake them, plus the Shade Turrets and Wraiths, and bring down the base itself!

Legendary Tactics

You may need a little extra help on higher difficulty levels; instead, send a Vulture or two and a Locust to help with the demolition.

☠ Pain Train

By now, you should have spotted some Bomber Forms drifting in from the west toward the central base at Waypoint 5. To reach your goal of slaying ten of them, move your Vultures west, past Waypoint 1, and search out the cluster of Bomber Forms in this location and the Den that is producing them. Don't destroy the Den until you've popped the last Bomber, then take the **Pain Train Skull** floating atop the tentacle-clad Forerunner shaft.

[**6** and **7**] Heal & Repair your Scarab, and send it plodding northeast up the hill from Waypoint 4, ignoring the nearby base for the moment, as there's a Covenant Summit at the hill's top that's lightly guarded. Rake the enemies and then destroy the Summit, as this is where the Banshees are being produced. This lessens the number of air attacks that your base receives. You may also try this plan out with your Vultures.

With the Banshees' building facility destroyed, stay on this higher ground and aim down at the third Covenant base at Waypoint 7. Vultures are especially useful here, as they can attack the base from this height, and the Covenant troops aren't in range to retaliate. You may spot a couple of Spirits dropping in Elite Honor Guards, but the Guards can't strike airborne troops (as they will understand when you massacre them).

8 Take your squadron of Vultures and swoop past Waypoint 8 (which is where the second teleport is located if you've unwisely decided to use ground troops). Take them around to the upper plateau where the final base is located. Beware of some nasty Covenant vehicles, including another Scarab. Lay down a Vulture barrage to finish it, then back off before any Vultures are destroyed and Heal & Repair them. Then tackle the Scarab, before laying waste to the base and optionally the two Summits—the other two locations where you should expect Banshees to appear from. When all four bases have changed hands, the mission is over.

📦 Black Box 13

Waypoint 8 is also the location of **Black Box 13**, hidden on the hilly ground that an infantry unit, a Warthog, or a flying vehicle can access. Grab the item before attacking the final Covenant base.

Awards and Summary

GOLD	SILVER	BRONZE	TIN	Best Objective Score	Best Combat Bonus	Best Time Bonus
🏅	🏅	🏅	🏅	✔	👊	⏱
40,000+	25,000-39,999	15,000-24,999	0-14,999	3,500	x10 (35,000)	x5 (17,500)

Theoretical Best Score	56,000 (3,500 + 35,000 + 17,500)

Mission 01   Mission 02   Mission 03   Mission 04   Mission 05   Mission 06   Mission 07   Mission 08   Mission 09   Mission 10   Mission 11   Mission 12   **Mission 13**   Mission 14   Mission 15

Basics   Factions   Campaign   Multiplayer   Appendices   Art Gallery

137

14: REACTOR

Anders's plan to utilize the Spirit of Fire's FTL Reactor Core to nuke the Shield World is about to be put into action. After two Pelicans fail to drop the Core into the World's Apex Base, it falls to you to transport the Core through hostile environments to the plateau atop a series of ramps, where the Core can be attached.

OBJECTIVES

Win Condition:
All Primary Objectives met.

Loss Condition:
Loss of the FTL Reactor Core.

Par Time:
15:00–30:00

PRIMARY OBJECTIVES

■ **Build and Attach Elephant to FTL Reactor Core**
Completion Score: 500 Points

The FTL Core is heavy, but an Elephant should be able to drag it to the Apex.

■ **Use an Elephant to Tow the Core up to the Apex Base Site**
Completion Score: 1,500 Points

Destroying the Shield World is the only way to deny the Covenant its secrets. The FTL Core must be towed to the Apex.

OPTIONAL OBJECTIVES

■ **Kill 20 Vampires [20]**
Completion Score: 750 Points

Vampires are very effective at destroying UNSC aircraft. Counter them with Wolverines.

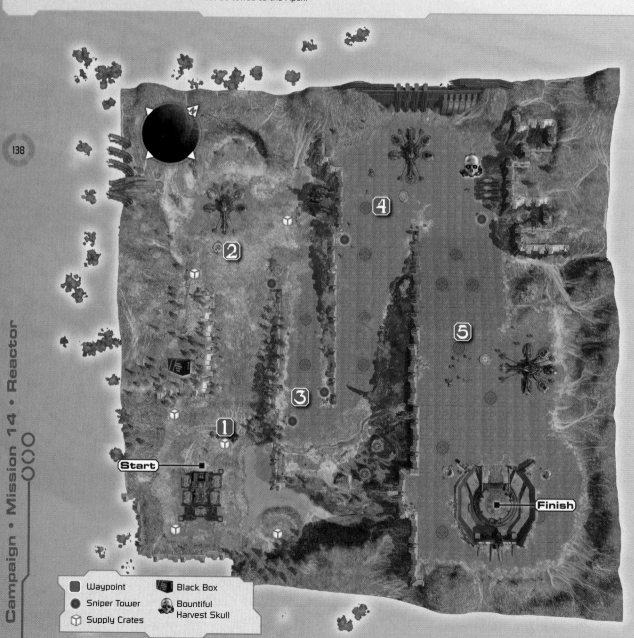

Start

Finish

	Waypoint		Black Box
	Sniper Tower		Bountiful Harvest Skull
	Supply Crates		

Difficulty Modifications (compared to Normal)

Easy: All enemy units have 50 percent less Health Points and inflict 50 percent less damage.

Heroic: Covenant advance their Ages more quickly.

Legendary: All enemy units have 25 percent more Health Points and inflict 25 percent more damage. Covenant advance their Ages much more quickly.

MISSION COMMENCEMENT

SPARTAN 130 - ALICE
Spartan - Machine Gun

(**Start**) You're tasked with moving the exceedingly heavy (and precious) Reactor chamber from the base of the mountain to the summit, while avoiding being overrun by Covenant forces along the way. You must first take your troops and move them to the vicinity of the fallen Reactor Core. Protect this Core from any encroaching enemy as you build up your Station into a fully functioning Fortress. Haste is important here, as the Covenant are massing forces at several choke points along this zigzagging peninsula.

Quickly build your base and insert the two Turrets nearest the lake to quell the few floating Flood Forms and the intermittent Banshee attacks. There is an immediate threat at the top of the grassy ramp northwest of you, so don't delay; build two Reactors, three Supply Pads, and a couple of Scorpion Tanks. Then take the assembled force, with your Spartans leading, and head up the hill.

1 Either before or after you reach Waypoint 2, tether the Reactor Core to a vehicle strong enough to drag it to the top of the mountain. Fortunately, your Fortress base produces Elephants; construct one and then upgrade it so it moves at a quicker rate (do this after you build the Elephant). Trundle the Elephant across to Waypoint 1, where the Reactor Core is waiting, and couple the Core to the Elephant. Then bring this contraption with you up the ramp, following well behind the initial forces attacking Waypoint 2.

Legendary Tactics

If you wait too long, the Covenant forces at Waypoint 2 are much more problematic to dispatch, as they reinforce the base quickly and easily. You must drive up to this base as soon as you can.

TIP

When upgrading the Elephant, choose the additional speed upgrade, but don't worry about the extra Turrets; you aren't going to be locking the Elephant in place unless the rest of your forces aren't fighting to their true potential!

2 Take your ragtag band of brothers up the ramp to the base, cutting down the scattered Covenant

139

Mission 01   Mission 02   Mission 03   Mission 04   Mission 05   Mission 06   Mission 07   Mission 08   Mission 09   Mission 10   Mission 11   Mission 12   Mission 13   **Mission 14**   Mission 15

Basics   Factions   Campaign   Multiplayer   Appendices   Art Gallery

infantry troops as you go. When you reach the base, demolish the foes at the Sniper Towers so they don't fire on you, and beware of enemy Vampires whittling your health down as you try to destroy this base. Call on two MAC Blasts from the Spirit of Fire to help take out this base quickly and effectively. Once the base explodes, bring the rest of your squad up to this location.

Legendary Tactics

▮ On lower difficulty settings, you can Rush the base at Waypoint 2 from the very start, without waiting. On harder difficulties, there isn't really time to wait for tanks to build, so send up your Spartans to clear the infantry and Sniper Towers, and ferry in vehicles to a Rally Point just outside the base's Turret range. Build up your forces as Scorpions become available and then strike, upgrading to Canister Shells just as you're in the middle of fighting with two or three Scorpions.

Once you wipe the Covenant base from the grassy hillside, quickly call in and deposit a Firebase. It is important to claim each base as your own and create additional bases to stop the Covenant from rebuilding. Once you claim this base, you're periodically attacked by Flood Bombers, so erect two or three Turrets to shoot down these foes, and upgrade the Turrets with Missile Launchers in case Vampires arrive here.

TIP

To claim the **Didn't Get to Second Base** Achievement, it is important not to claim each base as your own and keep only your original Firebase as the source of your units as you ascend. Construct Vultures from your original base to quickly catch the rest of your team.

TIP

Choosing buildings for this base is important, as long as you can do it while continuing up the hill. Drop in a Supply Pad, another Reactor so you're at Tech Level 4, and then another Vehicle Depot or Air Pad, and a Field Armory. Building vehicles or aircraft allows you to make specific vehicles farther along the path so they have less distance to travel. Remember to fix a Rally Point at a spot farther along the ramps where you'll need reinforcements.

Black Box 14

When your second base is well under construction, send an infantry unit south along the rocky promontory to the side of the grassy ramp you just climbed. Nestled in a tree-lined clearing is your penultimate collectible crate: **Black Box 14**.

3 The remainder of this mission involves ferrying the Elephant with the Reactor Core up the ramps to the top. However, before this occurs, move your offensive line up the second long ramp to Waypoint 3, and engage the Covenant in this area. Place Spartans Jerome and Alice in the Sniper Towers at this location, where the Flood are accumulating, and then launch all your salvos at the Flood Den and the troublesome Launcher embedded in the hillside. After you defeat these, head around to the next ramp.

Legendary Tactics

▮ To receive a perfect Time Bonus, you must judge when a fight is about to end and have the Elephant move up behind to join your troops immediately so it isn't too far away from them ascending (and can be picked off by aerial foes) or too close to the fighting.

TIP

There are two types of vehicles ideally suited to this mission: Scorpions and Vultures. Vultures take longer to build but are quicker to reach each subsequent base and knock it out at a slightly faster speed. Scorpions are quicker to produce but are slower on the ascension. However, as you have to use an Elephant to reach the mountaintop, either vehicle works well.

4 Trundle your mechanized division up to the next Covenant base at this Waypoint, and lay waste to it. If you're having difficulties, call in a MAC Blast from the Spirit of Fire, or upgrade your Scorpions or Vultures and launch fearsome secondary ability attacks into the base, taking it down as quickly as possible. Once the base has been removed, repopulate it with a Firebase and quickly upgrade it to a Station. Add two Turrets to guard against any stray Bomber Forms or Vampires.

5 The plan is identical as you reach the top of the mountain ramps, with a final Covenant base to destroy. With a sizable army (remember you can build Vultures down below and quickly send them up as reinforcements without zigzagging up the ramps like Scorpions have to), this base should be leveled in moments. Begin with the Covenant's Turrets, and then launch your entire barrage of firepower into the base center. There's little point in taking down the building clusters connected to the central spire, as this simply takes you longer to reduce the base to rubble.

Legendary Tactics

This should be tried only on Easy difficulty, but an adept player can upgrade the Elephant's speed at your initial base, clamp it to the Reactor Core, and tow it to the top using only his starting units for company and passing all the bases en route! However, again, this doesn't quite pan out if you're playing on a higher difficulty.

(Finish) Anders's plan is about to be put into effect. Drive your Elephant toward the Apex Site, and it automatically reverses in and completes this mission. Clear the area of Covenant first so there are no foes in the vicinity of your Elephant as you reach the site.

Cooperative Advice

This mission is significantly easier if you have a second player studying and defeating the Flood Forms and Vampires heading to your base, building up the bases quickly, sending up reinforcements, and letting the other player know of incoming foes. Meanwhile, the other player has to focus on the battles for each base, on Elephant and Reactor Core safety, and on bringing the pain on the Covenant.

Bountiful Harvest

Weigh the pros and cons of completing the Kill objective before this mission starts. To complete the objective, you must wait for Vampires to appear, as they aren't built at a base. They periodically head toward your base or toward your troops ascending the mountain ramps. They always appear in twos. To defeat them, construct Turrets with Missile Launchers at every base. If you wish, build additional Wolverines to help bring down the Vampires. Wait for Vampires to fly in, and keep this up until all 20 are downed.

The **Bountiful Harvest Skull** is located close to Waypoint 4, in the middle of a circle of Forerunner stonelike objects to the north. Grab this on your way to the mountaintop, or leave a unit here to take it if you're trying to keep as much of your Time Bonus as possible.

Legendary Tactics

Obtaining the **Bountiful Harvest Skull** is a problem here, as there's no possible way you can achieve the Kill objective (defeat 20 Vampires) without incurring a Time Bonus penalty, which negatively affects your ranking. If you're determined to get Gold, ignore this Kill objective and the Vampires, and complete the mission in under 15 minutes (the quick Par Time); your score is actually higher if you leave the Vampires alone.

141

Awards and Summary

GOLD	SILVER	BRONZE	TIN	Best Objective Score	Best Combat Bonus	Best Time Bonus
30,000+	20,000–29,999	10,000–19,999	0–9,999	2,750	x10 (27,500)	x5 (13,750)

†*Due to the length of time it takes to complete the Kill objective, this theoretical score is almost impossible.*

Theoretical Best Score 44,000 (2,750 + 27,500 + 13,750)†

Mission 01 · Mission 02 · Mission 03 · Mission 04 · Mission 05 · Mission 06 · Mission 07 · Mission 08 · Mission 09 · Mission 10 · Mission 11 · Mission 12 · Mission 13 · **Mission 14** · Mission 15

Basics · Factions · Campaign · Multiplayer · Appendices · Art Gallery

15: ESCAPE

After a frantic battle with the Arbiter, Forge successfully fends off the beast, but the Reactor Core's on-board timer is destroyed. While Forge takes the core from the Apex up into the Shield World interior light source, you must fight to open six giant doors allowing the Spirit of Fire to finally exit the Shield World interior. Evacuation of all UNSC troops is of paramount importance.

OBJECTIVES

Win Condition:
All Primary Objectives met.

Loss Condition:
Any door remains closed when the timer ends.

Par Time:
20:00–33:00

PRIMARY OBJECTIVES

■ Open the Portal
Completion Score: 1,000 Points

If Spirit of Fire is going to escape from the Forerunner structure, the door must be opened. The unlocking mechanism appears to be some sort of giant puzzle.

■ Clear Out All Enemies Near the Interlock Tower
Completion Score: 500 Points

The enemy units near the interlock towers appear to be preventing them from working. They function if humans are nearby, but other life-forms must be cleared from the area.

■ Activate the Interlock
Completion Score: 500 Points

The nodes appear to be laid out in some sort of pattern. If they can be activated in the correct sequence, the portal door sections may open.

OPTIONAL OBJECTIVES

■ Kill Three Scarabs [3]
Completion Score: 2,000 Points

A heavily armored walker designed to smash through enemy armies, the Scarab is a nearly unstoppable killing machine. If one appears on the battlefield, the best counters are Scorpions and Cobras.

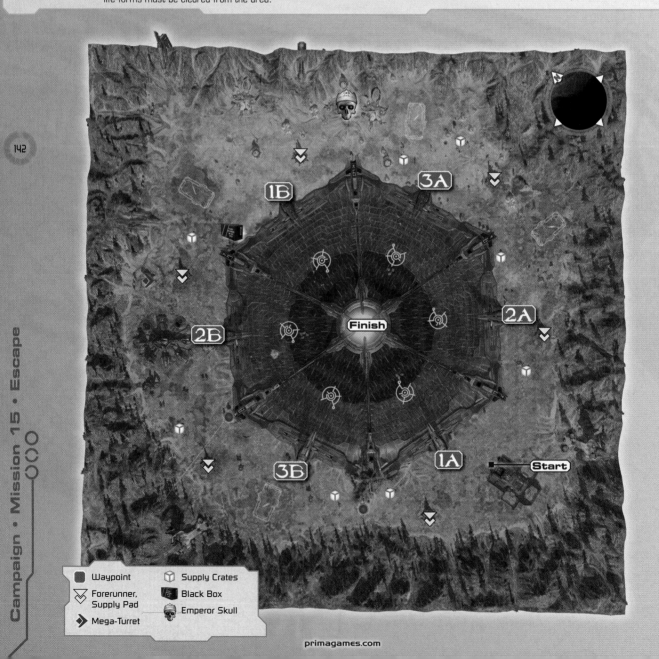

Legend:
- Waypoint
- Forerunner, Supply Pad
- Mega-Turret
- Supply Crates
- Black Box
- Emperor Skull

Difficulty Modifications
(compared to Normal)

Easy: All enemy units have 25 percent less Health Points and inflict 25 percent less damage. Least aggressive enemies, and enemies have low-level upgrades.

Heroic: All enemy units have 25 percent more Health Points and inflict 25 percent more damage. Enemies have high-level upgrades. You begin with half the supply resources.

Legendary: All enemy units have 50 percent more Health Points and inflict 50 percent more damage. Most aggressive enemies, and enemies have highest-level upgrades. You begin with only 1,000 supply resources.

MISSION COMMENCEMENT

(Start) The endgame begins now! This mission, with its time limit and puzzle, is initially confusing but more straightforward than you'd think, and there are some sizable shortcuts to try along the way. To begin, though, you have an initial wave of attacks to repel. After you defeat this initial incursion, you can follow the onscreen prompts to open the portal. Or, you can try the tactics detailed below, which ignore some of the prompts but allow you to finish with an impressive score. The choice is yours. Whatever your decision, you should immediately improve your Firebase to a Station, build Supply Pads and a Reactor, claim the nearby supply crates, and eventually turn this base into a Fortress with an Air Pad, four Reactors, and a Vulture squadron at the ready!

Your base improvements are going to take some considerable time, so while this is going on, move the infantry that you began this mission with to the left and right, heading to the two Forerunner Supply Elevator Hooks close to Waypoints 1A and 2A. Man both of these Supply Elevators so you need build only two or three Heavy Supply Pads at your base. This also adds to your economy quickly. You should be grabbing both these Supply Hooks immediately after fighting the initial attack wave.

When you've built up an initial force, begin a killing spree that lasts for a while, moving counter-clockwise around the map. Your goal is to clear the Covenant, UNSC, and occasionally Forerunner foes around the circumference of the portal. First, however, it is sometimes wise to move clockwise, heading past (or around, onto the portal doors and back onto the grass) the Sniper Tower to the empty base and claim it. If you're too slow in your troop buildup, you may encounter a Covenant base here; if this occurs, you may be completing this mission too slowly.

Your task is to open the portal, which involves clearing the six Waypoints shown on the map. An example door is shown in the adjacent picture. The order is important if you want to claim all objective points. Access each of the portal doors to open a menu, which appears only when there are no enemies in the vicinity.

NOTE

Your Population cap has been bolstered for this mission only. You can now train a total of 40 troops, or 50 if you upgrade your Population using the Field Armory.

Mission 01 Mission 02 Mission 03 Mission 04 Mission 05 Mission 06 Mission 07 Mission 08 Mission 09 Mission 10 Mission 11 Mission 12 Mission 13 Mission 14 **Mission 15**

Basics Factions Campaign Multiplayer Appendices Art Gallery

143

After the initial base pad—which should be immediately improved and held with Turrets and a mixture of ground and air add-ons—there's the small issue of the real problem area, the Covenant base. It is heavily fortified, but you must take it down. If you're after the Kill objective bonus, don't take the base down immediately. There are two options available to you: fly in with Vultures (or a massive number of Scorpions) and raze the entire base, or send in a Vulture to ascertain the location of your first Scarab and unleash a terribly cunning plan to complete the Kill objective.

[**1** A and **1** B] The portal-opening begins now! Move an infantry unit close to the portal door at Waypoint 1A and open it.

While keeping your base clear of enemies, fly your Vulture squadron directly north, on a straight path away from your starting base. Hover near or around Waypoint 1B, the portal door on the opposite side. By now you should have spotted your first Scarab. Annoy it with some Vulture fire, then speed toward Waypoint 1B with the Scarab following you.

Make sure there are no enemies near Waypoint 1B, and then open the first set of portal doors. Ensure the Scarab is standing on either triangular door section between Waypoints 1A and 1B. When the doors are activated, these sections disappear; and the Scarab falls away into the inky blackness below! Congratulations, you've killed your first of three Scarabs without firing a shot! It is wise to order in a Firebase and secure it near Waypoint 1B.

Black Box 15

When your forces are clearing the area at Waypoint 1B, check the ground to the west for **Black Box 15**.

Each door is part of a pair, with its partner directly across from it beyond the center of the portal. To open the doors of a pair together, unlock the activation nodes for both doors.

> **TIP**
>
> The order in which to open the doors is shown on the guide map. Look at the Forerunner Glyphs on each of the six triangular portal sections. There are only three symbols, each repeated once. In order to figure out which is the first, second, and third Glyph, look at the tiny circle on the edge of each one, which indicates the number. The circle at "12 o'clock" is 1. The circle at "2 o'clock" is 2. The circle at "4 o'clock" is 4. Opening the Glyphs in the correct order grants you the **Thinkin' About My Doorbell** Achievement.

Continue heading counter-clockwise around the portal circum-ference. The Vultures' flight now becomes

incredibly important, as you can fly over the segments of the portal door that have opened, whereas ground units suffer from maneuvering on the grass, slowing your army considerably. Continue to Waypoint 2A, and open this door, prepping it for later. Then continue around to the map's eastern side, using your Vultures to cut down the troublesome Flood foes. Claim another base and optionally a supply elevator near Waypoint 3A.

> **TIP**
>
> As you head around this map, take as many bases as you can simply for the supply crates, which allow quick access to troop construction and Leader Powers.

Legendary Tactics

Send your Vultures out or Jack a Banshee, and fly across to the map's northwestern side, close to the Covenant's main base but without attracting attention. Do this as early into the mission as possible. The Covenant has a Mega-Turret, which is initially unmanned. Call in a Pelican Transport and lift some of your infantry (and optionally a Spartan) to land and take this structure. Leave the infantry to take potshots at the foes; the damage they can cause is considerable. The Mega-Turret is not available in Cooperative mode.

> **TIP**
>
> As you progress through this mission, remember you should have an abundance of supplies and all the Leader Powers. Use them to take down Scarabs, bases, and other concentrations of troops. In addition, the Cryo Bomb is excellent at instantly destroying, for example, flying units. Also, the Flood, Covenant, and Forerunner forces all attack one another. Watch for these fights, then mop up the survivors for a better Combat Bonus.

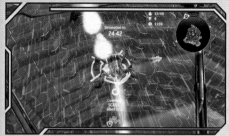

Continue to check on the Covenant base until a second Scarab appears. You can employ the same technique as before—opening the portal doors and letting the Scarab fall through—but you won't be able to open the portal doors in order, because you can't acquire Waypoint 2B with the Covenant base in operation. Instead, launch a Vulture attack on the Scarab, softening it with a MAC Blast. Execute this as soon as possible. Then wait until the final Scarab appears, destroy that, and finally launch a final, all-out offensive against the main Covenant base.

CAUTION

Once you begin opening the portal doors, the Scarab tends to walk around the triangular holes. This can lead it straight to your base. Keep an eye open for these behemoths!

CAUTION

You must kill your first Scarab as early as possible, as each takes several minutes to spawn. If you wait around for the last Scarab to appear, you'll lose your Time Bonus.

Emperor

When the final Scarab falls, move northeast to where the largest proportion of Flood reside. Fly in, grab the **Emperor Skull**, and flee if you haven't cleansed this area yet.

Legendary Tactics

As you near the point where you're about to attack the Covenant base, notice that the base sends out Wraiths, infantry, Locusts, and other troops. However, it also sends out Banshees as scouts. Kill the Banshees first and quickly so you avoid detection. If they spot your forces, the Covenant tends to send their forces to you, which can be problematic if you're engaging, say, the Flood or Forerunners.

Legendary Tactics

If you wish to perfect your Combat Bonus, let more Flood infections spawn from their lairs to the north of the portal instead of cutting out the Dens and other spawning holes.

Legendary Tactics

You can slog your way around the map and kill everything, or to win faster, you can use Pelican Transports to surgically take out each activation node site. Drop in and take out the bare minimum of enemies to turn each node on, then get out. This may not reward you with a perfect Combat Bonus, but your Time Bonus is likely to be perfect! Also use Transports to quickly reach the map's opposite side, especially if you're using infantry to open portal doors and none are nearby.

[2] A and 2 B] After an epic battle at the Covenant's base—where your Spartans may have taken over a Locust or two and turned them on the structure, your Vultures pulverized the base's shields, and you've called down all the Spirt of Fire's Leader Powers—move from the smoking husks of the base and open the portal doors at Waypoints 2A and 2B.

[3] A and 3 B] You have one set of portal doors left. If you're on foot, take a transport to locations 3A and 3B. You should have troops already stationed here, holed up in cover and keeping enemies away, or you should have a few Vultures dotted around, guarding these Waypoints so you can open all four doors in quick succession. As soon as this occurs, the portal is revealed. Escape, once a grossly optimistic thought, now looks imminent!

145

Awards and Summary

GOLD	SILVER	BRONZE	TIN	Best Objective Score	Best Combat Bonus	Best Time Bonus
30,000+	20,000-29,999	10,000-19,999	0-9,999	4,000	x10 (40,000)	x5 (20,000)

| | | | | | Theoretical Best Score | 64,000 (4,000 + 40,000 + 20,000) |

Mission 01   Mission 02   Mission 03   Mission 04   Mission 05   Mission 06   Mission 07   Mission 08   Mission 09   Mission 10   Mission 11   Mission 12   Mission 13   Mission 14   **Mission 15**

Basics   Factions   Campaign   Multiplayer   Appendices   Art Gallery

1 v 1 MAPS

2 v 2 MAPS

3 v 3 MAPS

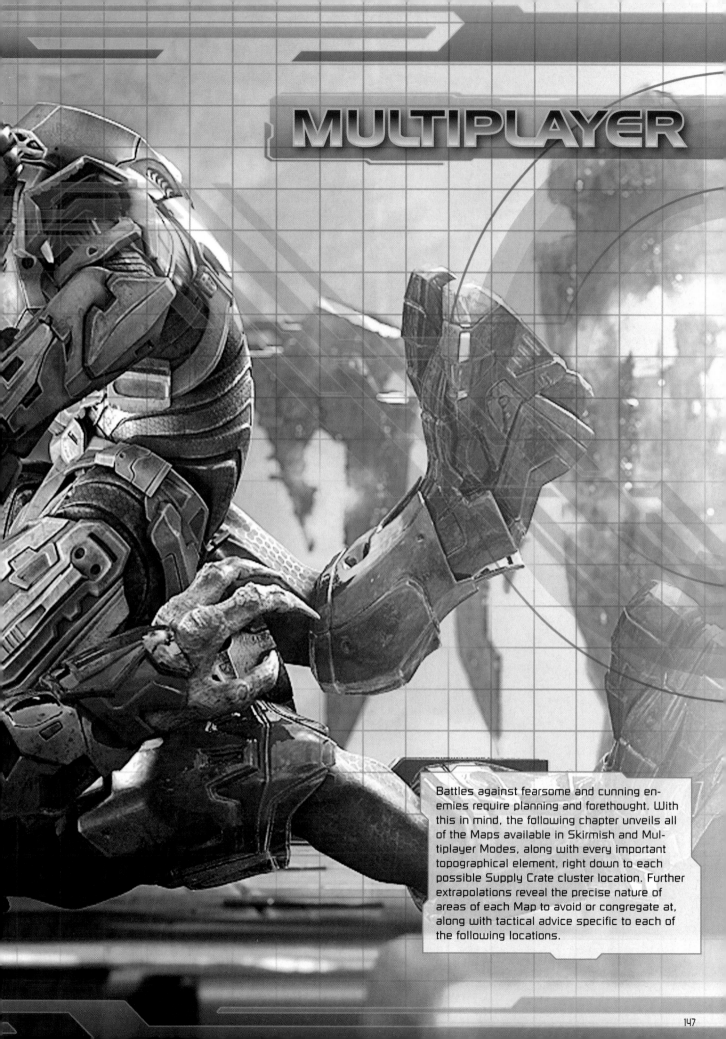

MULTIPLAYER

Battles against fearsome and cunning enemies require planning and forethought. With this in mind, the following chapter unveils all of the Maps available in Skirmish and Multiplayer Modes, along with every important topographical element, right down to each possible Supply Crate cluster location. Further extrapolations reveal the precise nature of areas of each Map to avoid or congregate at, along with tactical advice specific to each of the following locations.

1v1: BLOOD GULCH

A fast and brutal fight awaits in Blood Gulch. Teleporters allow for surprise attacks, while bonus Reactors offer opportunities for the aggressive strategies. This is essentially a flat central area stretching from east to west, with rocky upper areas to the north and south that house the Hooks and Sniper Towers.

AREAS OF INTEREST

Starting Bases: 2
Neutral Bases: 2

Teleporters: 2 (1 at entrance, 1 at exit)
Reactor Hooks: 2

Supply Hooks: 2
Sniper Towers: 6

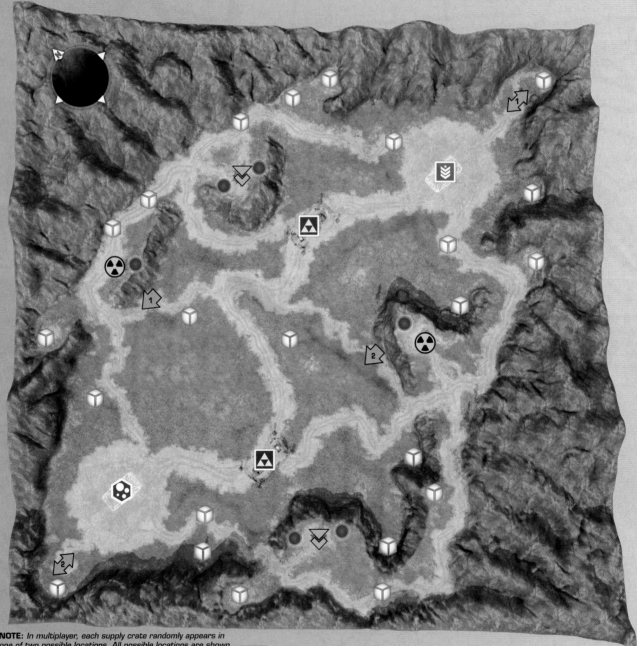

NOTE: *In multiplayer, each supply crate randomly appears in one of two possible locations. All possible locations are shown.*

✲	Starting Base	☢	Reactor Hooks
⬡	Starting Base	⬜	Supply Crates
▲	Neutral Base	▽	Supply Hooks
⇄	Teleporters	●	Sniper Towers

148

There are two Teleporters on this map. Enter Teleporter 1 behind the UNSC base and exit it to the west, just below the northern Supply Hook. Enter Teleporter 2 behind the Covenant base and exit it to the east, adjacent but below the southern Reactor Hook. If you're splitting forces, try sending some through the Teleporter to claim supply crates and the Reactor or Supply Hooks you're far away from. Teleporters are also a good way to transport forces (especially slow-moving ones) near to a foe's base. For this reason, keep a lookout for enemy troops at the Teleporter exits.

TIP

Another topographical feature to utilize is the dirt roads that crisscross the landscape. Until you learn the layout of this map, they provide reasonable routes, and you can easily learn the perimeter of the map by following them.

A key to commanding this map are the four Hooks, two on each side of the gulch. Notice there are two types: one adding to your Reactor total and the other giving you continuous supplies from an in-ground elevator. Depending on your play style, you may wish to secure one or both types (for example, Covenant forces have to spend many more supplies to raise Tech levels, but capturing a Reactor solves this issue quickly). Simply put, if you control the majority of these Hooks, you're likely to be victorious. Train infantry early on to inhabit these locales and the nearby Sniper Towers.

TIP

If you want upgraded, hi-tech units without the Heavy Reactor or Temple upgrade costs, then grab those Reactor Hooks as soon as you can! Better yet, you can upgrade your preferred forces, then leave or ignore the Reactors as the combat situation demands; only stay in a Reactor you need to defend (if a unit requires a High Tech to create, or you don't want the enemy taking it). Spartans make good Reactor and Supply Hook guards (before being replaced by Marines if you require Spartans elsewhere on the battlefield).

This map has a bounteous harvest of supply crates, and collecting these (perhaps starting with crates farther away by using a Teleporter) is of great importance while you build your base. Because of the wealth of supplies, this leads you to quickly build light, fast-moving forces (e.g., Warthogs or Ghosts). This, coupled with the proximity of the enemy, makes Rushing or Scouting on a large scale two very viable plans.

TIP

Another way to quickly take control of this map is to utilize the Pelican Transport or Covenant hot-drop abilities. Send your units immediately to reinforce Hooks on the map's opposite side; this also keeps your opponent fearful of your plans, as they see your forces dropping in and massing!

Nestled toward the map's center are two neutral bases; expect minimal resistance from either of them. These secondary bases can be advantageous but are risky to obtain because they are very close to your enemy. Instead, consider concentrating on the Supply and Reactor Hooks.

TIP

Alternatively, you can attempt to swarm one of the neutral bases (closest to your original base) as early as possible, and pour all your resources into defending it. If you're simultaneously capturing the Hooks to the north and south, you can effectively control an entire third of the map, reinforcing your original base later.

Although a wide variety of unit types work well in this gulch, of particular interest to Covenant players are the

Brute Infantry with the Jump Pack upgrade. Their ability to quickly leap up to the Supply and Reactor Hooks and man them (instead of plodding there on foot) allows you to easily control these strategically important areas and keep your opponent worried.

149

1v1: CHASM

This area is dominated by large mountains and chasms, but there are still many possible approaches to traverse the rugged landscape. Scattered Sniper Towers are positioned perfectly to defend key tactical locations. Aside from a central path, there are snaking roads on each side, all undulating and deceptively labyrinthine.

AREAS OF INTEREST

Starting Bases: 2	Supply Hooks: 2
Neutral Bases: 2	Sniper Towers: 8

NOTE: *In multiplayer, each supply crate randomly appears in one of two possible locations. All possible locations are shown.*

Starting Base	Supply Crates
Starting Base	Supply Hooks
Neutral Base	Sniper Towers

Of all the maps, this one places the opposing starting bases closest to each other, separated by the short central chasm road with the two Sniper Towers in the middle. For this reason, expect to be attacked earlier than normal, and plan your base-building and troop-training accordingly.

With such an easily reached target, your foe will usually attack with Rush tactics; if they don't, you should. Quickly send in a handful of infantry troops to the enemy's base early. This nasty surprise will keep your foe occupied while you concentrate on other key positions throughout the map.

TIP

While you're annoying your adversary with a few infantry troops, make sure you garrison the next wave of four units in the central Sniper Towers (or at least, the two nearest your base). Not only does this give you control of the main (and most direct) route to your enemy, but the infantry are better protected from this vantage point and act as an early warning of an enemy attack.

For such a small area, this map is dotted with dozens of supply crates. Grab the ones in the central main route before your foe can find them, then weave along the side paths to secure more. Split your fast-moving vehicles to claim these supplies as early as possible, and plan on attempting (or defending) a Rush or mass Scout strategy; both are very viable on this map.

The neutral bases are relatively safe to rake and destroy, then build up as your own, and they allow a much more flexible and fast-building army if you're attempting to draw out your battle. Another often-overlooked tactic is to rush to the neutral base near your opponent's starting base and take that over, harassing your hapless opponent from two directions! However, don't get caught by a foe attempting this on you!

Out of the way and easily overlooked in the map's corners are two Supply Hooks that provide additional unit-building materials once you defeat the neutral forces. Taking these is also extremely important, and after a fast-moving forward reconnaissance force has done the bulk of the fighting, station a group of Marines, Grunts, or Jackals in the Sniper Towers to better defend them (or to keep your foe at bay until you can bring in reinforcements).

TIP

Despite the map's small size, it is aptly named. The holes in the ground and narrow pathways make it somewhat cumbersome to maneuver large armies around. Counteract this problem by focusing on building air units, then close the gap without worrying about problematic topography!

TIP

Study the roadways of this map carefully, as there are numerous paths to your foe's main base that can cause panic and confusion in your enemy: Consider rounding a squadron of Hornets around and attacking from the rear, or utilize flanking attacks, with two sets of agile forces attacking from the sides. This often-overlooked plan works especially well if your foe is reinforcing the front of his base.

151

1v1: PIRTH OUTSKIRTS

The swampy outskirts of Arcadia's capital city features unclaimed bonus Reactors and offers alternate routes for attacks. The area is open and easily navigated, even by the most cumbersome and powerful vehicle. The starting bases are on the map's east and west sides, with a cluster of two other bases and a Reactor Hook to the north and south.

AREAS OF INTEREST

Starting Bases: 2
Neutral Bases: 2

Unguarded Bases: 2
Reactor Hooks: 2

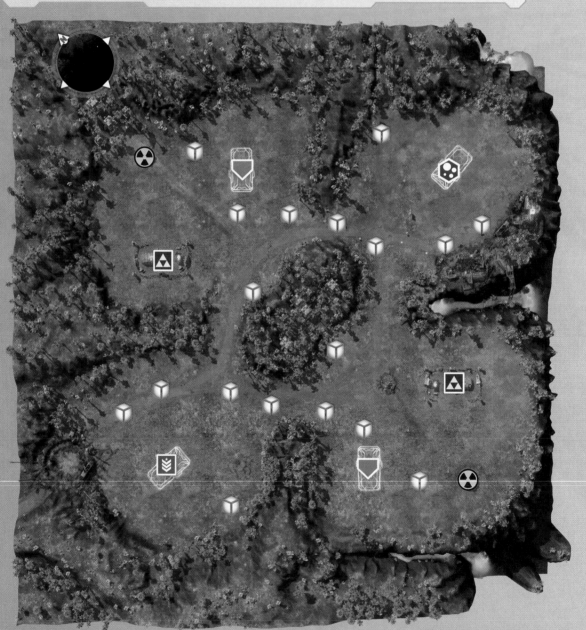

NOTE: *In multiplayer, each supply crate randomly appears in one of two possible locations. All possible locations are shown.*

Starting Base		Reactor Hooks	
Starting Base		Supply Crates	
Neutral Base		Unguarded Base (Empty Base)	

152

The two starting bases are located in a large flat area and are easily attacked, so expect the possibility of an early Rush. Take either curved road from one base to the other; they are the same distance. Because your foe may be preoccupied with capturing the three structures to the north or south, react accordingly and Rush. However, usually it is better to build up your base defenses and multitask by quickly foraging for supply crates, then taking the empty base.

Part of the tactical advantage you gain when employing a Boom or Tech strategy is further augmented by capturing one of the two Reactor Hooks on this map. There's yet another reason why taking the empty base as early as possible is a good idea: You can build a Turret close enough to the Reactor, improve it by adding on a Flame Mortar, and then lure the Reactor's guardians into its line of fire. This makes the Reactor much more easy to take. Don't forget to have Marines, Grunts, or Jackals waiting to claim the Reactor the instant it becomes secure.

The number of bases in this map is high compared to its size, so it stands to reason that you should occupy the empty base as early as possible, especially if you're employing a Boom or Tech strategy. With minimal resistance (just the odd band of neutral infantry to crush), you can have two bases working simultaneously before your foe has even finished foraging.

The ragtag neutral troops in either of the two guarded bases are very dangerous to take. If you see a foe attempt to tackle a neutral base early on, consider launching an attack on them, as they're bound to lose a few initial troops in the process. For this reason, leave the guarded bases alone until later; this includes building a front-right Turret in an adjacent empty base you just took, which attracts the neutral base's attention. However, this can become problematic if you're facing a dangerous foe.

TIP

Remember there are two empty bases; mix up your tactics and frighten your foe by capturing the empty base nearer to his starting base, if you have the supplies and forces necessary to defend it. Or, fake an attack to flummox him!

TIP

Due to this map's size, another excellent tactic is to build up your Warthog collection, or send in your Covenant leader and teleport in reinforcements and Rush early on. This can lead to devastatingly quick victories!

The end-game scenario for this map can be extremely satisfying (and explosive!), as the slower and more expensive units  (that provide you with a spectacular finish) are worth building, because they don't have much ground to cover. Mass a force, perhaps several lumbering tanks, and complicate your opponent's defensive tactics by flying in some airborne vehicles to attack his base from behind.

1v1: RELEASE

The Flood threatens to overrun this dangerous but crucially important region. Send units to activate the console near the enemy's base to unleash a nasty surprise. Note that the console is housed inside a Forerunner Relic, and each Relic controls one of two Containment Units. Also beware of three possible base locations, currently homes to a Flood Colony.

AREAS OF INTEREST

Starting Bases: 2
Flood Bases: 3

Forerunner Relics: 2

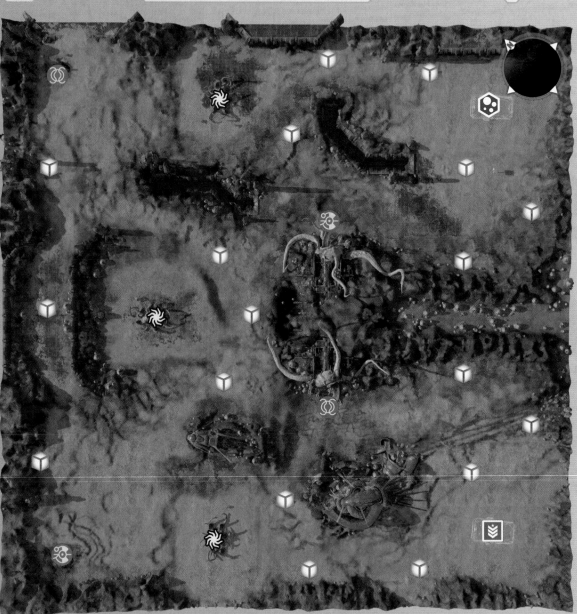

NOTE: *In multiplayer, each supply crate randomly appears in one of two possible locations. All possible locations are shown.*

Starting Base		Flood Base	
Starting Base		Forerunner Relic and Release 1	
▢ Supply Crates		Forerunner Relic and Release 2	

Although initially complex, this map is shaped like a giant horseshoe, with three troublesome Flood bases dotted from northeast to southwest. You begin your battle on either side of an ancient Forerunner Flood Containment building, which is covered in Flood Tentacles; you don't have to attack these. Because you're starting so far away from your foe, Rushing isn't a good idea; instead, begin a Scouting plan.

TIP

Because you are relatively far away from your foe, building up Scouting forces (e.g., Warthogs or Ghosts) and setting them off to claim the dotted supply crates is a great plan.

Scouting is only partly about securing as many supply crates as possible; there are two important Forerunner Relics in the map's north and western corners. These must be manned by infantry and are guarded by a Flood Tentacle. Once you Commandeer one of the Relics, you can opt to release the north or south containment unit. The north Relic opens the north unit, and the west Relic opens the south unit. Once opened, the following units spew out.

Containment Unit: First Release

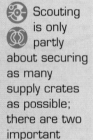

Infected Marines are spewed forth and stagger to their doom.

Containment Unit: Second Release

Infected Marines and Thrasher Forms tear through friend or foe alike.

Containment Unit: Third Release

Marines, Thrasher Forms, and Flood Swarms rampage about the infected hellscape.

TIP

Using the Flood to aid you is an excellent idea; try reaching a Forerunner Relic and defending it (taking infantry with you to man the Relic) while you also execute a Boom strategy. Send waves of Flood at your opponent's base to occupy him while you Tech up.

CAUTION

As the Relics open Flood Containment Units on their side of the map, it is important not to release Flood that immediately attack your own base! Combat this by Scouting to the farther Relic or by employing fast-moving vehicles to coax the Flood toward your enemy.

This map favors a slow buildup, with you pushing your forces toward the middle of the map at a measured pace. Therefore, when you attempt to tackle one of the three Flood bases, employ almost overwhelming force—the enemy is almost always nearby and is probably waiting for you to clear the Flood defenses before sweeping in and easily taking the base you worked so hard to conquer. Naturally, this "sweep-in" plan is a tactic you should try yourself!

More advanced tacticians have seen the topographical challenges of this map and have planned accordingly. Or to put it another way: try creating troops that fly! Jumping Brutes or aerial assaults are an excellent way to avoid the Flood, quickly arrive at your enemy's base, and slaughter them while your foe's tanks are still stuck in a world of swamps and tentacles! The good news is that you should have time to build these units too.

Another possible winning scenario is mixing your Scouting plans with some hard-hitting base assaults. Take a Warthog or Ghost squadron to the Forerunner Relic farthest from you, then attack the nearby Flood base before your foe realizes how close you are. Then pump out infantry to man the Relic, release the Flood hordes, and send in waves of Flood, your forces, more Flood, and more of your forces, and crush the opposition!

155

1v1: TUNDRA

A frozen pond and several craters channel troop movements into killing zones in this battle-scarred region. Use the structures to your advantage; tactical knowledge of the Sniper Towers and central Mega-Turret can turn the tide in your favor as long as you don't overextend your army gaining these locations. Central Sniper Towers also have barriers that stop vehicles but not infantry.

AREAS OF INTEREST

Starting Bases: 2
Neutral Bases: 4

Sniper Towers: 8
Mega-Turret: 1

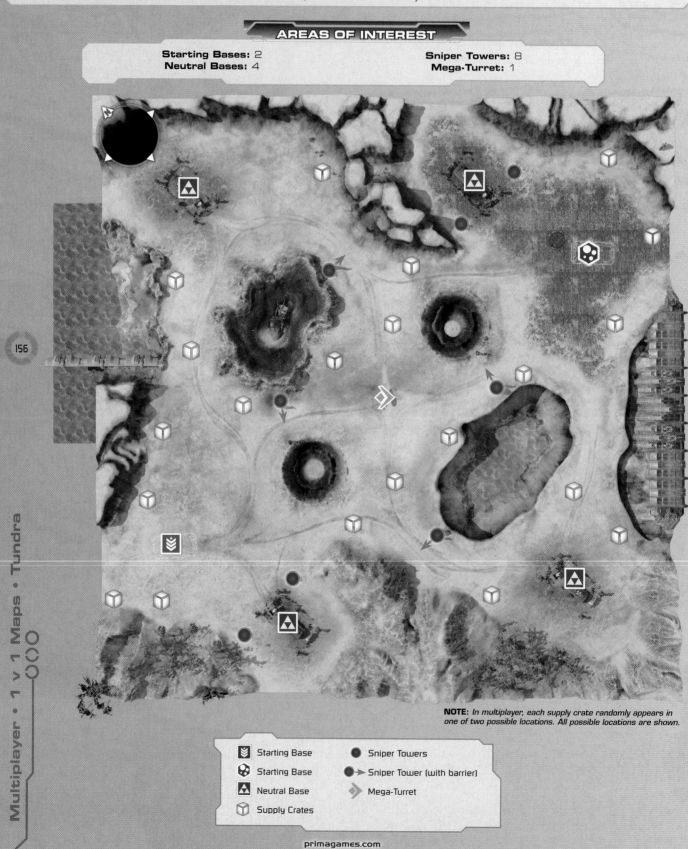

NOTE: *In multiplayer, each supply crate randomly appears in one of two possible locations. All possible locations are shown.*

Starting Base	Sniper Towers
Starting Base	Sniper Tower (with barrier)
Neutral Base	Mega-Turret
Supply Crates	

The neutral base adjacent to your starting base should be taken early, as it allows you to build up your economy quickly and effectively. The easiest way to quickly claim this base is to build a Barracks, an Elephant (UNSC), or a Hall (Covenant) and send in the infantry to tackle the base dwellers. Losing a few troops for this cause is a reasonable sacrifice, as the enemy is so far away.

Victory in the Tundra can come quickly, and it is easier to achieve if you control the central Mega-Turret, which is powerful enough to really impede your foes, even if they trundle in with heavier vehicles. Camp a group of your own vehicles here, and ready yourself for the fireworks! Conversely, if you let the Mega-Turret slip from your control, call in a MAC Blast or Disruption Bomb to soften up the target.

TIP

Sending in a large army of Flamethrowers to wrench control of the Mega-Turret gives you a huge initial advantage. Attempt this as quickly as you can.

The Sniper Towers in the middle of the map allow you to activate a barrier and can seriously impede your foe's progress. They are especially annoying if you plan a Scout strategy, sending in quick vehicles to the three Sniper Towers nearest the enemy's starting base. Have them guard the Sniper Towers until your infantry arrive. Cut off all ground travel at these locations, reinforce them (and the gaps to the northeast or southwest), and then tackle the Mega-Turret. When the enemy finally breaks through, they're in for a world of hurt!

TIP

Due to the high number of infantry needed to man and defend the Sniper Towers and Mega-Turret, you can optionally maneuver an Elephant or Covenant leader to keep the supply of trained foot soldiers coming.

CAUTION

It can be difficult to attack the enemy's main base when playing as the UNSC, because reinforcements tend to take much longer to travel across the map (they cannot teleport, unlike the Covenant). However, the plan below can negate this issue!

If the enemy tries to stop you from reaching their base or the Mega-Turret by employing the Sniper Tower Barrier, simply build airborne units. These are usually faster than land units, and they can head over the lava holes and other topographical anomalies and can easily capture a neutral base or launch an all-out attack on your foe.

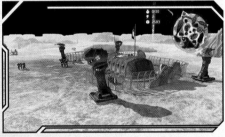

The other neutral base in the map's north or south corner is sometimes forgotten about in the race to secure the Mega-Turret. Although it isn't recommended to conquer this corner base until later into your match, it can provide a tactical advantage, because it's a straight shot to your opponent's starting base. In addition, the very fact that it isn't used much means your foe usually ignores it. Make sure you don't; quickly build up forces there and pounce!

TIP

If you're attacking the foe's starting base, and he's already commandeered the adjacent neutral base, be mindful of your unit placement: Attack so you're heading toward the side of his main base; that way you're only caught by two of his turrets. Don't park your forces in between both bases or you'll be savaged by both of them!

2v2: BEASELY'S PLATEAU

Bases in this region tend to have ways in and out. Controlling the center may lead to a larger-than-normal Population limit. A mixture of dirt and tarmac roads loop around the two middle neutral bases, between which resides a Forerunner Life Support Pod Hook that's extremely useful. Also be aware of the four sets of two "single pads and a turret base" Socket Hooks, guarded by neutral troops.

AREAS OF INTEREST

Starting Bases: 4
Neutral Bases: 6

Socket Hooks: 4
Life Support Pod Hook: 1

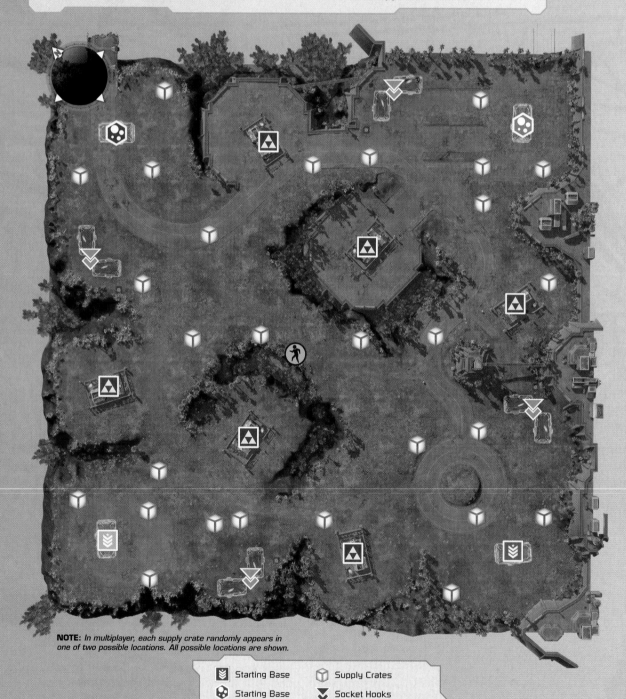

NOTE: *In multiplayer, each supply crate randomly appears in one of two possible locations. All possible locations are shown.*

⬙ Starting Base		⬡ Supply Crates	
⊕ Starting Base		⬇ Socket Hooks	
⧄ Neutral Base		🚶 Life Support Pod Hook	

The four starting bases are each located in a corner of this expansive map. Due to the long distances between these places, and the number of hostile neutral troops guarding their own bases, it is very difficult to support your teammate, especially early into this battle. You and your teammate should Scout immediately and ascertain what your enemies are up to, and build up your base.

TIP

Use this guide's map to roughly locate the scattered supply crates as you investigate one of your foes, optionally heading straight for their base, then backing up to claim as many crates as possible. Watch for neutrals during your crate pillaging.

Simply because it's initially difficult to back up your teammate, Covenant players can easily and

effectively execute a "double Covenant Rush." Each takes their leader and Rushes him to the same base for double the mayhem and builds troops like crazy to teleport in near the hero. This can catch a foe early and crush him quickly. Remember to try feint tactics, heading for one base, then looping around to swarm another. You can also split your attack, one leader on each of your foe's bases, but victory is less assured this way.

CAUTION

The UNSC can also try a "double Warthog Rush" using the same principles: build Warthogs like crazy and converge them on a single enemy base. This works well, except when your opponent builds Turrets, which demolish Warthogs easily. Therefore, a slightly more defensive strategy may work to an UNSC player's advantage.

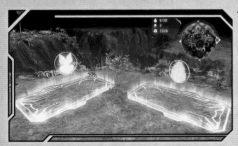

One of the interesting locations on this map is the Socket Hook. There are four, and each of them identical and guarded by two neutral squads. The Socket Hooks offer exceptional help early into your battle. They offer two Base Pads, on which you can build any structure you wish; a Turret, which is UNSC when constructed, even if you're

a Covenant player; and some defenses for infantry to hide behind. Think of Socket Hooks as more flexible versions of the Reactor and Supply Hooks you're used to in 1v1 confrontations. Send a couple of Flamethrowers (UNSC) or your leader (Covenant) to take a Socket Hook; this is an easy way to gain two extra Pads without having to throw troops at a fully guarded neutral base.

TIP

Gaining a Socket Hook is important, but so is keeping it. First, make sure some infantry are in cover. Second, quickly build the two buildings you need, such as an extra Reactor and perhaps a Barracks so you can pump local troops to guard the place. The Turret is extremely helpful too.

Conversely, the six scattered neutral bases are more difficult to destroy (at least early in a battle) but provide much more flexibility and protection when fully established than a Socket Hook. If you're constantly worrying about a Socket Hook, try taking and maintaining a neutral base instead; it has four times the Turret defenses and five more building Pads. As each player has three neutral bases within close proximity to the starting base, it is usually wise to take over the one on the same perimeter as your teammate; the enemy has more distance to travel to reach you.

TIP

This map, with its long starting distance between teammates, the U-shaped crevasses in the map's center, and other obstacles, make air units specifically advantageous over ground ones: Use airborne troops to quickly reach your teammate, and harass enemies as they try to reach a location; if your foes attack a base, wait until it crumbles, then swoop in, mop them up, and claim the base yourself!

Control of the Life Support Pod in this map's central area becomes essential. This is the only map that allows you to increase your Population by 10, on top of any additional Population upgrades you may have triggered. This gives a UNSC player a theoretical maximum of 50 and a Covenant player 60. Although it may seem cunning to take this early in the game to prevent adversaries from claiming it, this only becomes useful as you near your Population cap; by that time, you should have an array of troops that can easily wipe out the neutral forces. Get an upgraded infantry unit into the Pod, guard it, and then use it as a thoroughfare to cross diagonally toward your opponents' starting bases and crush them one at a time!

159

2v2: CREVICE

Bases in this region must be heavily defended when Flood Swarms emerge from their hiding places. Otherwise, this map is split from east to west by a crevice; to access the other side, you must go through a sunken central Forerunner plateau, or run the gauntlet past a Flood Colony and its Infected Forms and airborne beasts.

AREAS OF INTEREST

Starting Bases: 4
Empty Bases: 4

Flood Bases: 2
Reactor Hooks: 4

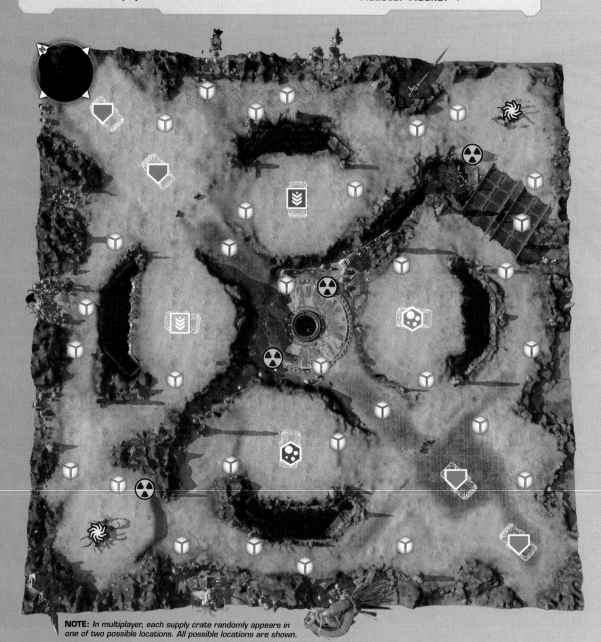

NOTE: *In multiplayer, each supply crate randomly appears in one of two possible locations. All possible locations are shown.*

Starting Base

Supply Crates

Starting Base

Unguarded Base (Empty Base)

Reactor Hooks

Flood Base

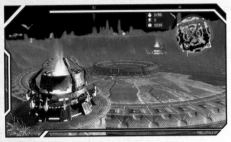

Beware! The Flood are active in this area. Expect vast Flood Swarms to attack from the air. There are two Flood Colonies—one on the far east and the other on the far west—to dodge or attack. These have numerous Infected Forms slithering around. For this reason and because of the gigantic crevice, Rush strategies are usually not planned—they are too difficult to employ early on, because your force must engage the Flood when maneuvering around the sides or up through the central Forerunner plateau.

The two Flood bases have a Colony on each, at the east and west corners of the map. These are worth defeating if you can muster enough firepower without your opponents learning of this plan (as they're likely to wait, then swoop in to claim the base afterward or attack your other locations while you're spread too thin). If you manage to claim them, you can control a main thoroughfare as well as a Reactor.

TIP

Every player has to deal with the troublesome Flood Swarms. Vehicles and troops automatically attack these nightmarish flapping fiends, but it helps to learn what to construct so you have to divert as little attention to them as possible. Refer to the "Factions" chapter, and choose vehicles and troops that are excellent at tackling airborne foes (e.g., build Wolverines or Vampires). Build them as more of a preference. Attacks that knock Flood Swarms from the skies are good, too, like Anders's Cryo Bomb. Normally, though, build base Turrets faster than normal and augment them with the Missile Launcher.

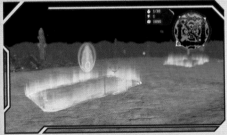

The unguarded empty bases that are in the north and south corners of this map are excellent places to quickly maneuver to and take over. You're not likely to be attacked, so you can quickly build up your defenses or choose one of your team to build and defend both bases while the other takes a more offensive posture.

The central Forerunner plateau is a key location on this map, but you must approach it with due caution. Be most careful if you decide to attack the neutral forces roaming this middle zone, as the enemy is extremely close by and may either ambush you as you try to hit the neutrals or wait until you've almost finished the job and move in to destroy your damaged forces. Try

counteracting this by having one of your team Scout and attract the opposition's attention, drawing forces away from the middle so you can claim it with the least fuss.

Once you've cleared the central plateau of neutral forces, it becomes essential to your victory and must be controlled at all costs. A large number of supply crates appear after you defeat the neutrals, and, more importantly, there are two Reactors within close proximity. This means you must keep a strong presence here, congregating before launching attacks on enemy bases. Obviously, man the Reactors, as the Tech level increase can result in your victory.

The topographical problem for ground forces on this map is another reason to pick air units, or, if you're playing defensively, choose antiair forces to predict this plan. Choose your hero with this in mind; Anders is an obvious choice for the UNSC. Now you can attack the enemy without facing any neutral or ground Flood units whatsoever. Sending in air units to constantly harangue your foe's starting base is a thoroughly rewarding plan.

This map can be confusing and needs a strategy to match the bewildering chasms, Forerunner Reactors, and Flood incursions (although don't try this strategy too often or your foes may expect it). As you begin, take your starting Scout unit to the map's other side via the perimeter (shrugging of Flood foes at the east or west Colonies) and claim an empty base, ideally the outer one, on the north or south corner. If your foes don't spot this daring land grab, you can attempt a delayed Rush, or at the very least, keep them distracted while your friend pursues openings; you're also denying your opponents an expansion base!

161

2v2: THE DOCKS

This densely built-up urban region of Arcadia features several Sniper Towers protecting key areas. Each team begins in adjacent grassy areas, separated by a large and impressive conurbation, inaccessible via the ground and running from the southwest to northeast of the area. The four Sniper Towers are the only gap between the two halves of the map; expect combat to peak in this locale.

AREAS OF INTEREST

Starting Bases: 4
Empty Bases: 2

Neutral Bases: 4
Sniper Towers: 4

NOTE: In multiplayer, each supply crate randomly appears in one of two possible locations. All possible locations are shown.

🛡 Starting Base		📦 Supply Crates	
🔵 Starting Base		⚫ Sniper Towers	
🔺 Neutral Base		🔻 Unguarded Base (Empty Base)	

In terms of ground access roads, this is a U-shaped map with the cluster of Sniper Towers at the choke point (which is the only way to head into your opponent's half of the map if you're not flying in), so plan your tactics accordingly. As you're relatively safe from early Rushes at your bases, you can attempt to gain control of at least your "half" of the map. Attempt this by taking and holding the four Sniper Towers by quick and forceful maneuvering. Try to halt your foe inside their half of the map.

Attempt to take the Sniper Towers by training groups of infantry as early as possible, and garrison them in all four of the Sniper Towers. The importance of this cannot be understated; use them to keep enemy troops from moving into your half, which also stops them from Scouting your base early into the battle.

The empty base on your half of the map is easy to take and bolster. It can also provide exceptional help to the troops you have mulling around the Sniper Tower area. Simply send your troops from this newly acquired base, perhaps keeping your starting base as a stronghold for supplies and Reactors.

TIP

A more cunning trick is to immediately Scout around the Sniper Towers, and claim the empty base that is on your opponent's side of the map. This is a highly effective Rush strategy—as you start pumping out the troops to really hamper your foes' efforts and put them into a defensive posture—and it leaves your colleague time to build up more impressive forces to launch a separate attack.

TIP

If you're utilizing the Covenant, another possibility is an early Rush using both Covenant heroes. The fact that both your opponents' starting bases are next to each other allows each hero to cover a base while you teleport in more troops to aid in this devious trickery. Extremely annoying to the foes!

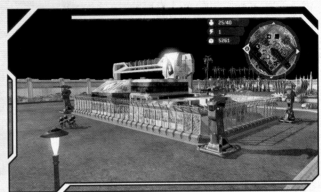

As the power struggle intensifies, you'll need to expand your bases. Although there are neutral infantry at the two neutral bases on either side of the map, these are usually easier to defeat than your foe, unless you're planning a Rush. While one of your team concentrates on maintaining enemy incursions from the Sniper Towers or building Turrets on the starting base nearest the middle of the southwest wall, you should pounce on both neutral bases. Then bulk up your forces and send them streaming into your foe's side of the map.

One tactic you should always watch out for are foes utilizing airborne troops. As air units effectively ignore all barriers, including the tall wall of buildings between both sides, they are exceptional for base raiding. They can effectively "guard" areas (especially inside your opponents' half of the map) until reinforcements arrive and generally cause a good deal of problems. Try building up a huge squadron of Vampires or Hornets and going for enemy base annihilation!

163

2v2: LABYRINTH

A maze of Forerunner structures creates a complex and challenging battlefield. The Forerunner Protector units may hold the key to victory. Both teams are separated by this strange complex, but there are ways around it, and the Protector Hooks on either edge augment your units with Healing, Combat, or Shielding capabilities.. Learn to control them and the central bridge for almost certain victory.

AREAS OF INTEREST

Starting Bases: 4
Forerunner Bases: 6

Protector Plant: 2
Sniper Towers: 8

Teleporters: 1 (1 entrance and 1 exit)

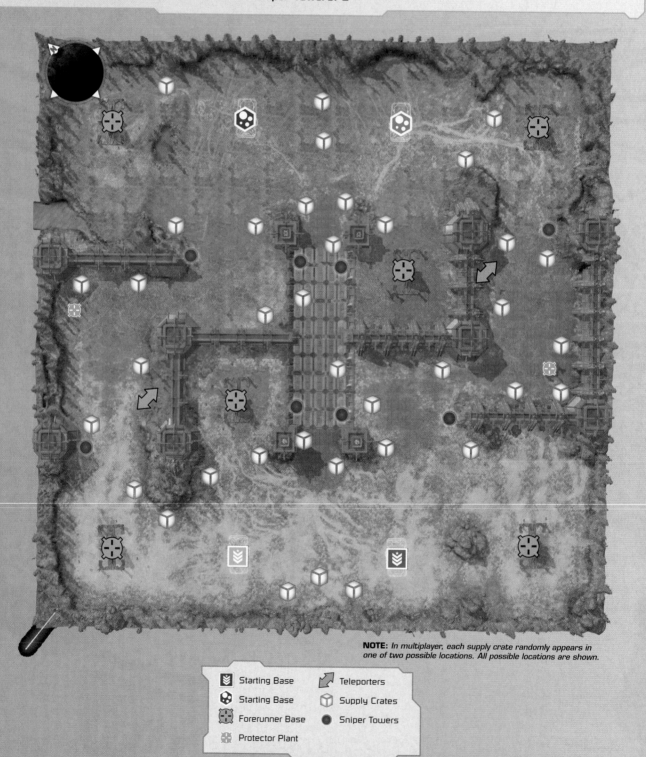

NOTE: *In multiplayer, each supply crate randomly appears in one of two possible locations. All possible locations are shown.*

Starting Base	Teleporters
Starting Base	Supply Crates
Forerunner Base	Sniper Towers
Protector Plant	

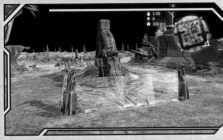

There are three Forerunner bases on each side of the map, and these are guarded by a few Sentinels and a fearsome Super Sentinel. These entities are violent when approached, and their laser technology from the craft and nearby Turrets is very damaging—the Super Sentinel's shots slow down your troops when they are struck. This means run-and-gun tactics are less certain. However, as your foes are facing the same problem, it might be wise for you and your teammate to band together, both tackling a nearby Forerunner base in half the usual time so you can crank out more troops, supplies, and Reactor levels.

Unique to this map is the Protector Plant. There are two available along the outer edges of the L-shaped path. Once you've defeated the Sentinels, you can build any of the three Sentinel Protectors listed below. Each adds 1 to your Population (be aware of this). You can only build one Protector of the same type at a time, but you can have all three building at once. Each Protector takes 30 seconds to build. The Plant does not require an infantry to man it. Simply keep a presence there and you can access one of the following:

Offensive Protector

Attach this to a single squad to have the Protector attack targets that are shooting the protected squad.

| 👤 1 | ⚡ 0 | 📦 100 |

Healing Protector

Attach this to a single squad to have the Protector heal the protected squad out of combat.

| 👤 1 | ⚡ 0 | 📦 100 |

Shield Protector

Attach this to a single squad to have the Protector generate a small shield around the protected squad.

| 👤 1 | ⚡ 0 | 📦 100 |

Naturally, a group of the same troops can be given the same or different chaperone Protectors. The Hooks are incredibly useful and are a great tactical location to hold, as the Protectors can augment your tough, friendly units such as Scorpions, Hornets, Vampires, or Covenant Leaders. Only one Protector can be assigned per unit, but having, say, a Healing Protector constantly keeping a Covenant Leader alive makes him even more dangerous. Similarly, assign a Protector to each Spartan, and they become incredibly adept at killing anything! Let your foes quake with fear as a Protector Scarab stomps over them!

Rushing is not recommended on this map, as both allies begin close to each other and can reinforce the other's base if it is attacked. You are better to wait or catch your foes unawares. Instead, using Turtling tactics is the most effective plan; simply lie in wait and build up your base (optionally Locking it so your foe isn't aware of how strong your forces are) until your foe mistakenly tries to attack you. If your foes are taking their time, gradually creep up and control the map until you meet resistance from them.

The central bridge with the labyrinth on either side is a great place to Rush to control and garrison some infantry troops in the four Sniper Towers. This slows down an enemy Rush and provides an early warning system that the enemy is on their way.

TIP

Don't forget the Teleporter, as this can allow your forces to flee pursuers, quickly reach the Protector Hook on the map's opposite side, or devise cunning plans: For example, have your friend bring a massive army up one side of the labyrinth's L-shaped path while you head up the other. Then instead of attacking from either side, head your forces into the Teleporter, and follow your friend up to bolster his units and crush with overwhelming force!

165

2v2: REPOSITORY

With many supplies up for grabs in the middle and dangerous enemies lurking everywhere, the fight for control of this region will be nasty, brutal, and short. The enemies in question are Forerunner Sentinels, which are adept at killing and guarding several bases and the central Sentinel Hook. Timing becomes paramount as you try to control the supplies and therefore the destiny of this battle!

AREAS OF INTEREST

Starting Bases: 4   **Empty Bases:** 2
Forerunner Bases: 4   **Sentinel Hook:** 1

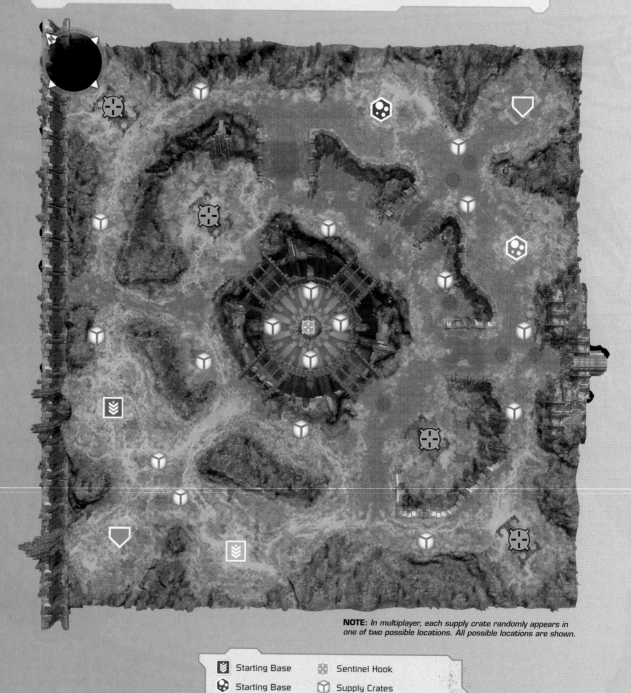

NOTE: *In multiplayer, each supply crate randomly appears in one of two possible locations. All possible locations are shown.*

Starting Base		Sentinel Hook
Starting Base		Supply Crates
Forerunner Base		Unguarded Base (Empty Base)

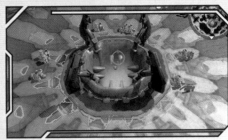

 The line of four Forerunner bases running north to south across this map are the toughest of the neutral bases to overrun and claim for yourself. With this in mind, it is always a good idea to watch what your opponents are up to: If they try attacking one of these bases, you should either sandwich them in and blast them; let them finish and then charge in to finish them off to claim the base for yourself; or head to a Forerunner base with enough overwhelming firepower to deal with the Sentinels, the Super Sentinel, and any sneak attacks from your foe. Try to get your friend to back you up, and aim for the outer bases first, because they have less traffic to worry about.

TIP

Before you head off to tackle a Forerunner base, choose a player whose job it is to provide supplies, and have them take over the empty base between your starting bases. Keep this as a supply or Reactor stronghold before you focus on the Forerunner bases or central platform. Or, you can grab the undefended base and execute a Boom strategy.

 An odd central platform with a Sentinel Hook dominates the central part of the map. It's advisable to send your finest Scouting forces (Warthogs, Ghosts, and infantry) in to defeat the Sentinels guarding it before massing some forces there yourself. Remember to either Scout and attack early (ideally with your friend backing you up), or wait for a foe to attack and then mop up afterward. The supply crates left here and the Supply Hook are a huge advantage. Take them!

There are also neutral troops in the eastern and western sections of this area; they release supply crates when defeated.

 The Sentinel Hook, which is unique to this map, allows you to construct two new units that are devastating and feature weaponry similar to that of a UNSC Hawk's. The Sentinel (which takes 15 seconds to build) and the Super Sentinel (which takes 30) are both excellent flying weapons; the Super Sentinel in particular is an outstanding asset to your offensive line. The Super Sentinel fires a powerful laser that slows down enemy vehicles; it is best utilized to back up troops when fighting enemy vehicles. Don't forget that Sentinels use up your Population like your other troops!

Sentinel

 A flying Forerunner unit, the Sentinels inflict corrosive damage with a dangerous beam weapon.

Super Sentinel

 The Forerunner Super Sentinel has the unique ability to slow down enemy units while also preempting their attacks.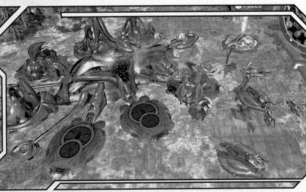

167

As you might have guessed by our recommendation of utilizing Super Sentinels, air units are the troop type of choice for this map. If you're attacking foes from the ground, the ridges and ramps are dangerous, and there are only three road entrances to each starting base. Instead, fly in and harass your foe into submission!

TIP

If you want to annoy your foes and therefore shake their confidence, try sneaking in a Ghost or Warthog to the map's opposite corner, behind both enemy starting bases. This is an even better idea if you're playing as the Covenant, because once you create a base behind (but in between) your foes, you can build a couple of Shield Generators and then crank out offensive troops or turrets to really hamper your enemies' expansion plans!

2v2: TERMINAL MORAINE

Sections of the map are accessible only by timed light bridges. Watch for the bridges to start blinking—any units on the bridges when they turn off are doomed. Time your journey across these bridges (to the northwest and southeast); each bridge turns off and on at one-minute intervals. Also of note are the four neutral bases on the outer corners and Sniper Towers at the edge of the bisecting road.

AREAS OF INTEREST

Starting Bases: 4
Neutral Bases: 6

Reactors: 2
Socket Hooks: 2

Sniper Towers: 12

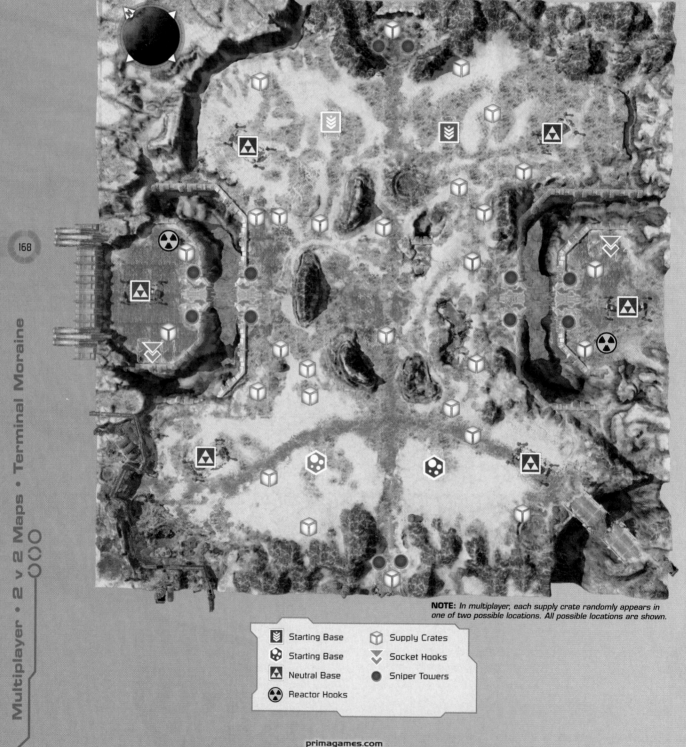

NOTE: *In multiplayer, each supply crate randomly appears in one of two possible locations. All possible locations are shown.*

Starting Base
Starting Base
Neutral Base
Reactor Hooks

Supply Crates
Socket Hooks
Sniper Towers

The lack of terrain, the straight road linking your bases to your enemies', and the fact that neutral forces are on either side of the main thoroughfare means that Rushing tactics work exceedingly well here; you should try them and prepare for them yourself.

Timing is everything early on in this map, and at least one team member should keep careful note of when the battle reaches the one-minute mark: After grabbing a supply crate or two, head to one of the light bridges and cross it, timing the drive so the bridge appears just as you reach it, thus letting you beat any enemy across. Once on the other side, avoid the Reactor and neutral base completely, and instead move to the Socket Hook and build two structures of your choosing: This is an easy way to gain an excellent advantage early on.

TIP

The Barracks is an excellent choice when you reach the Socket Hooks for another reason: There are four Sniper Towers, two on either side of the light bridge. Keeping upgraded infantry troops on these platforms is a great plan, but try this only if your foe is determined to reach you—you don't want to waste four of your Population if you're trying, say, a Rush strategy.

TIP

Air units are incredibly useful around the light bridges. They can be used to wipe out ground forces milling about, waiting for the bridge to appear; they can easily attack the neutral bases, providing fire support for infantry determined to take the nearby Reactor; and they can fly over the crevasse that the light bridge spans and head by the quickest means to any location necessary.

The six neutral bases on the map give you options, as they are the only way you can expand your bases aside from the Socket Hooks. The two bases, one on each of the "islands" reached by light bridge, are a

good way to send troops in if you've set up a Barracks, Vehicle Depot, or Air Pad (likely the first option). Creating a Barracks is additionally a great plan, because you can sneak infantry around the neutral base to claim the Reactor. If your opponent has done the same, the enemy will find it very difficult to counter you.

The other four neutral bases, one at each corner of the map, are spaced out far enough to be attacked easily and are a good second base if you decide not to try for the Socket Hooks across the light bridges.

CAUTION

There is a real risk of spreading yourself too thin on this map, due to "trapping" yourself on either of the light bridge islands. Counteract this by using air units, and make sure you haven't left any place poorly defended. Or better yet, find an opening when your foe makes a tactical movement error!

The two pairs of Sniper Towers on this map are rarely used, as they lead to a dead end, a few squads of neutral troops, and some supply crates. Clear out the crates, but the Sniper Towers should remain empty. The easiest (and most cunning) way to dispose of the neutral troops at the Sniper Towers is to take some vehicles or anti-infantry units and lay waste there before claiming the large rewards.

The large open tundra surrounding all four starting bases allows for a huge buildup of troops, and you can elect to Turtle and then send in a large force of upgraded vehicles. However, another possibility is for both teammates to create a vast army of Warthogs or Ghosts. These vehicles are helpful when controlling the neutral base sites, and a few of them can quickly be peeled off to help your cause; grab supply crates en route to a swarm into your foe's defenses.

3v3: EXILE

Impassable terrain creates a nested trio of rings that defines this large battlefield. More base sites are found on the outermost ring, but controlling the center is tactically superior. With an empty base for each player and a quartet of Reactors ready to be hooked to your bases, you have many choices when deciding what to take over. Boom, Tech, or Rush? Make sure your team knows your preferred plan!

AREAS OF INTEREST

Starting Bases: 6
Empty Bases: 6

Flood Bases: 4
Reactor Hooks: 4

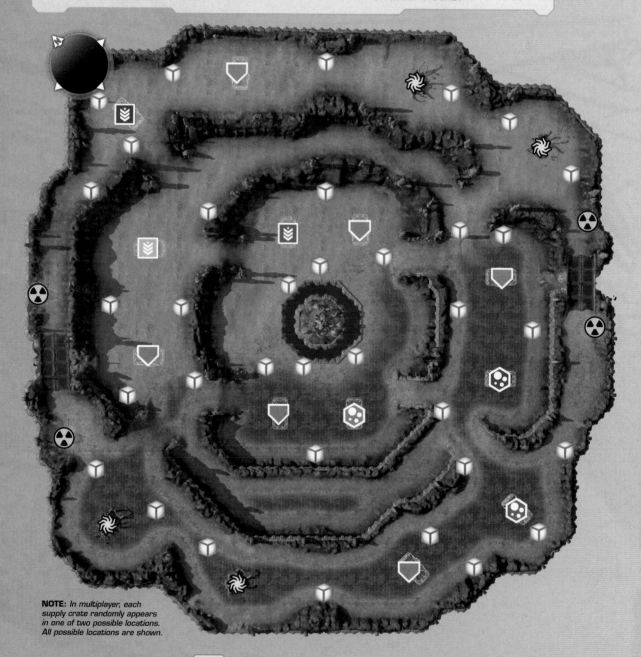

NOTE: In multiplayer, each supply crate randomly appears in one of two possible locations. All possible locations are shown.

▼ Starting Base		⬡ Supply Crates	
⬡ Starting Base		▽ Unguarded Base (Empty Base)	
☢ Reactor Hooks		🕸 Flood Base	

Each of your team-mates and your enemies begins at a base, and the closer it is to the map's center, the more dangerous the base. The farther out you are to the map's edge, the more you should consider providing fire support and supplies to the innermost colleague, who is separated from the enemy only by the central plateau with the indestructible "Flood Island" colony.

> **TIP**
>
> Your first plan as a team is to instinctively know which supply crates each of you are going for, and then snag them without everyone heading to the same crate cluster.

When you begin, grab the undefended base sites. Increase the chances of obtaining them by quickly sending two players' worth of forces during the initial stages of the battle to secure the empty bases closest to your foes, before snagging the empty outer bases. From this point on, the preferred tactics involve Booming and Teching; this map is designed primarily for this purpose.

> **TIP**
>
> Try sending in units before your foe gets the empty center base established, then waylay the build here while your allies Boom and Tech. Stopping your foes from increasing their forces in a streamlined manner is a good idea here.
>
> Also try the "sling strategy." Let the two allies on the middle and outer rings feed the central player supplies while he builds forces to overrun the enemy. This plan can really be effective if your central player can upgrade, build from depots and the Firebase, and send in troops to fight.

There are four secondary Reactor Hooks with a light neutral troop contingent guarding them. They are on either side of the outer ring path to the east and west and are easy to miss if you aren't Scouting the map properly. These should be immediately secured with Warthogs, Ghosts, and infantry. Try moving to the Reactor closer to your foes' side of the map and hold it; group forces here to dissuade them from attempting to take a Reactor. If you can claim all four Reactors for your team, you can seriously Boom and Tech.

> **TIP**
>
> Your foes aren't going to sit back and let you keep the Reactors you commandeer, so work closely with your allies about defending these structures properly. Pelican Transports (for the UNSC) or a Covenant Leader teleporting troops to these general Reactor Hook locations help to secure them. You may wish to give one of your team (either the player on the outer or middle ring path) the job of keeping these Reactors.

> **NOTE**
>
> The four Flood Colony bases are usually ignored, and although it is recommended you attack them later into battle, you can try establishing a base there early and launching a surprise attack from the map's east or west corner. However, the casualties make this plan viable only if your foes are in a weakened state or aren't being aggressive.

Aside from the Boom and Tech methods, this map is also excellent for Rushing tactics. If you can quickly call upon an ally (perhaps while your third teammate claims Reactors or empty bases or interferes with your foes' movements) to join you in the central plateau, you can Rush around the stagnant Flood Colony and batter the two opposite bases, taking care to learn and understand the areas where your foes' other allies are likely to head in from. A concentrated Rush early on can really be advantageous and allow you to capture the four central bases.

Air units and other troops that are highly mobile are extremely effective on this map, due to its large size and numerous

rocky outcrops that segment the paths into rings. Air units can quickly and efficiently control the Reactor Hooks, backing up the infantry on the ground by laying down supporting fire on those seeking to reclaim the Reactors.

> **TIP**
>
> If you're utilizing the Covenant, cultivate a force of Locusts and place them at long range (but within range of striking a foe's base), such as on upper pathways above a base. Be sure to back them up so your foe has to wade through other troop types, by which time your foe's base is likely to be in pieces. Locusts can inflict sizable damage this way, as long as they are supported.

171

3v3: FORT DEEN

Named for a famous UNSC colonel who broke a Covenant siege, this divided map features highly defendable lanes, but strategically placed teleporters offer clever attackers alternatives.

AREAS OF INTEREST

Starting Bases: 6
Neutral Bases: 8

Teleporters: 2 (2 entrance/exits each)
Sniper Towers: 10

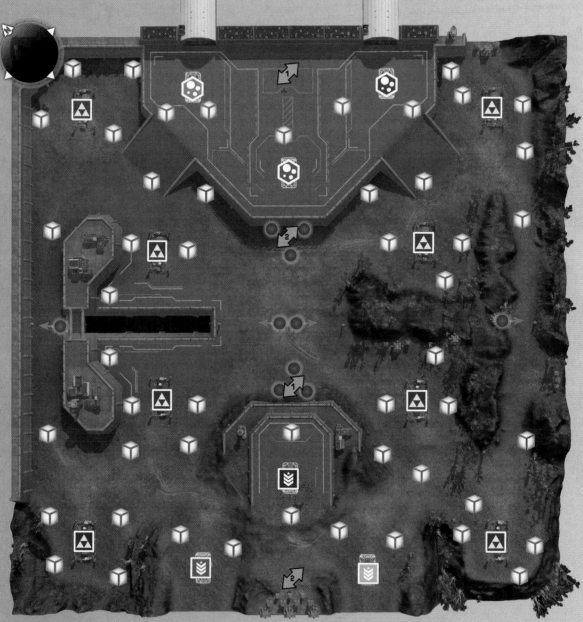

NOTE: *In multiplayer, each supply crate randomly appears in one of two possible locations. All possible locations are shown.*

Starting Base	Supply Crates
Starting Base	Sniper Towers
Neutral Base	Sniper Tower (with barrier)
Teleporters	

Chatting to your two allies is extremely important from the moment you begin battle. As your three starting bases are placed in a triangle and on raised ground to the northeast and southwest, you are afforded a little additional time to Turtle and Boom. The biggest consideration is the forward-center base. The player on this base can concentrate on building forces or sending additional supplies to the two outer bases. One player should move to man the three Sniper Towers directly below the forward base to avoid the enemy using the Teleporter. This pushes enemy attacks to the ramps on either side. The forward-center base needs no Turrets early in the game, as the two outer bases should catch incoming foes.

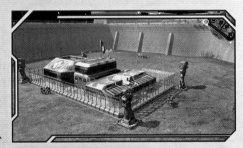

There are eight neutral bases. None of them are empty, meaning you must expend as many unit losses as your foes when tackling the neutral troops guarding them, a tactic you must try if you're attempting to Boom. Bring additional fire support from your ally to shorten the time it takes to tackle a neutral base; then take the neutral bases on the outer corner of the map's rear, as they are farther from your foe and less troublesome to defend.

As the conflict intensifies, your forces should gingerly advance toward the map's center. Have your preferred troop builder pour out vehicles and infantry to easily tackle one of the two neutral bases on either side of the central "barrier" zone. This allows you to maintain and hold the area before advancing across to take the other two neutral bases in the map's middle. Controlling all four of these central neutral bases ultimately decides the winning team during a protracted conflict, so make plans to head here and keep these bases.

TIP

Naturally, one way to do this is to venture as far into enemy territory as possible (for example, the neutral bases in the map's middle but on the enemy's side) and as early as possible. Claim and hold both neutral bases if you can, and then "backfill" the barriers and bases on your side of the map, taking them over afterward. This cuts off the enemy's movements and allows your third player to quickly build and attack neutral bases on your side of the map without enemy attack.

Rushing is extremely difficult on this map, due to the huge distance between opposing sides and the potential energy wall barriers across the map's middle. However, Rushing is perhaps the last plan your foe may be expecting, so use this to your advantage. It succeeds only if all three allies are working in tandem: Build a Warthog army as soon as possible. Have one ally Rush the left ramp or grassy bank and another rush the right. The third ally should Rush the Teleporters, appearing behind the middle base. After that, pick at least one base and hope for the best!

TIP

Later into a hard-fought conflict, air units are the troop type of choice, due to the long distances involved.

Controlling the Sniper Towers with the energy barriers that stretch across the map's middle can stop (or at least waylay) any enemy infantry units from crossing onto your side of the map. This is a great plan early on. You might want to order your two allies to each man two of the Sniper Towers with wall barriers. Once the walls are up, you can backfill your side of the map and take the neutral bases with some added protection.

Until your foes build air units, the only way infantry can be transported across the barriers is via a Pelican Transport. The Covenant can't afford this luxury and must rely on blasting the defenders from the Sniper Towers the barriers are attached to.

3v3: FROZEN VALLEY

A wide-open map, this cold wasteland features two bonus Reactors and a Forerunner Spire of Healing. The battlefield features large expanses of flat tundra with dotted rocky outcrops to trundle around or fly over, so expect your foes to encroach on the neutral bases that wreak havoc with early Rushes. If your enemies are relentless, they may be healing at the Spire and returning for more punishment!

AREAS OF INTEREST

Starting Bases: 6
Neutral Bases: 10

Reactor Hooks: 2
Spire of Healing: 1

Sniper Towers: 4

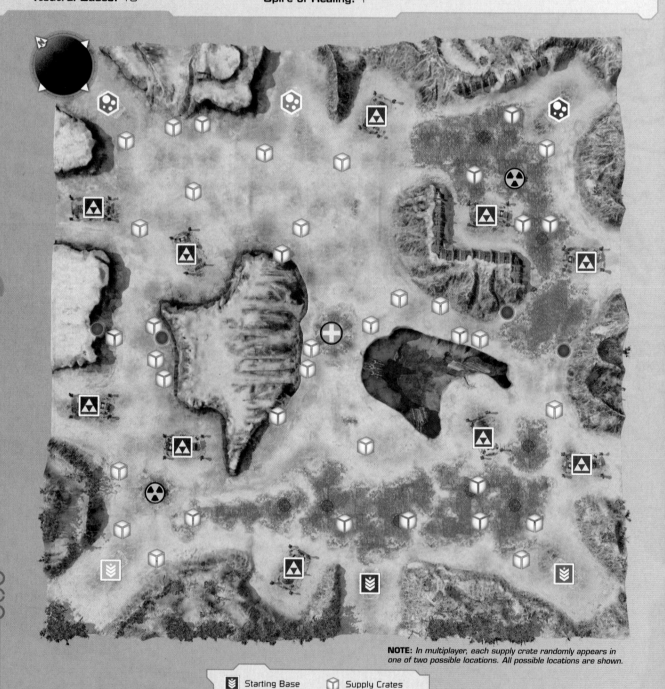

NOTE: *In multiplayer, each supply crate randomly appears in one of two possible locations. All possible locations are shown.*

- Starting Base
- Starting Base
- Neutral Base
- Reactor Hooks
- Supply Crates
- Sniper Towers
- Spire of Healing

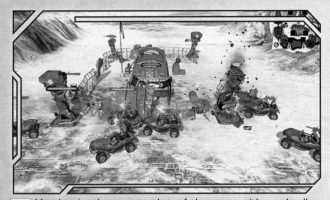

Hook. This is easy to take down, and it offers a simple way to Tech up. However, before you bring infantry to man the Reactor, destroy the neutral base's Turret that is nearest to the Reactor so it doesn't fire on you. You don't have to destroy the neutral base yet, just the Turret. Then lightly defend the Reactor with one infantry unit; the enemy won't reach you for a while. Now Tech up!

You begin along one edge of the map with each ally in a base along this edge. All three are very close to a neutral base. It is usually a good idea to each take a neutral base as early as possible. Consider Rushing, as the map has large flat areas for your Warthogs or Ghosts to dash through, but the lengthy journey means you'll likely be spotted and face retaliation. Alternatively, it is wise to Tech and Boom, with the ally adjacent to the Reactor Hook doing most of the building. The Sniper Towers aren't particularly useful, because they are too far from a location you'll end up defending; therefore, use them only as an early warning system.

Controlling the Spire of Healing is a straightforward and incredibly cunning plan, as your troops are constantly bathed in healing energy and can pick off damaged or wounded enemies as they try to reach this location. Keep a contingent here and reinforce it; the central location and large open areas mean reaching this location is easy.

As with other 3v3 maps, you should use a sling strategy to win a protracted battle. This involves funneling your supply resources to one ally, who spends his time creating a huge army with a high Tech level. Naturally, the receiver of the supplies should be the ally who has already Commandeered the Reactor Hook (so the Teching takes less time and supplies). Slinging works superbly, because your foes are far away and apart, and there are usually neutral bases between you and them, giving you more time to Tech up and less chance to face a Rush.

TIP

The other use of the Spire of Healing is obvious: engage the enemy and then retreat to heal before attacking again. This is much more proficient and quick than building additional troops to replace those defeated by your foes.

Scorpions and, to a lesser extent, Wraiths or any other vehicle or troop with a large number of Hit Points are much more useful on this map simply because they can be pulled from combat and healed at the Spire of Healing.

TIP

The troops of choice for a sling strategy? For the UNSC, the Teching player should be Anders, as her upgrades are half-price. Work on building an unstoppable army of Hawks! For the Covenant, a squadron of Banshees can really whale on your foes!

TIP

If you aren't about to wage a land war, take to the skies. Air units are effective at attacking the enemy's bases, located in mountainous terrain. Ground vehicles have difficulty reaching some of these locations, and the direct paths allow for easy and efficient escape routes that ground units cannot travel over.

The initial stages of battle should involve one of your allies almost instantaneously taking a Reactor

Secrets abound, from the Forerunner's hidden maps to the glowing skulls you collect as you progress. The following Appendices provide instant and gratifying knowledge of exactly what can be achieved, where all the Skulls lurk, the resting place of 15 Black Boxes, and offers a complete Timeline of events, with notes on how to unlock the Timeline elements where necessary. Classified information awaits.

APPENDIX I: ACHIEVEMENTS

	Achievement Name	Description	Points	Campaign-Related	Skirmish-Related	Live-Related	Misc.
	Meet Sergeant Forge	Complete Mission 1 on any difficulty (Secret)	10	✓	—	—	—
	Ice Warriors	Complete Act I on any difficulty (Secret)	40	✓	—	—	—
	Key to Pirth	Complete Act II on any difficulty (Secret)	50	✓	—	—	—
	Ugly Is Only Skin Deep	Complete Act III on any difficulty (Secret)	70	✓	—	—	—
	No Way Home?	Complete Act IV on any difficulty (Secret)	70	✓	—	—	—
	Adjudicate the Arbiter	Complete the Campaign on Heroic difficulty	30	✓	—	—	—
	Detour the Great Journey	Complete the Campaign on Legendary difficulty	50	✓	—	—	—
	Momma's Boy	Get a Gold medal on any mission	5	✓	—	—	—
	Crushed Colors	Improve your score in any Campaign mission	10	✓	—	—	—
	Mr. Punctual	Finish all missions under Par Time on Heroic difficulty	15	✓	—	—	—
	Own Worst Enemy	Get a Gold medal with all Debuff Skulls active	20	✓	—	—	—
	Wall of Recognition †	Get Gold medals in entire campaign	30	✓	—	—	—
	Epic Grinder †	Obtain a Lifetime Campaign Score over 1,000,000	40	✓	—	—	—
	Everything's Better with Bacon †	Mission 1: Ram 50 Grunts with Warthogs	5	✓	—	—	—
	Endless Fun †	Mission 2: Destroy every Methane Tank	5	✓	—	—	—
	Covenant "Hot Drop" †	Mission 3: Kill at least 5 Covenant units with the bridge	5	✓	—	—	—
	The Real Winner †	Mission 4: Save Adam	5	✓	—	—	—
	He's Got the Jack †	Mission 5: Jack 6 Covenant vehicles	5	✓	—	—	—
	Rhino Hugger †	Mission 6: Successfully protect every Rhino	5	✓	—	—	—
	Micro Manager †	Mission 7: Do not destroy any Power Nodes	5	✓	—	—	—
	Ramblin' Man †	Mission 8: Use Elephants to train 100 infantry	5	✓	—	—	—
	Sweet Naptime †	Mission 9: Put every colony in Hibernation mode at the same time	5	✓	—	—	—
	The Procrastinator †	Mission 10: Disrupt all tractor beams	5	✓	—	—	—
	Battened Down the Hatches †	Mission 11: Save all the Air Locks	5	✓	—	—	—
	Handy with Tools †	Mission 12: Repair the Power Core in less than 4 minutes	5	✓	—	—	—

Achievement Name	Description	Points	Campaign-Related	Skirmish-Related	Live-Related	Misc.
Beaming with Pride †	Mission 13: Destroy 25 units with the Scarab	5	✓	—	—	—
Didn't Get to Second Base †	Mission 14: Don't claim any extra bases	5	✓	—	—	—
Thinkin' about My Doorbell †	Mission 15: Open the doors in order	5	✓	—	—	—
Backscratcher	Complete any Campaign mission in Co-op mode	10	✓	—	—	—
OMG BFF FTW	Complete entire Campaign in Co-op mode	40	✓	—	—	—
Playin' the Field †	Win a Skirmish game with every leader	15	—	✓	—	—
Gallivant around the Galaxy †	Win a game on every Skirmish map	25	—	✓	—	—
Empire Builder †	Win a game in every Skirmish game mode	5	—	✓	—	—
Titan †	Get 100,000 points in any Skirmish game	15	—	✓	—	—
Big Al's Scooter	Win a Heroic Skirmish game against the AI in under 10 minutes	10	—	✓	—	—
My Virtual Friends Love Me	Win a 3v3 Skirmish game with 2 AI allies	10	—	✓	—	—
Walk-Off Winner	Use one of the 6 major Leader Powers to destroy an enemy's last unit	30	—	✓	—	—
2 Bugs are Better Than 1	Win a Skirmish game with dual Scarabs	10	—	✓	—	—
Penny Pincher	Get a winning high score with 10 or less squads against the Heroic AI	10	—	✓	—	—
NOOb nO MOr3	Win a Matchmade Skirmish game on Xbox LIVE	10	—	—	✓	—
So Lonely at the Top	Win and have the highest score in a Matchmade Skirmish game on Xbox LIVE	20	—	—	✓	—
Basically Naïve	Obtain the Recruit rank on Xbox LIVE	10	—	—	✓	—
Officer on Deck	Obtain the Lieutenant rank on Xbox LIVE	30	—	—	✓	—
Running the Show	Obtain the General rank on Xbox LIVE	50	—	—	✓	—
Alas, Poor Andrew Thomas	Collect your first Skull	5	✓	—	—	—
Graverobber †	Collect all Skulls	30	✓	—	—	—
Halo Academic	Unlocked 20 Timeline Events	15	—	—	—	✓
Halo Historian †	Unlock All Timeline Events	40	—	—	—	✓
Ready for the Sequel	100% completion	75	—	—	—	✓
24 Hours of Quality	Played Halo Wars for at least 24 total hours	20	—	—	—	✓

† Complete all Achievements marked with "†" for "Ready for the Sequel" Achievement.

APPENDIX II: SKULL LOCATIONS

	Mission	Skull Name	Skull Location
	01	**Look Daddy!**	Left side of the last battle area before you head into Alpha Base.
	02	**Grunt Birthday Party**	South edge of Alpha Base, inside the walls of the base.
	03	**Cowbell**	All the way back in the circular platform where you save Forge and Anders.
	04	**Wuv Woo**	On the map's right side, below the Covenant base. It is a little past the top of the stairs.
	05	**Fog**	The overpass on left side keeps going to the map's top left corner. It is on the overpass.
	06	**Sickness**	Just inside the big hangar behind your base.
	07	**Rebel Sympathizer**	Left side of map, on the edge of the battlefield area, on a ledge that juts out over a canyon, next to a Power Node.
	08	**Rebel Supporter**	Far right of where Echo is taken over by the Flood. On a small ridge.

	Mission	Skull Name	Skull Location
	09	**Rebel Leader**	Not far from the base on top of a plateau near a burning Covenant ship.
	10	**Catch**	On the island to the southeast. You need a flying unit to reach it.
	11	**Sugar Cookies**	Floating in front of the ship. You need a flying unit to grab this.
	12	**Boomstick**	On the superstructure on Spirit of Fire at the far end from the Power Core, above the main deck on a platform (must be reached with a flying unit).
	13	**Pain Train**	On one of the Flood vents. It is up where the Flood come from when you try to enter the first Pelican.
	14	**Bountiful Harvest**	Behind and to the left of the second Covenant base.
	15	**Emperor**	Behind the Flood base, way in the map's rear, northeast on the minimap.

APPENDIX III: BLACK BOX LOCATIONS

Mission	Black Box Location
01	Under the last bridge before you reach the back gate of Alpha base
02	Up in the area through the Covenant shield where you can get several supply crates. Top left of the map.
03	Over to the left of start point, near a Pelican crash site. Outside the Relic.
04	At the base of the elevator tower where you can save Adam. Near the controls to let Adam out.
05	Just off the main road down the first available ramp. It is tucked behind a destroyed Pelican.
06	The far side of the map, where you must transport the third Rhino by Pelican.
07	Right side of map, in a cavelike alcove with many supply crates.
08	Near the big Brute fireline at start. Up on the ridge to the right.

Mission	Black Box Location
09	Straight out from the base ramp on the map's other side.
10	It is with Bravo Platoon, the middle platoon that you must get picked up.
11	On the left rear of the ship, on the wings that slant down. You need a flying unit to grab this.
12	Left edge of the Spirit of Fire, not far from the Power Core building, along the Power Core's left side.
13	Up on a ledge near the second set of Teleporters. Behind the Covenant base.
14	Up and left at the top of the first ramp. It is on the edge of the actual ramp.
15	In the northern part the map, directly across from where you start. Between Covenant base and Flood area.

APPENDIX IV: COMPLETE HALO WARS TIMELINE AND UNLOCK CONDITION

16 January 2498

Unlock Condition: Complete a game on the Docks.
Arcadia Colony opens the DSRA (Deep Space Research Array), designed to research and study extremely high-gravity events, such as black holes and other areas that exploratory vessels cannot visit directly. The DSRA is eventually destroyed by the Covenant during the initial attack on Arcadia in 2531.

2506

Unlock Condition: Unlocked at the start.
Project ORION, the original SPARTAN project—the first attempt by the Colonial Military Administration to create and train teams of supersoldiers for covert military operations in the Outer Colonies—is deactivated. Though the Spartans are effective, their abilities fall short of original expectations, and they are far too expensive to develop and field. The soldiers in the program are reassigned to various special operations units.

17 August 2517

Unlock Condition: Unlocked at the start.
Dr. Catherine Halsey and her aide Lt. Jacob Keyes covertly inspect one of the first test subjects for the mysterious "SPARTAN-II" project. The prospective candidate—a six-year-old child named "John"—is ideal for the project. Halsey arranges for the subject to be covertly conscripted.

23 September 2517

Unlock Condition: Unlocked at the start.
Halsey's SPARTAN-II project begins, with primary research conducted on the planet Reach in the Epsilon Eridani system. Seventy-five children of both sexes are subjected to an intense program of physical and mental retraining and technological augmentation, including reinforced skeletal structure and improved musculature.

20 July 2520

Unlock Condition: Collect Black Box in Mission 04.
Captain Alexander, the last civilian captain of the Spirit of Fire, retires from active duty at the conclusion of the Verent mission. The ship is requisitioned by the UNSC and scheduled for refit.

1 September 2520

Unlock Condition: Collect Black Box in Mission 05.
Spirit of Fire completes an extensive refit at the Reach orbital shipyards before entering active military duty as a ground support vessel, initially detailed with providing ground support for the upcoming operation TREBUCHET.

Edict of the Office of the High Prophet of Restraint

Unlock Condition: Complete a game on Pirth Outskirts.
It is known the Kig-Yar ship Pitiless has brought forth an Unclean Being's corpse. Hear now, all Kig-Yar vessels are to be searched. Let faithful Sangheili lead teams of Unggoy to all Kig-Yar ships and seek further evidence of the Unclean. It is done.

Edict of the Office of the High Prophet of Tolerance

Unlock Condition: Collect Black Box in Mission 11.
Hear now that 500 teams are to be formed to study the language of the Unclean. Each team to consist of the most clever and most educated Unggoy and Sangheili. These teams to speak only the Unclean language among themselves. The Unclean language to be taught to all military strike teams, that the foe shall be vulnerable.

Excerpt from *The Punished Deeds*, Vol. III

Unlock Condition: Complete a game with the Prophet as your leader.
The youngest of the new Prophets, Regret ascended by manipulating and blackmailing those around him. Regret was one of the Prophets who visited the Oracle, an ancient AI, where it was learned that the humans were somehow connected to the Forerunner race and that the very foundation of Covenant belief was flawed. Their decision to eradicate humanity to hide these facts is debated to this day.

Edict of the Offices of the High Prophet of Truth

Unlock Condition: Complete a game on Chasms.
All within the Covenant, hear now and obey. Weapons and ships of war to descend upon the inhabited world of Epsilon Indi. Strike with all force. No intelligent survivors may remain, upon severest penalty.

3 February 2525

Unlock Condition: Unlocked at the start.
Contact with the agricultural colony Harvest is lost. Initial attempts to reestablish contact fail. The worst is feared. Meanwhile, in orbiting ONI facilities near Reach, surgical procedures to augment the SPARTAN-II candidates are about to begin. Many candidates will "wash out"—dead or crippled by the process.

Excerpt from *The Punished Deeds*, Vol. III

Unlock Condition: Complete a game with the Arbiter as your leader.
This new Arbiter did not fear death, but even he was afraid of what was inside the relics of the Ancients. Before he entered a relic, he would send in a squad of Unggoy to check for any signs of danger. If all was clear, they would live, but at the slightest sign of trouble, the Arbiter would detonate plasma bombs attached to the methane tanks.

20 April 2525

Unlock Condition: Unlocked at the start.
Contact with the scout ship "Argo," sent to investigate the problem on Reach, is lost. A larger, armed battlegroup is prepared in response.

Excerpt from *The Punished Deeds*, Vol. III

Unlock Condition: Complete a game with the Arbiter as your leader.
The new Arbiter was almost immediately tested. An installation of the Ancients near remnants of a massive space installation that was thought to contain a "key," an object that was believed could be used to activate technology. The installation was heavily defended by a growing faction of Elites who did not agree with the ways of the new Prophets. The Arbiter killed them in a battle that raged for days. A key was never found, but the dissident movement was silenced.

7 October 2525

Unlock Condition: Unlocked at the start.
Battle Group D arrives at Harvest and engages the Covenant but is forced to jump away back to Reach after two of its three ships are destroyed by a single Covenant vessel. An audio-only message was transmitted by the Covenant during this engagement: "Your destruction is the will of the gods...and we are their instrument." It is believed that because the message was transmitted in English, the Covenant have been studying humanity for some time.

1 November 2525

Unlock Condition: Complete a game on Frozen Valley.
The UNSC military goes on full alert and begins making preparations to move in and retake Harvest. All Colonial Military Administration combat forces are immediately placed under NavCom/UniCom "for the duration of the crisis." The SPARTAN-II project is accelerated to its final phase: MJOLNIR, a new form of powered armor specifically designed for Spartan use.

181

27 November 2525

Unlock Condition: Complete a game on Tundra

All SPARTAN-IIs are transported to the Damascus Materials Testing Facility on Chi Ceti-4 to be equipped with MJOLNIR armor. They only have a matter of hours to test suit operation before an alien vessel enters the system and attacks their orbiting support ship. In the ensuing battle, three Spartans board the enemy ship and encounter their first Covenant soldiers, capturing an energy shield gauntlet. One Spartan is lost in the engagement.

Edict of the Office of the High Prophet of Regret

Unlock Condition: Complete a game with the Prophet as your leader.

Hear now the infamy in Chi Ceti system. Due to lack of faith on the part of the crew of the vessel Unrelenting, a band of Unclean were able to board and slay. A Science Lance is ordered to be formed to study the captured weapons and armor that mitigation can be taken in future.

2526

Unlock Condition: Unlocked at the start.

At the Battle of Harvest, Vice Admiral Preston Cole's war fleet—one of the largest ever mobilized—engages the alien warship responsible for the decimation of the colony, scoring a victory. Only Cole's last-minute tactical inspiration turns the tide of battle. Upon his return to Earth, Cole is promoted to the rank of Admiral.

Edict of the Office of the High Prophet of Regret

Unlock Condition: Complete a game on Terminal Moraine.

Let the Victory of Epsilon Indi be celebrated by fasting and prayer. Unggoy and Kig-Yar food rations to be eliminated for the next three work periods. Sangheili and Jiralhanae to spend two rest periods in public prayer. All attend the public monitors at the sounding of five bells to observe the execution of those who failed their duty at the Victory.

30 January 2528

Unlock Condition: Complete a game with Cutter as your leader.

Captain Cutter turns down a command position on board the destroyer class ship The Prophecy. His decision to stay close to his family prompted an ONI psychological examination that determined that while fit to command, his family ties worked against any larger military career.

Incident Report 16-196901

Unlock Condition: Complete a game with the Brute Chieftain as your leader.

Security team called to Jiralhanae Chieftain's quarters at third bell, second shift. Team arrived at location to find quarters door torn from its frame and five chunks of unidentified biological matter in hallway (see attached diagram). Upon inspection, biological matter confirmed as parts of two Unggoy from Deck Four Kitchens. Chieftain was calm and responsive; stated that delivery of his midday meal was not to specifications (thorn beast overdone, dipping sauce insufficient). Maintenance crew notified; official reprimand of D4 Kitchen supervisor filed.

17 August 2530

Unlock Condition: Complete a game with Forge as your leader.

Sergeant Forge incarcerated for assaulting a senior officer. His career would have been over if Admiral Cole had not intervened and seen that the investigation was fair and aboveboard. The senior officer eventually faced a court martial, and Sergeant Forge was assigned to Spirit of Fire in an effort to keep the prior events quiet.

Professor Anders' Log, 30 January 2531

Unlock Condition: Complete a game with Anders as your leader.

Upon boarding The Last Gleaming, I was shown my quarters. On the door it read "Doctor Anders"—the name my mother wanted me to use in my professional career. I cannot abide being reminded of her wishes. This whole cloak-and-dagger trip has her fingerprints all over it.

Message from the Office of the High Prophet of Regret

Unlock Condition: Collect Black Box in Mission 03.

Return at fastest possible speed to the world they know as Harvest. We must learn the secrets inside the holy relic before the Great Journey can continue. The humans must not be allowed to enter the artifact; we will do whatever we must to deny them access. All must be resolute in this task, or face punishment.

4 February 2531

Unlock Condition: Collect Black Box in Mission 01.

The UNSC support ship Spirit of Fire enters orbit around Harvest. While Admiral Cole's fleet is engaged elsewhere, Spirit is sent to Harvest to investigate ongoing Covenant activity in the system and look for survivors from the missing UNSC Destroyer The Prophecy (previously dispatched to Harvest to investigate the same activity). Commanded by Captain Cutter, Spirit has been reassigned by FLEETCOM. ONI has placed Professor Anders onboard to lead the investigation.

6 February 2531

Unlock Condition: Collect Black Box in Mission 09.

Professor Anders writes her father what appears to be a detailed analysis of Homer's *Odyssey*. In fact, it is a coded message detailing her mission to Harvest and the result of the find there. ONI censors miss the cipher completely and the message passes unaltered to her father.

7 February 2531

Unlock Condition: Collect Black Box in Mission 02.

Spirit of Fire holds service for the crew of The Prophecy. The crew roster is read despite objections from ONI personnel. The Prophecy was lost with all hands on a first expedition to Harvest to investigate the Covenant interest in the artifact found near the polar region.

9 February 2531

Unlock Condition: Collect Black Box in Mission 07.

After engaging Covenant forces on the surface of Harvest, the UNSC vessel Spirit of Fire arrives at Arcadia—only to find that the Covenant are already there and attacking the colony. Spirit's ground forces assist in the evacuation and help fight the Covenant to a standstill on the surface of the planet.

Message from the Office of the High Prophet of Regret—CLASSIFIED

Unlock Condition: Collect Black Box in Mission 06.

Arbiter, you are the Hand of the Covenant—my hand. You know what must be done. Return to the surface and capture the human female—the one who managed to make fools of us on Harvest. She is the key to unlocking the secrets of the Ancients.

10 February 2531

Unlock Condition: Collect Black Box in Mission 08.

The capture of Professor Anders forces Captain Cutter's hand; Spirit of Fire pursues the enemy into Covenant space. The ship's AI projects an arrival at their destination in 312 hours. The ship remains on high alert for the duration, though nonessential crewmembers are briefly placed in cryo sleep.

11 February 2531

Unlock Condition: Complete a game with Forge as your leader.

Sergeant Forge confronts SPARTAN Douglas-042 over his recommendation to destroy the Covenant ship carrying Professor Anders. The altercation results in a broken chair, a seal malfunction on a bulkhead door, and a stern interruption by the ship's AI, Serina; 42 and Forge always eat together in the mess hall following this event.

14 February 2531

Unlock Condition: Collect Black Box in Mission 10.

Serina, knowing that the crew may be on a one-way trip, manufactures and delivers fake emails from family members to the crew celebrating Valentine's Day. She uses previous correspondence as a basis for the letters. No one ever suspects her of this deception.

Excerpt from *The Punished Deeds*, Vol. III

Unlock Condition: Collect Black Box in Mission 12.

The Shield World that Regret intended to activate was one of just a few that the Covenant had uncovered in the quest for the Halos. These treasure chests of technology enabled the Covenant to quickly gain access to advanced weaponry and space propulsion systems, allowing them to dominate the galaxy.

23 February 2531

Unlock Condition: Collect Black Box in Mission 13.
Spirit of Fire arrives at an uncharted planet swarming with strange alien life-forms. Within a day, the ship is drawn into the planet's interior, where the crew confronts the Covenant and eventually rescues Professor Anders.

Cutter's Log, 25 February 2531

Unlock Condition: Complete a game on Exile.
Pelicans engaged in ground operations on the outside of the shell planet failed invariably within four to five flights. The dust adhered to the intakes during entry into the planetary atmosphere in an almost defensive manner, as if the planet itself did not want any space vehicles descending down to its surface.

25 February 2531

Unlock Condition: Collect Black Box in Mission 15.
Thanks to Sergeant Forge's sacrifice, the Spirit of Fire escapes from the Forerunner Shield World. Spirit of Fire sets a course for home as the majority of the crew prepare to enter cryo sleep for a journey that will take years, if not decades.

Chief Medical Officer O'Neil's Log, 26 February

Unlock Condition: Complete a game on Release.
The decision to burn bodies infected with the virus was not taken lightly, but the danger to the crew and the sheer voracity of the infection made taking the bodies aboard Spirit of Fire impossible. Study of the virus and its effects also seems unwise given that we are not equipped with any quarantine labs or have the faintest idea how the virus spreads.

1 March 2531

Unlock Condition: Collect Black Box in Mission 14.
Chief Engineer Prescott finishes his assessment of damage to Spirit of Fire, and repairs continue to the hull. The FTL core reactor cannot be replaced, and plans to manufacture a spare from base reactor units is considered impossible. The decision is made to run the ship on a skeleton crew and place the rest in suspended animation.

Cutter's Log, 3 March 2531

Unlock Condition: Complete a game with Anders as your leader.
Professor Anders's captivity by the Covenant has made her the longest known POW in the war so far. She has never sought counseling or talked much about her time in captivity, but one can only begin to guess at the nightmares she went through during that terrible time.

Professor Anders's Log, 4 March 2531

Unlock Condition: Complete a game on Labyrinth.
The artificial construction of this "world" is far beyond the Covenant. Indeed, they seem to scavenge this technology for their own use and are unable to operate the machinery, either by design or advancement. The fact that my hand was required to unlock the device leads me to believe the original builders of this planet may have had some knowledge about humans.

12 March 2531

Unlock Condition: Complete a game with Cutter as your leader.
Captain Cutter walks the ship, stepping into medbay to check on the crew still recovering from the battle. He assures Nurse Hershey that a way will be found home and that she will get to see her fiancé again. He returns to his cabin and, after writing five more commendations, fourteen family condolence letters, and a note to his wife, sleeps for the first time in two weeks.

10 February 2534

Unlock Condition: Complete a game on Repository.
The UNSC designates Spirit of Fire as "lost with all hands." The previous designation of "missing" had given hope to family and friends. The reason for the change is classified top secret. A memorial service is held for the crew, but many prominent family members do not attend, holding out hope that their loved ones are still alive.

1 June 2536

Unlock Condition: Unlocked at the start.
The Siege of the Inner Colonies begins as Covenant forces swarm into human-controlled space. For several years, the war falls into a pattern: humans win isolated battles, typically during ground operations, but at horrible cost. One by one, the colonies fall.

9 September 2549—Black Tuesday

Unlock Condition: Complete a game on Beasely's Plateau.
The Second Fall of Arcadia. The Covenant left Arcadia alone after their first attack on the planet in 2531, but the humans mostly abandoned it, leaving the capital city Pirth to nature. Eventually, a small rural farming community started Abaskun, a rich farmland area on the continent of Mu. Although mostly lawless, the area provided much needed food supplies to the UNSC until the planet was attacked again by the Covenant in the fall of 2549.

Edict of the Office of the High Prophet of Truth

Unlock Condition: Complete a game on Fort Deen.
It is known that there is a delay installing Luminaries upon newly constructed vessels of war. On each vessel still lacking a Luminary, 1 Unggoy worker out of every 64 is to be executed. To preserve discipline between the Sangheili overseers and Unggoy, choice of victim and execution is to be by Kig-Yar death squads. This is to continue daily until that vessel's Luminary is installed.

27 August 2552

Unlock Condition: Complete a game on Blood Gulch.
Twenty-five of the 28 surviving SPARTAN-IIs, including SPARTAN-117, are recalled to Reach to be briefed on the Covenant threat and to receive their new orders: board a damaged Covenant vessel, use a "mission specialist" to crack the Covenant computer system, and locate the Covenant homeworld. Once accomplished, a covert team will be dispatched to capture the Covenant leadership and broker a truce by force. Despite recent successes, the human military is being systematically slaughtered, and this may be the only chance for survival.

30 August 2552—0400 hours

Unlock Condition: Unlocked at the start.
Reach, the home of ONI's CASTLE facility and the Spartan-II project, is attacked by an overwhelming Covenant force. The vessel Pillar of Autumn, commanded by Captain Keyes, transports Spartans into battle, hoping to seize a Covenant vessel. Though the Covenant are prevented from learning Earth's location, most of the Spartans fall in battle and Reach is lost.

30 August 2552—0500 hours

Unlock Condition: Unlocked at the start.
Pillar of Autumn, commanded by Captain Keyes, flees Reach with Covenant ships in pursuit. The ship is heavily damaged but manages to drop into Slipspace and escape. Pillar of Autumn carries the only Spartan thought to have survived the engagement on Reach.

Edict of the Offices of the High Prophets of Regret, Truth, and Mercy

Unlock Condition: Complete a game on Crevice.
Hear now, all personnel to spend today's second rest period in attentive watchfulness before display monitors. All display monitors to show the humbling punishment of the Sangheili Supreme Commander of the Fleet of Particular Justice for failure, cowardice, and lack of faith.

Edict of the Office of the High Prophet of Truth

Unlock Condition: Complete a game with the Brute Chieftain as your leader.
In recognition of the virtue of the Jiralhanae, it is ordered that all Sangheili aboard the Fleet of Profound Solitude, The Fleet of Tranquil Composure, and the Fleet of Inner Knowledge to be completely replaced by Jiralhanae. Each removed Sangheili is to be assigned other duties. In celebration, all imprisoned or criminal Jiralhanae to be released, rehabilitated, and pardoned.

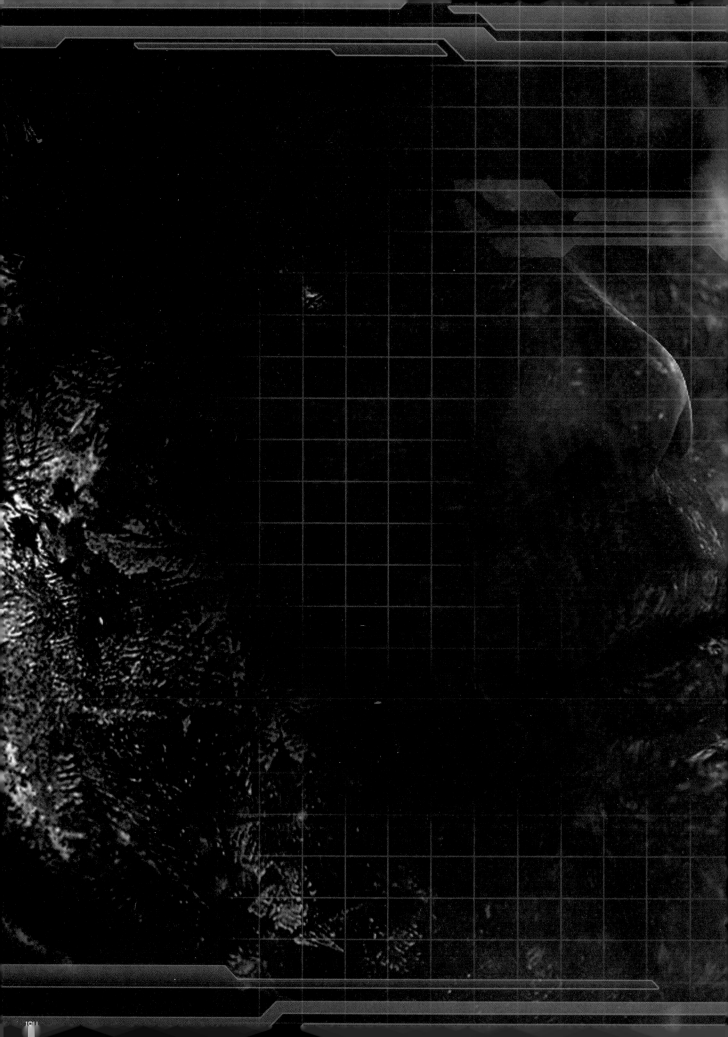

ART GALLERY

Creating Halo Wars was an enthralling challenge, and the creative minds at Ensemble Studios were tasked with remaining faithful to the original vision, but also to add to and extrapolate the unit backgrounds, storylines, and canon. The remainder of this book showcases some of the very best pre-production artwork from every facet of this game's creation. From the epic battlefield art to the character studies, the strange alien landscapes to augmentations for familiar troops and foes; the following is but a glimpse into the latest evolution of this popular franchise.

Art Gallery • Covenant

Let's face it—*Halo Wars* has some serious "badass" units. Preexisting units like the Arbiter and the Hunter are hard not to love. In conceptualizing these units, we gave them the attention that they deserved, treating them as if they were our own original ideas. When it came to re-creating units like the Brute Chieftain, the same rules applied. There was a lot of excitement and passion in the process from start to finish.

189

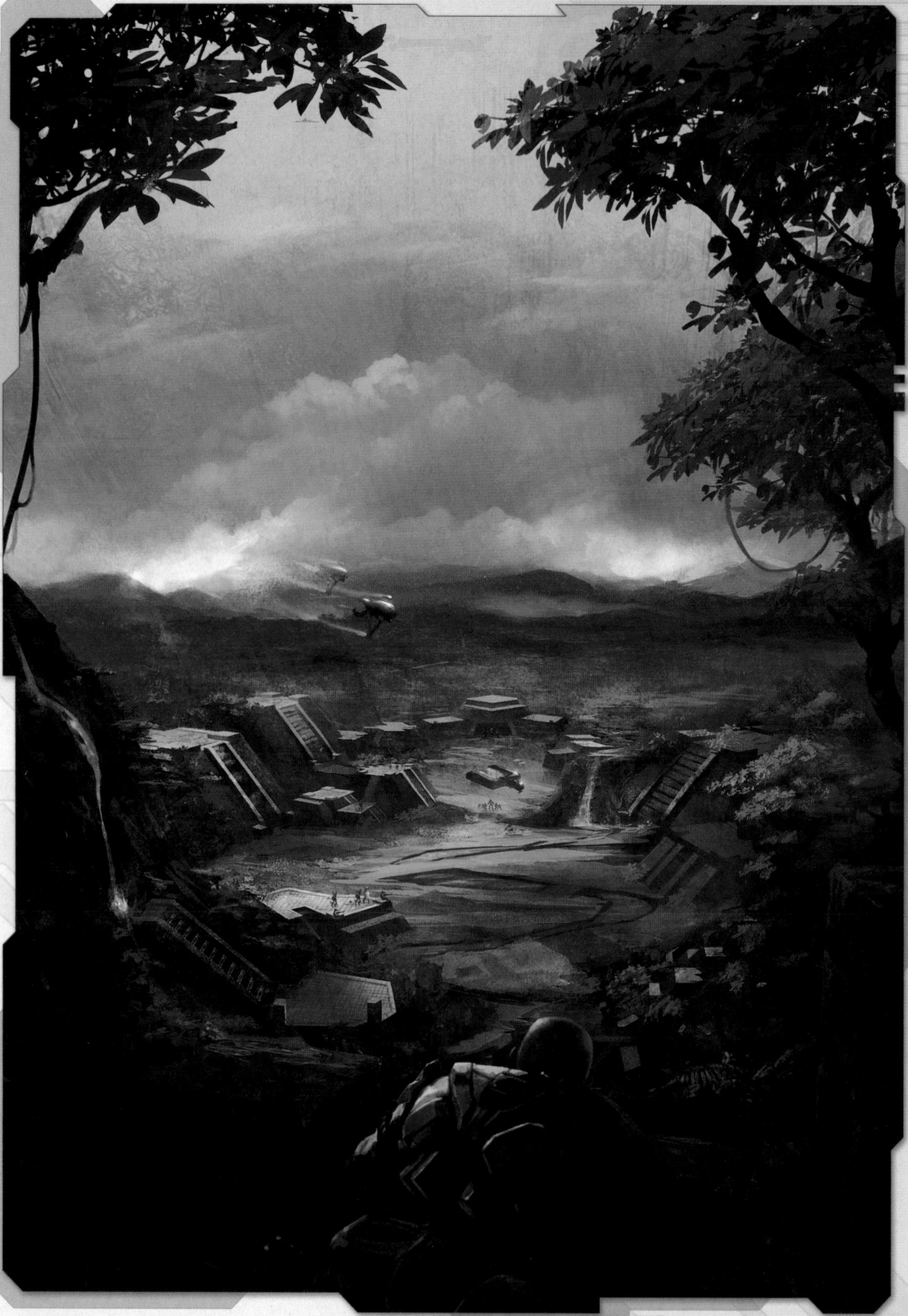

You can't have a *Halo* game without Spartans—it would be like having *Star Wars* without Jedi. In *Halo Wars*, we had the opportunity to introduce the Spartans before Master Chief's time, and in a first for a *Halo* game, we get to see multiple Spartans in combat on the world of Arcadia! We ended up with a ton of different Spartan images. Looking back over our inventory of artwork, it's clear just how cool the Spartans are, and it's easy to see the impact that Master Chief has had on other video-game heroes and characters.

191

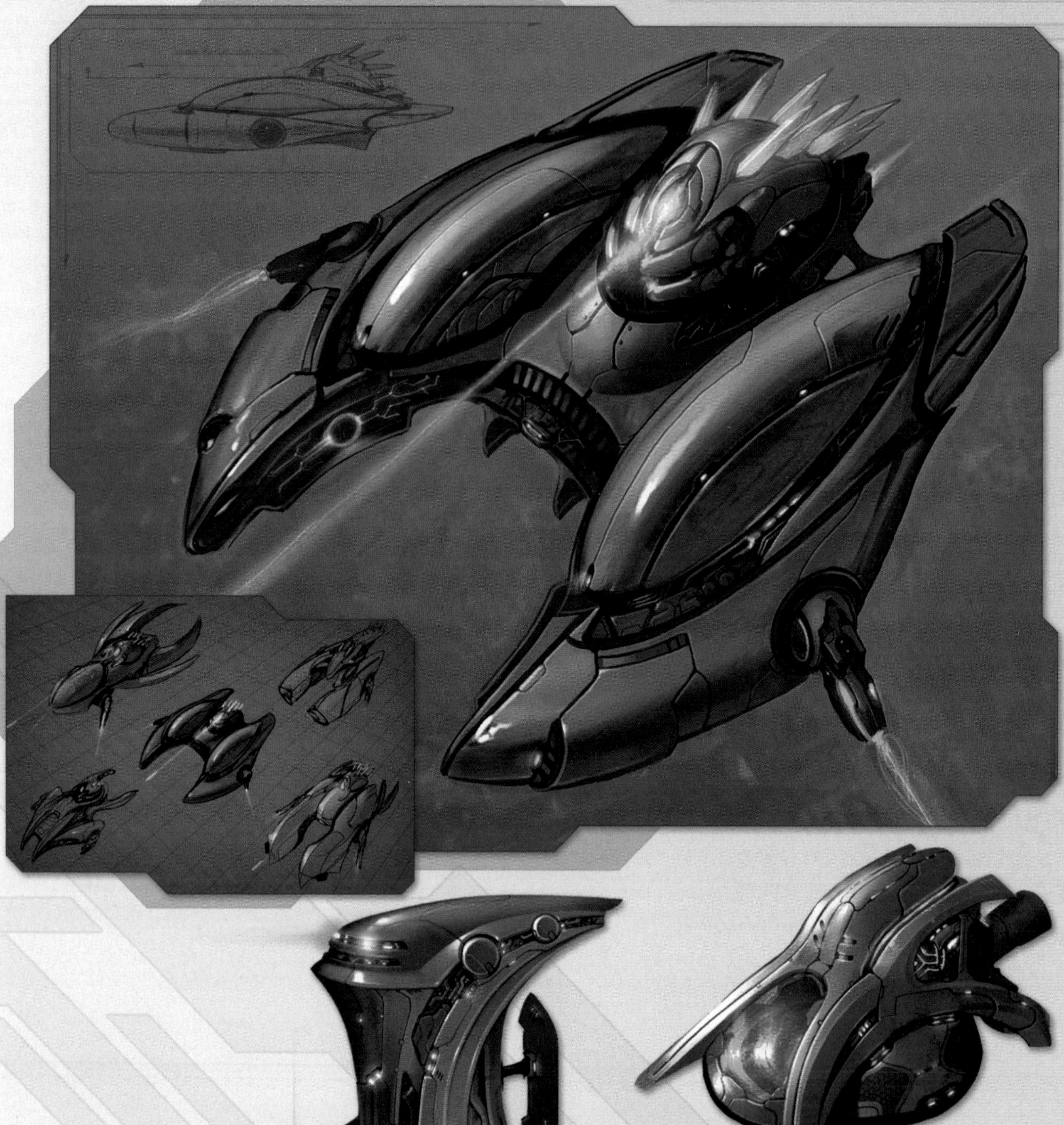

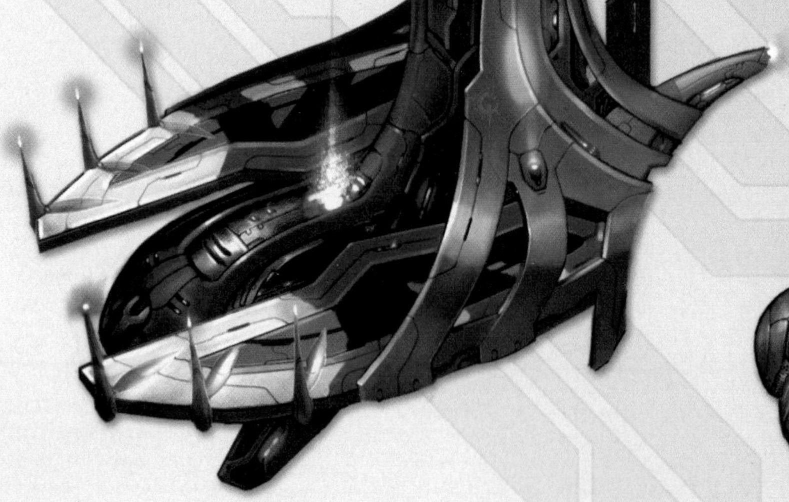

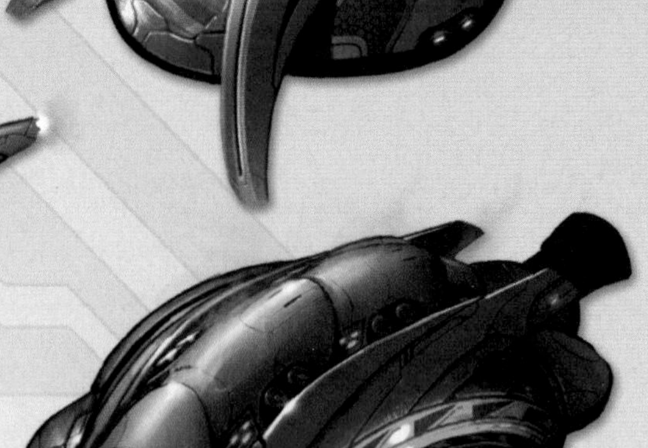

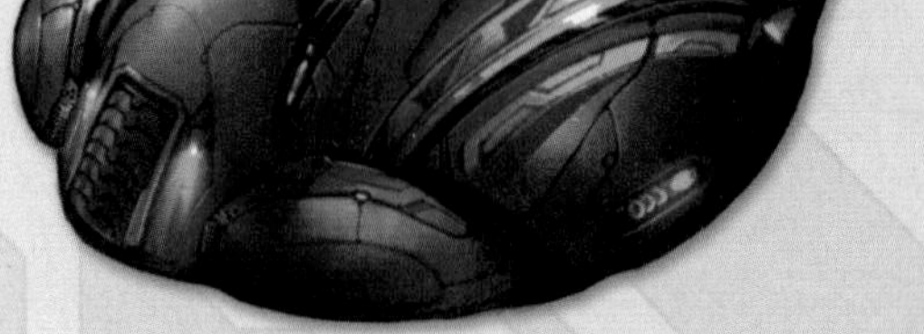

The biggest challenge from a conceptual standpoint was to develop new ideas while at the same time staying true to the successful foundation that previous *Halo* games had established. I'm a little biased, but I definitely think that we did a great job with these unique units, both for the Covenant and the UNSC.

197

Creating a variety of creatures for multiple environments was a blast for the art team. We were excited at the possibility of having animals with distinct and individual behaviors accent the various worlds of the *Halo Wars* universe.

198

While it goes without saying how much fun it was to work on the UNSC and the Covenant, with the Insurrectionists, we had a great opportunity to branch away from the traditional *Halo* factions. These bandits live on Harvest and Arcadia and salvage their equipment from UNSC vehicles, weapons, and civilian buildings.

STATIC DISH:
LIGHTS UP WHEN EMP IS
CHARGED AND FIRED.

"REAR VIEW"

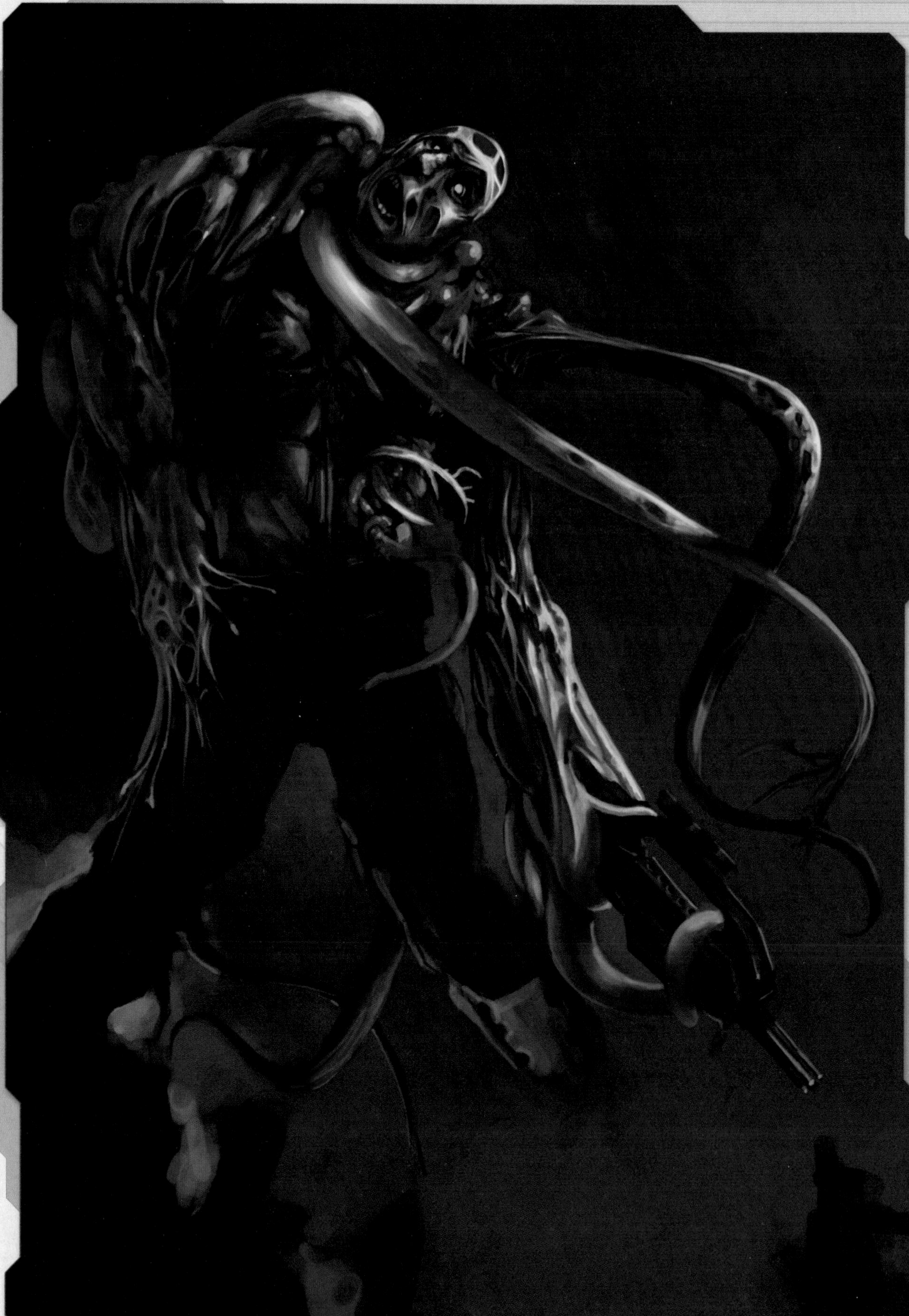

The Flood…'nuff said.

202

204

Here we explored new units while keeping some very recognizable UNSC traits. For the Flamethrower, Vulture, Elephant, and Grizzly, our goal was to add spice to the hugely successful *Halo* recipe.

205

IF THEY WANT WAR, WE'LL GIVE THEM WAR!

three factions, three objectives, three ways to play. command and conquer.

strategic battles, territory takeovers, total domination.

win the game before you can buy it
thestrategicconquest.com